Happy Travels

Adventures

of a Solo Traveller

2019 BC (Before Corona)

Stewart Alexander Noble

**TWO
FEET
WIDE**
PUBLICATIONS

To Catriona

Good Luck on your
Life Journey. . .

Acknowledgements...

Self-publishing is a misnomer. It's just not possible to do it by yourself. I must give thanks and also recommend these two individuals to other writers. As well as being incredibly efficient and professional, they also gave me a great discount for doing so.

I am grateful to my friend, Jacqui James who with laser like precision scanned every word and punctuation mark and corrected them accordingly. To any American readers, the word 'traveller' has not one but two l's and we don't like the use of 'Z' so much over here. It's an eazy mistake to make though. To any English readers, the occasional use of Scottish slang or expletive is inevitable and entirely deliberate. You should just be glad that I didnae write this book in Doric (my mither tongue!)

Jacqui James of Wider Horizons
(Editing and Proofreading)
Virtual Administrative Assistance
www.widerhorizons.co.uk
Contact: info@widerhorizons.co.uk

They say that you shouldn't judge a book by its cover but it's probably why you picked this one off the shelf in the first place. The cover design and artwork were beautifully crafted by Rosie Balyuzi, the 'Queen of Doodles'. It is even more remarkable that she managed to collaborate with me while on holiday lockdown in Corfu with a dodgy wi-fi.

Rosie Balyuzi aka Doodlehut
(Artwork and Graphic Design)
www.doodlehut.com
Instagram:@doodlesurferArtwork
rosie@doodlehut.com

Preface...

The book you are holding wasn't planned. Indeed, I never thought of myself as a writer or a teller of tales. Mrs Dow, my primary school teacher, made sure of that. My first attempts at writing were usually returned with more red over scores highlighting my mistakes than my own misspelt words penciled on the pages.

And so, like most kids, I left school with the embedded belief that I couldn't write, sing or dance, or do much else either. Despite that, life proceeded as it does and I was lucky to be fairly successful at most things I attempted.

Nearing pension age, I decided to spend a year on a solo journey around the world just to see what was 'out there'. Rather than spend valuable travel time sending personal messages to each of my friends and family back home, I posted regular weekly updates on my Facebook page mostly to let them know that I was still alive! I added collages of photos to these notes and so it began.

My friends encouraged me and gave such positive feedback that the inner writer (who exists in all of us) woke up and started to pay attention. And so, as my adventures unfolded, the writer simply watched and took notes as I stumbled about from country to country. I never knew what to expect and the stories really wrote themselves based on my experiences.

On returning home I printed out all 48 chapters and they appear here now with very little editing. Lockdown due to the Coronavirus happened soon afterwards and with so much time on my hands I had little else to do but to try and produce my first book. Initially I called it 'Two Feet Wide' - a senior's solo journey around planet Earth. The world has changed now, and so has the title of this book.

It is only now that I realise how lucky I was to have the opportunity to travel so freely. I hope this compendium of traveller tales will be a source of inspiration to other budding nomads and perhaps inform and entertain you also. It is my accurate account of the state of our world in 2019 BC (Before Corona).

I give my heartfelt thanks to all of my friends who encouraged me and to the wonderful souls who shared their lives with me along the way. I must also thank my spell checker and my 'Grammarly' app.

I'm sure that even Mrs Dow would be impressed.

"Thinking is the best way to travel" **The Moody Blues**

Contents...

1. Prologue...   10

2. God (and the devil) is in the details...   12

3. The Nomad Unclothed...   14

North America

 4. The Love Train...   16

5. Psi Chick and Del Ick...   18

6. Montreal   21

7. On to Toronto...   23

8. Niagara Falls & the Time Traveller...   27

9. The Calgary Cowboys...   31

10. Rocky Mountain Way... .   34

11. Dark and Light in Vancouver...   37

12. Portland, Oregon...   41

13. Bianca and The Giant Redwoods...   45

14. Whale watching in Monterey...   50

15. Rockin' the Fillmore...   52

16. Life's a Beach in San Clemente...   55

17. Carlos Santana plays Vegas on Halloween...   57

18. Mexico City on the Day of the Dead...   60

19. Quintana Roo - 7 Shades of Blue...   62

20. The Tale of Tecuintlicatl...   64

South America

21. The Colours of Cuba ...   67

22. Bogota, Colombia, and the Comedown...   71

23. Onwards and upwards to Peru...   74

24. The Sacred Valley, Machupicchu and Rainbow Mountain... 78

25. It's Hot in Chile...   81

Oceania

26. New Zealand (South Island) with Penguins...   83

27. New Zealand (North Island) with Hobbits...   86

28. Fireworks in Sydney, Australia...   88

29. Surf and Turf on Australia's East Coast...   91

30. Australia's Wild West...   96

Asia

31. Bali Highs...   99

32. Flores and the Komodo Dragons...   103

33. Hot Lava in Java...   106

34. Singapore Sling...   109

35. Sick in Saigon...   113

36: Cambodia is Kampuchea...   118

37: Smoke and Water with Tigers in Thailand...   126

38: On the Road to Mandalay...   132

39: South India: Inside the Golden Golf Ball...   138

40. Delhi Delights and The Taj Mahal...   142

41. Nepal - On Top of the World...   148

Africa

42. Qatar - Land of the Car...   153

43. Nights over Egypt...   156

Europe

44. A Greek Tragedy...   159

45. Sicily - Living on Lava...   161

46. When in Rome...   163

47. Epilogue...   165

48. Happiness Around the World...   169

49. About the Author...   177

50. Other Publications...   178

Prologue...

They say that everything starts with an idea. Well, like most ideas, this one arrived in a flash but took so much time and sustained effort before it even started to take shape.

"You're getting on", it said. "You'll be collecting your pension soon. What else can you do with your life while you are still able? So far, you've learned some good lessons about yourself and others, about how things work and how to get things done. Perhaps it's time now to take this to a new level?

So, why not go around the world, carrying only what you really need, inside you, and in a backpack? See those places that you have always dreamed about, get lost and found again like you did before during earlier solo adventures."

Those trips showed me something new and profound. Being alone and vulnerable brought about experiences I still cannot understand or easily explain to you. It was simply this. When I followed my heart instead of my head, something magical always seemed to happen - remarkable coincidences, synchronicities, being in the right place at the right time.

I met some of the kindest and most wonderful people and had some amazing adventures. Love always replaced fear. I became aware of a new connection with something much, much greater. I was like an actor in my own personal movie but who was the Producer? Was it my 'Higher Self', the Soul of Humanity, perhaps it was God? I don't know. Whoever or whatever was

guiding and protecting me was awesome. I was hooked and I wanted more. I had so far, received only two instructions...

1) Don't be a tourist - Fly overseas but not over land. Meet local people and feel the earth change through your bare feet as you go. Stay grounded!

2) Budget 10% 'alms tax' to give to the kind souls you will meet along the way.

I imagined that I would be creating my own 'world wide web', sprinkled with random acts of kindness.

In spring 2017, the idea returned, germinated, and took root. At that time, I didn't have enough money, but I had already learned a key life lesson. I must give what I hoped to receive. I needed worldwide friends and places in to stay. So, I joined AirBnB and offered a room in my house to strangers from wherever.

They came from all over the world, each one with their own remarkable story. They too were world travellers and they gave me tips, ideas, inspiration, encouragement, and money. They came as strangers but left as friends. I pledged to try and meet them again and spend it back, if not with them personally then with someone from their country.

The idea grew and blossomed. I stuck a map of the world on my wall and each guest was invited to stick a pin on it locating their own home. When I was ready, I would run a thread around the pins to determine the journey I was to travel.

One hundred thousand miles long but just two feet wide.

At the top of my list was New Zealand and that was exactly where my first guests came from! A good start. Over the next 18 months, my map filled up with over fifty pins and the journey started to reveal itself to me. The next question was simple - East or West?

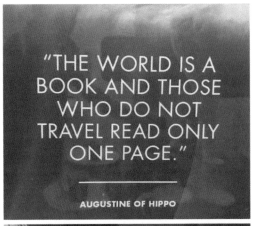

As I needed to travel light, I had to follow the sun and try and stay in 'T' shirt and sandal weather. I planned to leave in September, so this young man chose West. In this way, I could imagine my feet helping to turn the planet on its axis (instead of slowing it down!) It also meant that I could build confidence in English speaking countries before wandering into more exotic lands.

So far, this part of the planning process was easy. Then came the hard bit. Getting myself ready - body, heart, mind, and soul. Putting my house (and garden) in order. Letting go of commitments, de-cluttering my past (and my attic), getting rid of a lifetime's 'stuff' and creating healthy new habits, getting fit, practicing mindfulness and being alone. Sometimes it felt like dying.

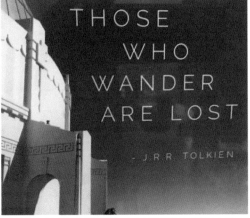

They say that proper planning prevents problems. I hoped they would be proven right. Only time would tell.

At this point in time, I am getting just a faint glimmer of an emerging idea of what this journey could be about. This is an opportunity for me to take stock of the nature and condition of humanity as it presents itself to me at this time. You might see it as a global report through the eyes of one of us.

We all see the world through different eyes. Could it be that our experience is determined by our own beliefs? As subjective perceptions seen through the prism of our own personal story so far. Or is it more than that? I tend to see the good in people and seem to experience the best from others. Can I still do that in foreign lands, with different humans from diverse backgrounds and walks of life? We will see.

And you, dear reader, will be the first to know what happens and how this story ends. I hope it inspires you on your own soul journey one day and you too make it back in one piece.

God (and the devil) is in the details...

"Plan for the best but prepare for the worst, said my dad. So, what's the worst thing that could happen then? My more pessimistic friends were quick to suggest a few possible scenarios...

"You could die!"

So, I got travel insurance. I discovered that it's four times more expensive for me compared to someone half my age! I wrote my will and end of life plan, pre-ordered my willow coffin from and left instructions to where the silver birch tree was to be planted.

"Leave nothing behind that you don't want others to find!"

I decluttered my house, room by room, one cupboard and drawer at a time. This was followed by lots and lots of trips to the recycling centre where it was sent to that great landfill in the sky. Then I sold my car. In the process, I discovered that letting go of the past is one of life's great presents. I felt lighter than air.

"You could get kidnapped and tortured and held to ransom!"

OK so listen carefully family and wealthy friends (joke). If you get a message from a business person in Nigeria or a drug dealer in Columbia instructing you to send them money.

Just don't. OK?

I will simply let them see this blog and that will be that. Anyway, a bullet to the head is a much better way to end my story rather than slowly decaying in the local overpriced nursing home. When you lose your fear of death, you also lose your fear of life and that's exactly what I intend to do. Live. So that's that out of the way.

"You could pick up some deadly virus from those weird people and places!"

Did you know that our once free UK National Health Service now charges for many vaccinations? I got the basics free (Yellow Fever, Hepatitis A, Tetanus, Polio, Diphtheria and Typhoid) but they wanted another £640 for three of the more exotic private brands!

More research revealed that the affected countries often give these for free or for far less cost. I learned that I have 24 hours to get a rabies jag if the monkeys bite me and I start foaming at the mouth. Expensive, short shelf-life malaria tablets can be bought locally where and when needed. And of course, I will avoid drinking sewage and swimming in paddy fields.

"Your stuff could get stolen and you will have nothing."

We all now live in a digital world apparently, so my life work, contacts, photos, videos, music, messages, publications, documents, passport, tickets, financial records, and audiobooks have now been copied to that mysterious place in the sky called 'The Cloud.'

Yes, the life and work of Stewart Alexander Noble born Sept 2nd, 1955 is now reduced to one little number - 1.2 TB (that's terabytes to you), and it can be accessed from any internet device, anytime and anywhere. A trusted friend now has the four-digit number password, the key to my digital life of secret treasures.

"There could be a general election or a second Independence referendum while you are away!"

In that case, I will be back in a flash on the next flight home to mark my cross before returning to where I left off.

But the worst thing that could happen - the worst thing I can imagine? Perhaps there won't be a second referendum and Brexit will leave my country isolated, unrecognisable, and unaffordable. It's people, my friends and family, struggling and downhearted, my hard-earned state pension of just £20/day shrinking like the crappy plastic paper it's now printed on. The unicorn still tethered to its chain.

What then eh?

Well, I might have to cash in my chips, emigrate and tough it out on some remote tropical island beach, playing "Wish you were here" on my guitar while being fed fresh fruit and coconut milk by my jungle princess.

"Swimming in a fish bowl
Year after year
Running over the same old ground
And how we found
The same old fears
Wish you were here."

Pink Floyd

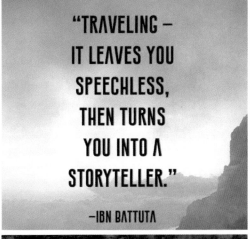

The Nomad Unclothed...

What are the most important things in life? Of course, we all know that they are not things at all, but when travelling with a backpack, less is certainly best. Determined to avoid those long queues at the airport to collect my hold luggage and then for it to arrive bashed and broken, I resolved to travel with only a carry-on cabin-sized pack and keep my stuff to the bare minimum.

They say take half as many clothes and twice as much money, so that's what I tried to do. On the second attempt to pack my luggage it weighed in at only 29 lbs. - not enough to break my back and my budget was slightly more at £65 per day - just enough to break my bank.

My inventory:

Backpack - This *'Osprey'* one has a zip on day pack and wheels (but unfortunately no engine!).

Laptop and I-Phone. These are both synchronised to the cloud and contain telephone, camera, television, video, music machine, 500 albums, books, notepads, maps, and calendars - a virtual ton of things which weigh nothing at all! Isn't technology wonderful?

Inflatable world map (also useful as a beach ball).

Documents and Scottish Passport

Lucky travel charms and whistle (useful for scaring wolves, witches, and other potential predators and of course for refereeing the occasional football match).

Hats and headscarves.

Selfie stick, tripod, and torch.

Neck pillow, blindfold, and earplugs (when I want to switch the world off for a bit).

Rain jacket and day pack bag.

Specs and shades.

Mosquito net (this completely covers my head and may also be useful to disguise my age when trying to enter nightclubs).

Life straw (for clean, bacteria-free water). They say that it's even possible to drink your own urine with this device - yeuch!

Toiletries.

Tech bag. (Travel Adaptors, Cables, USB back up drive)

First Aid Kit.

Trousers with zip-off legs - waterproof, mosquito proof and pickpocket-proof - yet to be proven.

Shirts and T-shirts x 6.

Sandals, sandal socks (yes there is such a thing) and boots.

Jacket.

So that's it. My life support system in a nutshell. The bare essentials to life on the road. And if I discover I have missed anything, there is always a Tesco in Timbuktu, right?

Travel Tip No 1: Before you set off, lay out the contents of all your luggage and travel kit and take photographs of all your stuff. This will be invaluable if you need to make an insurance claim online and en-route. Also take photographs of the receipts of expensive items such as your phone and laptop.

This one tip could save you more than the price of this book. Other tips might even save your life.

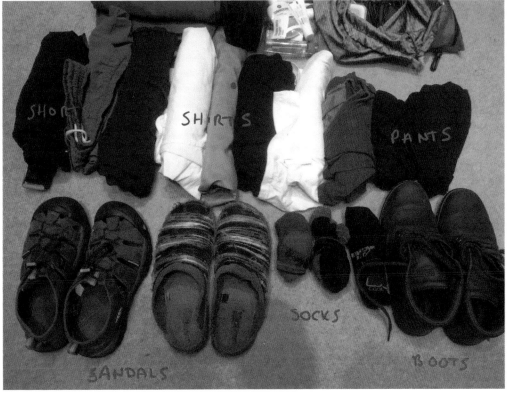

The Love Train...

September, Days 2-4: 3,484 miles

The story starts here.

A friend kindly drives me to *Inverness* Airport at 5 am. I am in *Manchester* at 10 am. A hop skip and a jump and at 11.55 am, I'm in *JFK, New York*. Isn't time travel amazing!

I catch the subway train to *Manhattan*. In my carriage, I see a whole bunch of us - a smorgasbord of humanity. People of every skin colour, race and age, bobbing along together through dark tunnels towards the city. Many are asleep, many glued to their devices. Some have dead and empty eyes and seem lost in their own inner worlds. Somewhere a rapper is singing his song.

A sad and battered young guy walks through the carriage lamenting the end of this sad and battered world. He holds out his hand for money. People look away and watch through the safety of the reflections in the windows.

Directly across from me there's a slim Latino guy. Well, he looks like a guy, but he has breasts. He looks a bit fierce and strange, so I too look away. I am sitting next to the door as the train stops in Brooklyn. A heavy woman in an electric wheelchair is struggling to board the train. There is an eight-inch step and despite many attempts, she just can't get on. Someone holds the door open while she tries repeatedly.

I am tempted to try and help but just then the scary Latino guy jumps up and cursing, starts to try and push the chair on. "Where are we people?" he shouts. "This is not my fucking world." A few of us get up to help him and before long the wheelchair jumps into the carriage and the overweight lady plugs in her earphones and starts jiving to her music.

Something has shifted in here. I smile at the Latino guy and give him a thumbs up. Others start looking at each other and some even converse. This one act of kindness has changed everyone's perceptions. Prior judgements dissolve and there is a real sense of safety, of community. We are all in this train together.

There is a lesson for me here.

I get off at *Penn Street Station, 8th Avenue*. For some reason, my phone won't work, and I can't get in touch to let my friend know when I will be arriving. Despite all my clever preparations with my laptop, iPhone, and smart apps, I can't even make a bloody phone call! Is technology wonderful? There is just enough time to grab a McDonalds and try and use their free Wi-Fi. No success. And no big apples either.

I catch the Amtrak train with seconds to spare and journey on up the Hudson River. Soon the city is behind me as we travel through wooded forests. Grand wooden mansions rise up to show off through the trees as the train clatters along the valley.

A very frail old lady stumbles past me on her way to the toilet. When she emerges, she stands to hold on to the handrail. The train is rocking from side to side and she is trying to time her step to make it safely back to her seat. Without hesitation this time, I get up, take her arm, and slowly guide her back to her seat. She is so sweet and grateful - a beautiful lady who politely thanks me.

Her name is Barbara and she is heading home to celebrate her sons 65th birthday. People smile at my gesture. They look me in the eyes now and somehow, seem more familiar. We are kind. We are safe here. When I leave to get off, they acknowledge me with a friendly nod. I feel good but also a bit anxious at the thought that my friend may not be here to meet me. I needn't have worried.

We hug and spin around on the platform. "How did you know to be here," I ask. "Hm, I just had a hunch that this would be the train you would be on," she said. I call her Psi chick and we both laugh as we drive home to her beautiful house in the forest.

We have been friends for many years and, although it has been four years since we last met, it seems just like yesterday. We quickly catch up with our life stories and despite the distance of space and time, we seem to be on exactly the same page.

Soon the effects of time travelling catch up with me and I go to bed and fall into a deep sleep.

"People all over the world
Join hands
Start a love train, a love train
People all over the world,
Join hands
Start a love train, a love train"

The O'Jays

Psi Chick and Del Ick...

September: Days 2 - 4. 3,421 miles.

Upstate New York is nothing like the movies. It's surprisingly green and teeming with wildlife. On the road home, we pass deer, squirrels, and chipmunks. Wild turkeys strut and gobble in gangs along the roadside and eagles fly overhead.

We stop off in town to grab some supplies from the health food store. As we park, I notice a frumpy middle-aged woman standing anxiously next to the parking lot meter, waving a $10 note. "Can you change this?" she asks. I rummage around my pocket for loose coins and offer them to her with an open hand. "Aw, you don't have enough" she bemoans. I tell her to just take what she needs. "But, but I can't pay you," she replies. I turn my cheek and invite her to kiss me, which she does with a nervous peck. "There, we are even now," I say grinning.

"But, but this is America we don't do this here. Folk here just take and you can't trust anyone these days." She was really gob smacked and clearly out of her comfort zone. "Well I am not from here," I tell her. "I'm from Scotland. Listen," I say "If you are still uncomfortable with the few dollars I gave you, just pay them forward to the next one of us who needs them more than you. It's easy. No problem." She walks away, mouth open and I wonder what she would tell her friends about our encounter.

"Well you are clearly off to a good start on your journey Mr Noble" laughed Psi. And yes, for less than the price of a cup of coffee we had enjoyed this random act of kindness shifted someone's reality, and I had given myself a nice wee story to share. Priceless.

Psi and Del are health care professionals who now live alone with their two German Shepherds, Comedy and Tragedy, and a stray cat which occasionally graces us with its presence. Their fridge is full of fruit, vegetables, and jars of strange but healthy concoctions. "We are really into mycelium just now," says Del. "You know the health benefits of mushrooms are really significant. Plant medicine is catching on. We forage and dry our own now and use different ones for skincare, gut care and mind care." Their bathroom is also full of dozens of bottles of tinctures of plant medicine from all over the world. I just can't find the soap.

In the morning, we meditate together in a room full of Buddhas. Then Psi shows me some good yoga moves to help keep me stay supple on my travels. Tomorrow I'll show you some breath work she says. But today I am going to treat you to a float. Let's go.

Soon I am naked, in a pitch-black room, my ears plugged with wax and I'm floating in a bath of body warm water mixed with Epsom salts. I am weightless, without gravity, touch, sound, taste, smell or sight. My muscles and mind relax. I feel like *Neil Armstrong* floating in space. It is wonderful.

In this state of sensory deprivation, my mind is free to wander, and it melts deep into the cosmos. My brain images a sea of colour. I am surrounded by webs of iridescence, countless crystalline strands of vivid reds and emerald green particles. All moving in straight lines in a fractal journey through time and space. I wonder if this is cyberspace.

Countless binary data streams flicker and pulse, travelling far into the distance. Somewhere, someone clicks a button. At lightning speed, the code instantly converts into ones and zeros. Through the keyboard it shoots, the router, the servers, 2G, 3G, 4G, 5G networks joining up and connecting the dots. Returning more dots to be re-assembled into a word, an image, a map, a friend. My thoughts are travelling at nearly light speed along the information superhighway.

Gee whiz.

The house sits alone in six acres of wild old forest. We must dress for dinner says Del as he hands me a green working Scottish kilt and a white waistcoat. After dinner, we sit on the boardwalk, sip green tea, and look down across the organic garden and deep into the forest. The Sun, our Solar King and Sun of God turns liquid bronze, its golden shards radiating through the branches. They glisten as they touch the leaves of the Aspen trees which shiver in delight as though in nervous anticipation of the impending night.

Soon the sounds of billions of insects fill the air. They rise and fall as if there is some invisible conductor guiding their song. The Orchestra Insecta. The Hexapod family is in full chorus. I hear a cry above me and watch a golden eagle as it glides across the rooftop. The moon grows brighter as she adorns a beautiful rainbow corona. The sky becomes star-studded with silver jewels, ruby red mars glowing brightly. Satellites and other aircraft zoom by as the stars do cartwheels in the sky.

The Hi-Fi blasts the sounds of Buddhist monks chanting, the haunting nasal sounds of Mongolian throat singers. It's like they are right here in the room. It changes. Next, the sounds of French accordions transport us to another world, and we dance. Psi spins like a snowflake and Del, the magician flicks a switch to turn the tree canopy into a canvas of spiraling laser lights.

Everything is connecting, everything is moving and everything seems alive. I watch as tiny ants drag leaves across the wooden floor, the paint slowly blistering. Even the metal balcony is slowly transforming into rust. The fruit bowl erupts into a cloud of tiny fruit flies which move in unison, like smoke across the room. I am lost in a sea of movement and swimming in awareness.

There is no I. Only particles of light, condensing into a multitude of forms, always changing and interconnecting in the most beautiful and timeless cosmic dance. I head for the bathroom and look at my reflection. The dogs never take their eyes off me and true to their name, shepherd me everywhere I go.

"Who am I?" I ask. "Who's asking?" it replies.

My face seems to melt like wax, changing shape. I am sad, I am happy. Through these lenses I see my face, I am old, I am young, I am a baby, I am my mother, I am my father, I am me, I am you, I am eternal, timeless. Tragedy gives me a gentle nudge and reminds me that I am actually here in the bathroom.

I head through to the lounge to lie down and then drift into a lucid dream. Comedy licks my toes and I resurface. I am lying with eyes closed as Psi spoon feeds me carrot, ginger, and coconut soup. I seem to sense when the spoon is close and open my mouth in hungry anticipation. It is warming, delicious and I feel it flow deep into my body radiating heat and nutrition. "Yum, I remember this." I say aloud. One spoon at a time, my mother is patiently and lovingly scraping the drips from my chin. Open wide, here comes the choo-choo train.

I cry like a baby.

Psi hands me a wooden staff. It's an authentic native spirit stick. Deerhorn has been spliced into one end and the stem has been inlaid with beautiful crystals, sacred turquoise Hopi stones at the tip. A golden rattlesnake is painted on the base along with other mystical symbols. It feels so familiar, comfortable and balanced in my hands

Who am I? Who's asking?

"We skipped the light fandango
Turned cartwheels 'cross the floor
I was feeling kinda seasick
But the crowd called out for more
The room was humming harder
As the ceiling flew away
When we called out for another drink
The waiter brought a tray."

Procol Harem

Montreal...

September, Days 5-7: 3,993 miles

The train from upstate New York follows the grand Hudson River upstream where it gets wider and wider until it becomes Lake Saint Louise on which the *City of Montreal* was founded. We travel through fertile agricultural lands, a tapestry of fields ripe with corn, peach, and apples.

A tornado has ripped through the valley and twice our train has to stop while ground crews are summoned to clear the line. It's a long journey and I fall asleep. I am wakened at the Canadian border by two cops with guns asking rapid-fire questions. "Where are you going and for how long? Where are you from? Where are you heading to? Are you re-entering America again?"

My brain slowly wakes up and I tell them that I am going around the world, and I'm not sure for how long I will be anywhere really but probably 15 - 20 days ish in this lovely country. They both look at me bewildered and take my passport.

Chris, my seat companion is led away. An hour later he returns to his seat looking nervous. He tells me that they led him off the train to a building for interrogation. "They put on their rubber gloves," he says with wide eyes. "I nearly shit myself. I'm so glad they didn't take their enquiries any further."

Apparently, their data had alerted them to his drinking and driving charge 25 years earlier, his one and only criminal offence. He was advised to bring the relevant paperwork with him if he wished to return to Canada in the future. Others were less fortunate and were directed to the nearest bus stop to try and return to where they came from.

I look up to see one of the cops walk menacingly down the aisle towards me. I gulp. He smiles as he returns my passport. "Have a great trip he says." Phew. This is not America.

The 9-hour journey stretches to 11 hrs. and I arrive at my AirBnB late into the night. My host Muiz is cooking dinner for his brother Machmud, and his cousin Taha. He invites me to join them on the balcony where they generously share their food and beer. Their family fled Libya after the war, and they are working hard to make a life for themselves here.

Machmud described his harrowing five years working as a medic during the war. Deep trauma is still carved on his expressionless face. "Libya was not good under Gaddafi" he said, "but the country is really dead now. NATO just walked away when they took the power and the oil. I have seen things no human should ever see but Canada has been great to us. We love it here."

Taha had come over from Ontario to stay with his cousins. "The whole town went down with the tornado last night. No electricity, no trains, and no radio or internet for 28 hrs. Folk were really freaking out," he says. So, he decided to brave the high winds and drive over to visit his cousins.

Montreal

Montreal is a bit like New York - same rich human diversity, a mix of old and new buildings paint the skyline but it's cleaner, artier, more civilised and more *'chic'*. People here have smarter clothes and a better class of iPhone. Most folk *'parle le francais'*. Indeed, this could easily be Paris. I admire the French architecture as wafts of freshly baked baguettes infused with the creamy smell of garlic ooze out of *les restaurants* and my stomach reminds me that I need breakfast.

I decide to follow the tourists to the *Old Port* and partake in the local delicacy of *Poutine avec le bacon*. (Chips, cheese, and bacon swimming in gravy in a brown cardboard box). Perhaps not the healthiest way to start the day but so delicious. It would make a great hangover cure.

I contemplate my next big decision. Do I go on the big wheel carousel, humiliate myself on the kiddies' choo choo train, or confront my lifelong fear of heights on the 1000' high zip wire? No escaping that one then. I just hope I don't drop my iPhone or chuck up my chips. Wheeeeee.

Later, I get lost in the streets. I head towards the sounds of a commotion and find myself at the head of a climate change protest march. Thousands of polite and pleasant folks with placards and drums walking slowly in the sunshine, as if in a funeral procession.

"What do we want? You to be like us.
When do we want it? Now!"

The streets are surprisingly quiet without huge crowds anywhere. It's as if the city architects had optimistically planned for a more heavily populated citizenship but the citizens have disembarked. Of course, I realise, just like where I come from, and just like you right now, they are all probably at home lost in cyberspace or with their heads in a good book.

It's Saturday night and there's a Picnic in the Park - an electronic picnic. I join the stream of beautiful young ones as we are hypnotically drawn towards the stage to the beat of the drum. DJ's weave their sonic sound textures, the crowd moves with the grooves; they simultaneously whoop and raise their arms high towards the setting sun. At some hidden prompt, clouds of marijuana billow into the sky as everyone lights up. It's going to be legal here in the next few weeks, I am told.

These kids are the new shiny ones. Wealthy, united, cool, successful, and full of optimism for the future. They are probably the grandkids of my own Woodstock generation. Aware that I am the oldest guy here, I stand under a tree and partly hidden by its branches, watch as I drink my plastic bucket of beer, with added wheatgrass and red bull. They sing together in some collective anthem. "Somehow, somewhere, we will find a way, someday." This is the new cool and the young people of Montreal are its foremost crusaders.

"Somehow, Somewhere, we will find a way, Someday."
Anon.

On to Toronto...

September, Days 8-10: 4,329 miles

I take the Megabus to *Toronto*. With a population of 3 million, it's the 4th biggest city in North America and it's only around 150 years old. It was clearly designed when city architects still used graph paper. The entire city is a grid divided east and west by Yonge Street, which at 54 miles long, is the longest straight road in the world.

The buildings are mostly square boxes. Stone boxes replaced by brick and then sandstone and now steel and coloured glass. I wonder if these too will soon be replaced with virtual shopping malls and offices. Digital avatars replacing office staff and shop assistants.

Toronto is more *Blade-runner* than *Gotham City*. The impressive shards of glass towers reach high into the sky but at street level, it's tired and grimy. I see many homeless folks sitting on pavements or lying asleep in doorways under dirty blankets. I am very grateful that I am staying in an AirBnB in the posher part of town.

Here, huge blocks of pretty apartments sit in cleanly manicured gardens with neatly trimmed bushes. Trees line the streets and there are squirrels everywhere. Their population exploded when barbecue squirrel sticks became unpopular. Middle-aged joggers in colour coordinated neoprene run by like prancing gazelles. They even wear matching dogs.

In the morning, I head out for downtown Toronto and buy my travel pass which should last for three days. "This will allow you to use all public transport services," advises the friendly ticket clerk. "Trains, subway, trams and buses. This is not London, you know. We still own our own schools, health care and transport services. Everything is integrated and works well together".

The subway train is clean, slick, and very high tech. I am sitting in a blue and white plastic earthworm - each carriage is a segment and connects to the next with a cleverly engineered plastic bridge. It smoothly snakes its way through the underground tunnels.

When it's on a straight piece of track I can see forward and back down its full length of maybe 20 carriages. It's one long articulated tube. The lights on the doors change from white to green when they open and turn red as they close to the chimes of a perfect octave (the first two notes of the song; *'Over the Rainbow'*).

I get off at *Union Square* and it's raining torrents. Torrential torrents Toronto style. I'd rather watch wet than get wet, so I head for the aquarium. *Robert Ripley's' Aquarium of Canada.*

I queue with dozens of small Japanese tourists having a family day out with their tiny tinseled tots. Eric serves me at the ticket desk. "How long does it take to walk around?" I ask. "That depends on how much you love fish" he replies with a cocky smile. "Not sure about fish," I say, "but I am rather partial to prawns." Eric is not amused. I bet Eric is a vegan.

Inside, there are lots of.... fish! Big fish, little fish, jellyfish. Fish with great names; Boggle eyed Goliath groupers and French grunts lustfully eye the delicate damselfish. Flamboyant cattle fish chase sleek unicorn fish through the corals. Long-nosed gars, Pacific spiny lumpsuckers, pen point gunnels, scaly headed sculpin, black belly rosefish, and decorated war bonnets cruise through the fleshy sea glow pens as tiny sea stars and strawberry anemone crawl and electric eels crackle. There are even some fish named after our Nicola. I couldn't find the one called Wanda.

I wonder who named all these fish and if the fish even care. There must be people whose ancestors are responsible for naming them. Ironically, no-one knows who they are.

The stars of the show are the sharks and the giant stingrays which swim over and around us as we walk through the sparkly glass tunnels. A big green turtle makes the occasional fly past, a welcome distraction from all those fish.

Later, I stroke the face of a stingray. It loves it and smiles. I'd like to say it was a load of pollocks, but fish really are much more beautiful when they are not battered in newspaper.

I pass under the iconic *CNN tower* which thrusts its manhood upwards, its tip disappearing into the clouds, like a giant dildo with hula hoops. Feeling hungry, I head for Chinatown and its street-lined cafes, bistros, and restaurants.

I decide to pass on Sushi due to my newly found respect for fish. But the Maki My Way 'Custom Sushi Experience' did rather appeal. The street signs draw me in with names such as The Greedy Duck, Gaby's Grill, Fred's Not Here Steak bar, Social Kitchen, and my personal favourite - Fat Bastard Burrito Co, which claims to sell 'freakin huge burritos.'

So many smells and so many choices. Why do I have only one stomach? Cows have three. I opt for a new place called *Landing Noodles* and a nice but nervous elderly Korean woman serves me a big bowl of noodles with sliced beef, chili and broccoli.

I have never mastered the art of using chopsticks and trying to eat wet spaghetti with them proves utterly hopeless. There's a large wooden ladle like the ones you see in the sauna, but smaller, thankfully. However, that too proves difficult as the noodles just slide off in a splash. I revert to lifting the bowl to my mouth and just tipping them in. Mmmm. I still have to use my napkin to clean the mess from the table though.

I head out for the open street market and turning a corner I see Spider-man crouched high on a street sign. He looks like a comic character – Marvelous! He points at me and reels in my attention with his sticky web. "Dip the tip in the bin man," he shouts. A cop car appears on the other side of the street and he nimbly shimmies down and, grabbing his tip bin, disappears up an alley.

His friend and minder is sitting on the street wearing a black hoodie and a bright blue tarpaulin, like a caped crusader. A can of Innes & Gun in his hand. His old boxer dog sits next to him with sad and sullen eyes. I ask him for a light, and he hands me a yellow lighter. "Here, just keep it man. I have pockets full of them."

He is known to his friends as Irish; O G Irish and his dog is called Karma. I ask him what the O G stands for and he says, "Original man - I am Irish the original." I introduce myself as Scottish. Stewart the Scot "Let's go and find an Englishman and make a joke," I say.

We walk up the street together with Karma trudging along beside us. He asks me what I work at. I tell him that I don't work anymore, I just play. And now I am playing at travelling around the world collecting stories. What's his?

Irish left his home in *Westport* when he was 19 years old. He was escaping the law and looking for work. He tells me that he is 46 years old and he has been living on this block on the streets for 21 of them. "I been shot, stabbed and run over man" but I got to stay alive for my daughters, right? "Where do you sleep when the snow comes," I ask. "I hang out with my brothers," he replies.

"They are First Nation people and we have known each other for a long time. We trust each other. They are my family now. They drink sherry. If you ever meet them, you need to know the word for thank you. It's *'Nina s kum tin'*. If it's too cold I get in jail. I am a POI man (person of interest) and they won't let me fly home. I know everyone here and they know me. I look after everyone man.

We pass a big building, *CAMH* (Centre for Addiction and Mental Health). Outside are lines of fat people in wheelchairs, some without legs and they are sucking on their cigarettes like there's no tomorrow.

Irish leans over a fruit stall, grabs an apple and throws it at me. "Food is free here for us when the market closes". He tells me. "So how much do you and Spider-man make on a good day?" I ask. "$10, maybe $20 man." He replies. He reaches deep inside his many hidden pockets and takes out a pair of Ray-bans. "Look, I found these today." He puts them on and smiles. "They suit you," I say. "You look like Clint Eastwood."

"I'll get maybe $20 for these man, today's been a good day." "What would you do with $20?" I ask. "Buy a bottle of sherry and dog food. Sherry for my brothers." I slip him $20 and thank him. "That's for the lighter you gave me and for your good company." I say. It quickly disappears inside one of his pockets. "Come on let's get drunk with my brothers," he replies.

We walk on and other street people appear from alleys, like lost ghosts. Billy is sitting on the pavement rocking back and forth. His eyes flicker around inside his head and he stammers. "Irish, I I lost my b b bag man and my b b blanket." "Come on," says Irish, "Let's get drunk and I'll help you find another." I take my leave and keep walking.

Later, as I pass a supermarket an older guy shouts over at me.

"Hey brother, have you got a light?" His hair is long and jet black and his face rugged and brown. I recognise him as a First Nation person. "Sure," I say, "Here you can have this lighter." I give him the yellow cigarette lighter that O G Irish had given me earlier. "How you doing?" I ask. "I'm tired man, really weary. I try and teach my brothers, but they just don't listen to me. They are lost." "Well I'm listening," I reply. "Come on, let's sit down and smoke and you can tell me all about it."

I pass him my *Natural American Spirit* tobacco pouch. "You smoke good shit brother," he laughs. He continues, "They just want to take and take, get drunk and bed their women. I try and tell them that we are not here to take, we are here to give. We were once a proud people, but they will always be poor, they just don't understand."

He then reaches across the bench and tries to give me a fistful of dollars. There must have been at least $20 in coins in his big brown hand. "No thanks," I say. "I don't like that stuff, it's too heavy. Where's home?" I ask. He looks down to the ground and then deep into my eyes "Where I grew up as a little boy all gone now. My family all gone. No past, no future. There is only now, and this is my home. He clenches his fist and slaps his chest. "I understand," I say, *"Nina s kum tin."*

"Hey, little brother." he says, "How you know Cree language?" I recount the story of O G Irish and how I gave him $20 earlier. It was clearly trying to return to me already. We laugh. "You understand man," he says. "We got to give if we want to receive." The only other native words I know are *'Mitakuye Oyasin'*. "Yes," he says, "we are all connected. Now I will teach you another word. *'Boom boom pee '*- it means I'll see you later." We shake hands and smile into each other's eyes and I walk on.

After a mile or so my satnav comes back on and I realise that I have been walking in the wrong direction. Cursing, I turn around and walk back the way I had come. Steven is still sitting outside the supermarket. "Hey, Steven" I shout, "You were right!, *Boom boom pee*."

So, this is the second time I have got lost with the satnav. Tomorrow I will buy a map and a compass, a pocket notebook, and a pen. I will pay more attention to the sun and the skyline and less time looking down at this damned phone.

The street sign says *'Blue Jay Way'* and a song comes into mind. I zip up my jacket , step across the tram tracks and walk wearily home.

Travel Tip No 2: When heading to a new destination, pay close attention to the direction of your first few steps.

"There's a fog upon L.A.
and my friends have lost their way
Soon will be the break of day
Sitting here in Blue Jay Way."

The Beatles

Niagara Falls & the Time Traveller...

September, Day 9: 4488 miles

Just around the corner from my apartment is a trendy grocery store. They sell an eclectic mix of health foods, delicious deli snacks, coffee to go and tobacco! I tell the shop assistant that they sell the best cheese and ham sandwiches that I have ever tasted.

She gleams as she proudly tells me that she makes them herself. "It's best, smoked ham," she tells me, "with local cheese and organic tomatoes. I chop salad finely and then smother it with mayo." It's all carefully layered in an artisan bun and wrapped in cheese paper and it's as heavy as a brick. "One of these keeps me going all day," I say.

Her name is Karina and she moved here from Lithuania three years ago. She is young, blonde, wears a toothpaste smile and has those cool steely blue Russian eyes. "In Russia, everyone's a bit, you know.... samey," she says. "My friend is from Latvia and we share a flat. For the first two years, we went everywhere and were excited about meeting so many different kinds of people, but it wears off after a while.

Now I just walk between my flat and my work. In here I just walk between this counter and that kitchen." She pouts and makes a funny rasping sound with her lips. "What's next?" I ask. "Hopefully meet a nice guy," she laughs, "settle down, get a nice house, have babies, you know - live the dream."

At Union Station, there's an exhibition titled *The Time Travel Capsule*. I am intrigued but just don't have the time. My Green Go train is leaving soon and I hurry down to the platform. I meet Sandra. "Does this train go to *Aldershot*?" she asks. She tells me that she is 6th Nation and is heading back to the reservation. "I have just done six weeks in rehab," she says proudly. "I can't wait to get home and see my babies. I have six." My jaw drops.

She seems like a slip of a girl who surely can't be more than 25 years old. I say so and she laughs aloud. "You look young and shiny to me," I say. "Good luck and remember that the first hit has a long chain of others hiding behind it. Stay focused and be happy." She nods in acknowledgement and thanks me. "It's nice to meet you," she says. *"Boom boom pee."* I reply.

I find a seat with a view on the top floor of the twin-deck train. Soon the high towers of the Toronto skyline are behind me. The train skirts around Lake Ontario and I change seats to see what's in front of me. I plug in my earphones and doze off. I wake up, look up and there's a circular rainbow around the sun. This landscape is strangely familiar.

The conductor announces that this is the end of the line. I get off and find myself at the exact same spot I started out from three hours earlier. *Platform 5, Union Station*. I'm bewildered and confused. Am I dreaming? Is this Deja vu? Like Groundhog Day?

I finally realise that I must have slept through my station in both directions when the train had reached the end of its line to return to Union Square. The Go train is ready to go again, and I don't know if I am coming or going! But *Niagara Falls* has been on my bucket list for a long time and I've pre-paid my tickets and booked a dinner reservation on the top of *Skylon Tower*. So off I go again.

From the train station, I catch the bus, but it unexpectedly terminates 15 miles before Niagara. There's a taxi outside the bus terminus so I jump in. Miguel my taxi driver is from Mexico has three kids and two jobs. His wife also works. "It's hard work," he says, "but life is pretty good here. It's crazy busy in the summer months but it's starting to get quieter now."

He tells me that Niagara plays host to over 30 million visitors every year. They come from all over the world. Mostly the US of course but everywhere else also. There are three waterfalls and they flow between New York State and Ontario forming part of its border. There is a bridge which also acts as a border crossing where you can move between both countries. "You'll be queuing for hours if you attempt that," he says. "Who's got the biggest falls?" I ask. "Well us Canadians obviously," he replies and we both laugh. Miguel drops me off at the welcome centre and gives me his card. "You might need this later," he says. I'm so glad he did.

As soon as I step out of the car, I am struck by the sheer size of this impressive natural spectacle. I can hear the thunderous rush of water as clouds of spray erupts into the sky like steam. The sun creates rainbows all around. Inside, we are given our 'complimentary souvenir raincoats' which are basically yellow bin bags with hoods. Like a bunch of bananas, we head down the elevator to walk through the tunnels behind the falls.

It's slippery underfoot and it smells like a damp cellar, but we obediently follow Gladys our Falls guide through each photo opportunity. I am not out of place with my selfie stick as the click-click of a hundred cameras resounds through the tunnels. We are told that 175 million gallons of water crash down every second. If that were beer, I reckon that everyone on the planet would get a pint and a half every minute. Now that's a sobering thought.

Where there are world wonders there is also wonga and the tacky tourist shops are milking it for all its worth. If you can think it, someone has stuck an image or a logo on it and is selling it at triple price. Not just the usual T-shirts and hats but every kind of merchandise imaginable; films, music, books, cutlery, toys, fridge magnets, golf gear, hockey sticks, sweets and yes there is even *Niagara Viagra*, presumably for those elderly gentlemen who couldn't get back up the tunnels.

You can buy a full-size stuffed Moose toy for just $8999.99 but you might have a problem getting it in the car or on the plane home. I bump into Phil and George from *Bristol, UK*. It's their 25th wedding anniversary today and they have dreamed of coming here for soooo long. They bought the handy pocket size moose to take home.

On my birthday three weeks ago, I had decided to treat myself to dinner in the revolving restaurant at the top of the Skylon Tower. I walk through the crowds lining the streets and make my way up the hill to the Disney World style 'town' at the top. I make it just in time to stand in another long queue for my turn to shoot up the elevator in no time at all.

I had carefully timed my reservation so that I could catch the sunset and I was, for a change, spot on. I am led to my table on the circumference of the restaurant. "Hi, I'm Maureen and it's my pleasure to be your wine stewardess for this evening," she says in mono scripted tones. "What can I get you?" I'm tempted to say, "Out of here," but I settle for the Merlot, large. I order the Sea Scallops 'St Jacques' with crab on a bed of spinach with oyster mushrooms and Gruyere cheese served on a shell of course. The scallops are the size of Tunnocks tea cakes and it's creamily delicious. If they could put this in a pie, I would have one for breakfast every day.

One full turn of the wheel and I see the world turning away from the sun for the night. It drops down to its bed and the sky becomes a fiery blanket of crimson, orange, and gold. For the main course, I opt for the Fillet Mignon Béarnaise. My glass is empty from all that spinning around so I order another. I feel like Rockefeller briefly, but hell I'm worth it.

Down below I see the city of tiny lights wake up and twinkle brightly. The Casino sign blinks in red white and blue, the carousel spins and the dinky little cars look like dancing fireflies from up here. The three waterfalls become illuminated at night and I am lost in awe and wonder and wine. The piano players' fingers dance lightly on the keys as he reels off versions of Ellington, Gershwin, and Porter. His rendition of *Maple Leaf Rag* seems lost on this audience though.

This is the high life I muse to myself. Much easier to sit here and watch the world go around than taking my body around the world.

Maureen returns with the bill and the dream collapses into the harsh reality of hard cash. The card reader displays $100 but with a couple of little clicks, the auto service charge sneakily adds on extra numbers along with the sales taxes. $150 all in. Oocha.

I'm running late and take a short cut straight down the steep hill through the woods. I miss the boat on its last journey to the falls but watch from above as the *Maid of the Mist* bravely battles the currents on her journey upstream. The American Falls turn scarlet and I think about all the blood shed on this piece of land and elsewhere. In stark contrast, the Canadian Falls turns into a massive rainbow of light which reflects the diversity and tolerance of this great country.

The welcome centre is no longer welcoming and the staff has hurried home. The car park empty and desolate. The last bus left at 9.17 pm and it's now 10 pm. No buses, no taxis and I'm 89 miles from my train station to take me back to Toronto. Oops. I remember Miguel and call him up. He arrives quickly to my rescue and much to my relief.

"How much to take me to Burlington train station Miguel?" He plays with his dash computer and hits me with the bad news $140. I show him my wallet. I only have $90. I plead and we haggle. Eventually, he agrees to switch the machine off and stuffs the cash on the dash.

"You have to get me there in 90 mins." "OK amigo," he says, and we speed off down the highway.

Ariba, Ariba.

Travel Tip No 3: When travelling on public transport...

A) Find a seat near the map

B) If there is no map then sit near the tannoy or near the driver.

C) Don't wear headphones if choosing option B

Travel Tip No 4: If you must take a nap then ask a fellow traveller to give you a nudge at the required destination. Or set an alarm.

Travel Tip No 5: Always get the times of the last bus and train home.

"Like a tunnel that you follow to a tunnel of its own
Down a hollow to a cavern where the sun has never shone
Like a door that keeps revolving in a half-forgotten dream
Or the ripples from a pebble someone tosses in a stream
Like a clock whose hands are sweeping past the minutes of its face
And the world is like an apple whirling silently in space
Like the circles that you find in the windmills of your mind."

Noel Harrison

The Calgary Cowboys...

September, Days 11-13: 6,500 miles

I travel across another two time zones from Toronto to *Calgary* in the West. I had vowed to try and travel overland rather than take flights. However, it costs $1200 by train travelling for four days and I would have to sleep in a corridor. The flight costs just $200 and I am there in only five hours.

Curtis on AirBnB is my host. He is a folk musician who's seldom here. One of his long-term guests, Paul, kindly shows me around. This is a cool place in a suburban street lined with small wooden bungalows. The furniture and artwork on the walls are up-cycled, retro and funky. There are guitars on the walls and a piano in the lounge. I feel at home. The cushion on the sofa is embroidered with the words 'Love is not getting but giving.'

There are not one but two Volkswagen campers outside. The backyard has a fire pit and a cool seating area under an apple tree smothered in fairy lights. The jewel in the crown is an outside double garage which Curtis has beautifully renovated into a music recording studio and rehearsal space. There is a band inside playing a Neil Young cover which I recognise. A wild mountain hare crouches under one of the sun loungers in the garden. It too seems to know a safe place with good vibes.

In the basement flat lives *Jasmine Lovelle* who is as lovely as her name. We quickly realise that we have a lot in common and we share our recent experiences and revelations about life, relationships, the universe, and everything in between.

A guy appears around the side of the building carrying a large black hold all over his shoulder. He looks like a pizza delivery man. "Is that your dinner?" I ask. "Yeh, these are my greens," she laughs. She is given a pretty little purple bag with string handles and pays the delivery guy $10. She opens it to reveal a vacuum-packed bag of green Sativa buds, another of Indica and some CBD lozenges. "You can order this on the internet now," she informs me, "and it's delivered straight away."

I spend the next day taking it easy. Travelling is demanding work and I need to pace myself. The following day I head to downtown Calgary. This is another huge cosmopolitan city and is now the financial and commercial centre of Canada's oil industry. Although it's Saturday afternoon, the streets are deserted. Despite its dirty business, the streets are squeaky clean but it's sterile, has no soul and seems lifeless to me.

The City is still steeped in the western culture that earned it the nickname *'Cowtown,'* evident in the Calgary Stampede, it's massive July rodeo and festival that grew out of the farming exhibitions once presented here. The horses have long been traded in for 4 x 4's and Jeeps. The Stetsons by baseball caps. Petrol is cheaper here and so are the baseball caps.

I have been trying to book my transport to *Canmore*, but the Greyhound bus website is playing up so I decide to head over there in person. It's a long walk out of town through construction sites. Light snow is starting to fall and it's freezing cold.

Bus stations can be sad and sorrowful places and this one is no exception. There are signs everywhere by 'The Management.' 'No parking here;' 'Stand in Line.' 'No loitering.' 'Don't lean your feet against the wall,' and my favourite; 'No excessive idling.' I decide to idle and loiter a while in the waiting area, but not excessively.

As I am trying to book my ticket, a young guy comes over to me. He smells really bad like he hasn't had a bath for ages. "Excuse me, sir," he says meekly. "Can you help me, please? The woman at that ticket office is not being nice to me and she says I must get my ticket online. Could you try and do that with your phone please?"

His name is David and he tells me that he was staying with his brothers' friends in Calgary. His brother got drunk and started a fight and they were kicked out. "I spent last night in a bus shelter. It was so cold I couldn't sleep. I just want to get home to Vancouver. I have $70." He tells me that his care worker had promised to buy his ticket and send it to the ticket office, but the ticket lady wouldn't help him.

We try on my phone, but the website keeps crashing so I take him back to the ticket desk. The ageing clerkess looks remote, uninterested and she won't look me in the eyes. "Excuse me," I say "What's the problem here? Can we get this guy home please?" "You must book online." she snaps back, never taking her eyes off her own PC. "If we could book online, we wouldn't be standing here in front of you and you would probably be unemployed like David," I say.

She tuts and frowns and eventually informs me that he doesn't have enough money. "Just give him his ticket," I say, "and I'll pay the difference." She has a face on her like she is chewing a wasp and disapprovingly hands me the ticket. "Give it to David please," I say. David is so grateful and with tears in his eyes, he vigorously shakes my hand. "Thank you, Sir, thank you Sir." he repeats. "This means so much to me." "Please don't call me Sir," I reply. "My name is Stewart. Now don't miss your bus."

I arrange to meet Paul downtown and he takes me to *'The Cask'* - a huge pub which sells over 100 draught cask ales. We didn't get to try all of them though. Later we stagger to a club nearby. It's *Depeche Mode Tribute Night*. Paul is slightly younger than me and was a teen during the punk era. We are probably the only two people in here who were around when new wave was the new thing. I am feeling decidedly more old wave now and more old age than new age. Paul knows all the words to all the songs and can sing them pretty well too.

The clientele is an eclectic bunch, but the dress code is strictly black. Fifty shades of black including Gothic black, charcoal black, light black and dark black. My favourite fashionistas are a guy with dreadlocks who wears a long black coat down to his ankles and sports a matching black eye-patch.

His girlfriend towers above him balancing on six-inch heels and she is wearing black tights with unicorns on the knees and black cats' ears on her head. He has to look up to keep an eye on her. I affectionately call them the Pugs - Pirate Guy and Unicorn Girl.

We have a great night and fueled by beer, show off our 'this is how we used to dance to this shit back in the day' moves. Paul insists on paying for the Uber Taxi home.

Next morning, he cooks me a welcome hangover cure of bacon and eggs and again insists on paying for another Uber cab for me to get to the bus station. "You don't need to do that Paul, you have already been too generous," I say. "Well maybe it's catching." he replies. "You helped get one of us home and now I'm helping you."

I say. "Thank you, partner," and ride out of town on a greyhound.

"Feeling unknown
And you're all alone
Flesh and bone
By the telephone
Lift up the receiver
I'll make you a believer
Reach out and touch faith
Your own personal Jesus
Someone to hear your prayers
Someone who cares."

Depeche Mode

Rocky Mountain Way...

October, Days 14-15: 6,575 miles

If Canada is like a pancake smothered in maple syrup, Canmore is like a triple decked black forest gateau lightly sprinkled with icing sugar. It is astonishingly beautiful.

It has been one of my lifelong ambitions to see the Rocky Mountains. That's what watching Yogi bear on television can do to a kid. My favourite song back then was *Burl Ives* version *of 'Big Rock Candy Mountain.'*

My alpine styled hostel sits nestled amongst spruce trees with a breath-taking panorama all around. I am 5,000 feet above sea level and yet these huge mountains tower up all around me. The early light sprinkling of snow highlights their ravines and crevices. In this light, they shine like silver.

Big *Bert McFadden* taxis me in his 4 x 4 up the steep and rough forest track to the hostel. "My ancestors came over from your Western Isles during your highland clearances," he says proudly. Many Canadians share the same story. "Yes, we are all Jock Tampsons bairns," I say. "That Jock had some cock" he crackles. He then warns me to watch out for the grizzly bear as the early winter snap has brought them down from the higher ground and a few have already been seen around town.

I have managed to time my visit to see the famous fall foliage. I drink in the fiery reds and golden yellows of the aspen trees contrasting so strongly with the dark green spruce which look like giant Christmas trees. Trees scrape the skies much more beautifully than buildings ever could.

Canmore is in the *Banff National Park* and it's a popular destination for wealthy tourists, hikers, and rock climbers. The cheapest AirBnB I can find is £150 per night so I decide to rough it with the hikers in a backpacker's hostel for just £40 per night. There are four of us crammed into a bunk room which is smaller than my bathroom.

Still, there is a fully equipped shared kitchen space and a great common room with an open fire. The views from this Swiss-style chalet in the mountains are better than any Toblerone advert.

There are 30 folks staying here and most of them are young people funded by BOMAD. (Bank of Mom and Dad). After a dinner of beans and rice, I sit in the communal area plugged into the free Wi-Fi system.

Some of these girls look like athletes and I'm guessing they are rock climbers. They have bodies like hourglasses but with deltoids and pecks on them worthy of any arm wrestler. They are doing impossible stretches and yoga moves on the floor next to me.

Bruce from Australia is talking, "I did Kilimanjaro last year." Ella from France is tres impressed. "Wow," she replies. "That is so cool. Have you been to Thailand?" "Yeh" says Bruce, "I helped with the elephants." "Wow," says Ella. "Do you scuba dive?" asks Bruce.

"Oui," says Ella. "I swam with the great white sharks off Fuji." "Wow," says Bruce. And so it continues as they share their respective worlds of wonders.

I have booked a seat on the more serene Hop-on-Banff bus tour for the next day. It's a new young company which rents local distinctive yellow school buses to take sightseers on a guided tour through the mountains. It leaves Banff at 8.30 am but I must get over there first. I set my alarm for 6.30 am and on wakening, discover that my roommates are already up and gone on their respective treks. Wow!

At the reception desk, they are selling bear spray for $35. The thought of facing up to a 700 lb. grizzly with a can of hair spray does not reassure me. Instead, I'll just have to find a walking partner who can't run as fast as me. That's going to be difficult here. Anyway, I have my whistle.

The snow has fallen through the night, transforming the woods into a winter wonderland. Robert kindly offers me a lift down to the Highway, which ironically travels along the lowest part of the valley. He is completing his Mountain Guide training. "Get paid for what you love doing, right?" he says. "That's the good life," I agree.

After he drops me off, I realise that I am no longer on my planned route recommended by Google maps. It tells me to take a shortcut through the forest. However, no one told Google about the hungry grizzlies, so I decide to walk on along the snow-covered road.

Bear in area
Travel with caution

Ours dans le secteur. Advancez prudement

My fitbitch watch buzzes to let me know that I have done my 3 miles for today. And it's not even 8 am! Go me. After a few wrong turns, slips and slides, I finally, make it to the bus stop just as the local *Roam* bus arrives. There's a big box of free books to borrow and a bike rack full of bikes.

The clouds are low, and the snow is falling. The mountains look like they are covered in big fluffy white bathrobes. Every so often they reveal a tantalising glimpse of their majestic forms.

We sell bear spray at the front desk:

$35

Our first stop is the famous *Fairmont Chateau* at Lake Louise. It's a really posh 500-bedroom hotel and spa which looks out over the lake with the Victoria glacier at its far end. "This is the highest settlement in Canada," says Tyler, our tour guide. "It was originally built as a base for outdoor enthusiasts in 1890." It's now a shopping Mecca for the rich. There are spectacular views from the dining room, but not today.

Thick pile carpets and elegant furnishings welcome me into the cosy Grand Foyer. On the walls, the glass eyes of moose, deer and caribou look down lifelessly on the guests and tourists below. There are posh boutique shops and a brassiere, but I don't have enough brass to buy anything. I grab a coffee in the deli cafe for just $5.

Half of these folk are Chinese and Japanese. (The face masks and umbrellas are a dead giveaway.) Don't they know that the air here is crystal clear and that umbrellas are just so silly under these soft snowflakes? And how do they eat so much and still stay so small?

Cameras click incessantly. I imagine that at some time in the future, Google will piece them all together in a virtual 3D jigsaw of this wonderful world. If we mess up this one, they might be able to recreate a holographic replica. Perhaps they already have, and we just think that this is the real deal.

I hop on the next school bus and soon I am hiking up the gorgeous *Johnston Canyon* with its sparkling waterfalls of turquoise blue. Further on we visit Moraine Lake. It's featured on the Canadian $10 banknote, but the view is priceless. Today, the colours of the sun have been filtered out into monotones. However, the lake below us still shines in iridescent blueness.

"It's a spectacular illusion of nature," explains our guide. "Tiny mineral particles are ground down like flour by the powerful glacier and then flow down into the lake. Only the blue part of the full rainbow spectrum of the sunlight is reflected back to us." But to me, it's simply magic as it looks like *Wicked Blue* Vodka.

We have had to climb high to get this view from above and coming back down, the icy path is steep and treacherous. Strangers join hands to prevent each other from falling. The bigger ones at the front will serve as a bouncy cushion if we slip. "My wife just turned eighty," informs my handheld companion. "Like wine, she just gets better with age."

I have always felt that there is something very spiritual about mountains. And have heard it said many times that people feel closer to God at the tops of them. Life's' dramas, which may seem huge from below, seem to shrink into oblivion when viewed from a higher perspective and a slower time frame. Simply being around mountains helps remind me that at least some things in our rapidly changing world seem constant and eternal. As do the stars above them. And that our own lives are just a short blip in time compared to theirs.

This place is a tonic for the soul. The air, pure and clean with just a hint of pine and berry. With the snow falling gently, it looks and feels like Christmas. A million Christmas trees line the roads wearing elegant white petticoats. They curtsy as we pass. The snow clouds evaporate to reveal the towering mountains, chiseled, dark and full of mystery.

High in the sky, I can see the victory flight of the snow geese heading north to their breeding grounds in the Arctic Circle. Tomorrow these two feet and my *Osprey* bag are heading south.

"Oh, the buzzing' of the bees in the cigarette trees,
The soda water fountain,
Where the lemonade springs and the bluebird sings
In that Big Rock Candy Mountain."

Harry McClintock

Dark and Light in Vancouver...

October, Days 16-19: 7,215 miles

Another two feet of snow has fallen overnight and the roads are gridlocked with stranded cars. No one expected this much snow so early in the season. My bus is running three hours late and I make conversation with the only other patient traveller at the bus station.

Roselle is carrying two rucksacks and a huge black bag. "That looks like a really big guitar," I quip. "Ha-ha, it's my skis," she tells me. "It looks like you might need them now," I reply. She tells me that she has been home visiting her mum who is unwell. She is heading back to *Salt Lake City* where she works, planting trees. "It's demanding work, but I love being outside and we will need to plant many more trees if we are to help slow this climate change."

"I have never met a Stewart before." she laughs. "And I have never met a Roselle before." I reply. "But look, we are wearing the exact same boots. Brown *Dr Martins* with yellow thread around the soles." They leave the exact same footprints in the snow. "What are the chances of that?" I ask. "Yes," she says, "We are all connected, and maybe through our souls." she laughs.

Our bus finally arrives, and it races bravely down the frozen mountain roads trying to make up time. It's a 13-hour journey to *Vancouver* and we arrive at midnight. I am wondering if West coasters are fundamentally different from East coasters, everywhere, all over the world. Do early sunrises encourage the more industrious early birds and

conversely, are beautiful sunsets preferred by the more sociable ones. Like larks and owls? If so, then I should feel more at home here.

I've been looking forward to getting to the West Coast and staying in the same time zone for a while. Vancouver is another huge city with more than 2.5 million people and its renowned for its scenic beauty and mild temperatures. My AirBnB host is Ray, a sprightly, blue-eyed 72-year-old who sports a long white wizard's beard. "You're just 100 yards from our sky train," he says. "It will take you to every part of town and your travel card also works on all of the bus routes."

I am tucking into my oats and berries in *Tim Hortons* (Canada's healthier fast-food alternative to *MacDonald's*). Right outside my window, there's a middle-aged woman on her hands and knees scraping the dirt and cigarette butts from between the flagstones. She is wearing blue rubber gloves and is using a metal toothpick to scrape the bubble gum from the slabs. She is so hardworking and smiles broadly to every passer-by.

Feeling remorseful for every cigarette butt that I have mindlessly thrown away, I decide to repent with a small offering. "You are working so hard and seem so happy at your work." I say, "I want to give you this in appreciation." Her name is Jane and she mumbles and smiles as she stuffs my offering into her pocket and carries on scraping.

I head for the City library, a good place to plan my

itinerary. It's on eight floors with a newly opened garden rooftop cafe. It's designed like the *Colosseum in Rome* and it's colossal. How have we created so many books with only 26 letters of the alphabet? I muse. And here's me now adding to the sum of human verbiage. There's a lift and I jump in.

The eighth floor is pleasantly book and bookworm free. Instead, there are shrubs in the sunshine and wonderful views across the rooftops. I decide to head for *Stanley Park,* a massive public area on an island straddling North and South Vancouver. There's a statue of *Robert Burns* here, and the first purpose-built library, the Carnegie, was paid for by Scotland-born U.S. industrialist and philanthropist *Andrew Carnegie.* The Scottish influence is very noticeable across Canada but especially here.

The musty smell of damp earth and the sweetness of ripening blueberries draw me into the forest. This smells just like home. Pine trees, birch and maples surround Beaver Lake in the centre of the park. My sandals scrunch through the dried maple leaves as squirrels play in the trees above. A cheeky chipmunk darts across my path, pausing briefly to look at me, its cheeks stuffed with hazelnuts.

Somewhere in the distance, a lone piper is playing *'The Skye Boat'* song. This even sounds like home. In the forest, saplings sprout upwards from the decaying stumps of their ancestors, recycling nutrients harvested in the past. Nothing is ever wasted here. Life constantly regenerates in an endless flow, cycles of birth and rebirth. I walk into a clearing filled with totem poles, a tribute to those who came before. We too stand on the shoulders of giants.

A hydroplane thunders above me, flying tourists over the *Lion Gate Bridge.* There are water taxis here too. It's getting late and Google maps indicate the best way home is by bus. I start walking and stop in past a run-down corner shop for cigarettes.

As I enter, the smell hits me. "Do you sell weed here?" I ask curiously. "No, but I do!" a voice behind me proclaims. I turn around and am looking up to a tall bald guy with a huge grin and big ears just like Mickey Mouse. Funnily enough, his name is Mikey. "I guess I am a walking advert" he laughs. "Come around to my place and you can have some."

I know this is risky, but I trust him and follow him around the corner through a discrete door and into another building. We pass through dirty narrow corridors with dozens of brown doors leading off them. This must be like a prison, I think, but dirtier.

Mikey's' room 123 is on the first floor. There is no window and it has barely enough space for his single bed, a table, and a chair. And for this, he pays $500 a month. "That's half of my benefits cheque," he tells me. "At least this one has a lock on the door." There must be a thousand rooms in this eight-storey building just like this."

"I came over from Toronto after my wife died from an overdose," he says. "It's warmer here and the weed keeps me off the crack. I'll be Ok if I can just keep it together. We talk about grief and letting go. "I was in Toronto and met a guy called Irish." I say. He looks at me astonished, "O.G. Irish? - he is a friend of mine!" It's a small world.

He opens a drawer to reveal huge bags of grass. "My oils are sold out. This is Kush, which is strong, I have some Indica to help you sleep or some Sativa?" I offer him $20 and he weighs out enough to fuel a rock band. "Listen Mikey," I say. Just give me a couple of buds and keep the change." "Cheers man." he shakes my hand and I wish him well with his self-medicated rehab.

He guides me out of the rabbit warren and back into the street. I head east and there's a skirmish across the road, angry voices shouting. Further down the block, I see the homeless ones starting to line the streets. Like birds finding their roosts for the night, they are fighting for the best spots, squabbling over newspaper and cardboard to sleep on. My bus stop is down that block, so I hide my phone and start walking.

On both sides of the street, they are gathering. Not hundreds but thousands. Not one block but four. This is *East Hastings* and I am walking through the valley of the shadow of death. Sodom and Gomorrah. I am not afraid, but I am deeply shocked at the scale of this apocalyptic scene. It's the Night of the Living Dead. People in rags, many with missing limbs. Smoking crack from beer tins and helping each other fix-up. Crazy laughter and angry shouts fill the night.

A woman stumbles past me poking her eyes with her fingers and muttering "I hate these eyes, I hate these fucking eyes." An empty bottle spins across the sidewalk towards me. I realise that I am the only person here with decent shoes and a backpack. I need to get away from here fast and find that bus stop. There is only one way out and that's forward.

A good friend once gave me some sound advice before I left. "When you find yourself in a dodgy neighborhood, just walk like a boss, like you own the place and know where you are going. And never look a mad dog in the eye."

I stride on purposefully, eyes forward and away from the depravity that surrounds me. My inner warrior stirs and I glance back. There is a guy who I saw earlier a few blocks back. He is slightly better dressed and fitter looking than the rest. I am sure that he is following me. I stop and look in a dirty window and he stops too, looking down and shuffling his feet. I walk on and he continues to shadow me. I pull my backpack strap tight, find my whistle, raise my frequency, and put my adrenaline on standby.

At last, I see the bus shelter. From its relative safety, I turn and face him. I narrow my eyes in my best *Bruce Lee* impersonation and slowly shake my head. The shadow is revealed, and he turns back down the street disappearing into the darkness. Phew!

Next morning over coffee, I recount my experience to Ray. "Listen Stewart," he says gently. "I know you were trying to be kind helping that street cleaner but your $10 is already in the hands of her crack dealer. You are naive, my friend. What you saw is classic crack behavior. It makes you crazy and you obsess over tiny details. There are hundreds of people like her on the streets. I know because I was one of them. OK here's my story..."

"My father was a brutal and angry person. He would beat my mom and he would drive me and my brother to school with a bottle of whisky between his feet. Glug, glug, glug. Every time we stopped at traffic lights, glug, glug, glug. One day he stopped the car in a layby and threw the half-filled bottle away. "Boys," he said, "That's the last time you will see your daddy drunk."

"He was 42 years old and he is now 91. He is still a bad bastard but a sober one," he laughs. "Thirty years later and I am going down that same road. Glug, glug, glug. I kept losing jobs, my wife left me and, at 42 I tasted my first crack pipe. The moment I felt it, I thought, this is the drug for me. Only two words kept repeating in my brain for the next 18 years. "More. Again. More. Again."

"Every cent I could find went to the crack dealer. I lost my home, my family, my clothes, and my dignity. More. Again. More. Again. I even stole my mom's jewellery to pay for it." Tears welled up and fell from Ray's eyes as he continued his story.

"Eventually I stopped eating. I even gave up alcohol to buy that shit. More, Again. More. Again. At the age of 60, I gave it all up; crack, meth, heroin, alcohol, weed, even tobacco. I have been clean for the last 12 years. It's all poison for the soul man. People everywhere are choosing poison over life. Not just drink and drugs but they do it with food, money, sex, gambling. It's life or death and the choice is ours. It's that simple."

"What turned you around?" I ask. "I got pulled over for a series of driving violations and sent to jail for 12 months. Inside, I started to recover enough to request rehab and I did another six months there. It's on an island off the coast. We had the best treatment you could imagine. I went fishing a lot but there was even a golf course in there.

The food was better than any hotel, 'T' bone steaks every day. And I got the best group therapy and started to talk about what had happened to me. In Canada we don't see drug users as criminals but as victims.

I was raped at the age of six and that's the same story for lots of them. I am one of the incredibly lucky ones," he says, "I'm one in a thousand. Nine hundred people have died on that street this year and it's only October. It's the road to hell my friend. It's the last stop before death. The road to revelation can be a long and painful one."

Next morning Ray knocks on my door at 5 am. "I have booked and paid for your taxi," he says, "and breakfast is ready." "That's not part of the deal Ray" I protested. "You see" he laughed. "You're just like me, you can give but you just can't take. Now shut up and eat your omelette."

Another hug and then I empty my pockets of cigarettes, the remaining weed, and the yellow cigarette lighter that O. G. Irish gave me. I throw them straight into Ray's garbage bin. He nods solemnly and smiles at me with his twinkly blue eyes.

"I've seen the needle and the damage done ,
A little part of it in everyone ,
But every junkie's like a setting' sun."
Neil Young

Portland, Oregon...

October, Days 20-25: 7,553 miles

Anneka meets me off the train in *Portland*. She is the daughter of a dear friend of mine who passed on some years earlier. Just like Ken, her dad, she is full of enthusiasm and has my visit all planned out. "You are staying at my Uncle Bills, she says excitedly. "You'll love him. But first, you need to unwind from your travels."

We drive up the magnificent *Columbia River Gorge* and stop for an herbal refreshment. The mountains here are extraordinary and rise up like tall brown Panettoni. We pass the *Multnomah Falls*. A stunning 600-foot silver stream of water pours from the cliffs above. There is a beautiful walking bridge halfway up.

According to Native American lore, the Waco tribe who once lived here were dying from a devastating plague. The daughter of the chief jumped from the top of the cliffs as a sacrificial offering to appease the Great Spirit, and the tribe recovered. When her father asked Great Spirit if his daughter was safe in the afterlife, a silvery stream of water started to cascade down the mountain. Some say that in winter her spirit can be seen. Dressed in white she stands and looks upon the place where she gave her life for her people.

We arrive at *Carson Hot Mineral Springs*. Xavier shows me around the facility. It was built in the 1930s and has seen better days. The smell of sulphur and minerals is strong and the sounds of gushing water echo around the concrete walls. There are massage beds and a dozen white enameled bathtubs with claw hammer feet.

A few fat old men sit around naked, sweating and farting. Some of them have bellies bigger than my rucksack. Whatever the health benefits, weight loss isn't one of them. I am soon submerged in the smelly hot water and all my aches and pains just melt away. Aaaaah My skin soaks in the minerals washed down from *Mount Hood*; Sulphur, Magnesium, Potassium, Calcium and Sodium permeate my pores and work their magic to my core.

An ice-cold bath follows and then I lie down on one of the beds. "Would you like a tight wrap or just a covering," asks Xavier. "Oh, just cover me up" I reply shyly. "I'll tap your toes in 25 minutes and then you can have a cool drink of water or a coffee. I bet it's *'Camp.'*

Aurora is a quirky small town. There is something strange here which I can't yet fathom. It reminds me of that weird 90's TV series *Twin Peaks* by *David Lynch* which I later discover was filmed nearby. The pumpkins must have ripened early this year. Their scary faces leer out from the windows of houses and shops. Outside the doors are spooky specters, vampire bats and skeletons. Halloween must be a hoot here but I'm glad I will miss it.

I walk into the only *Colony Pub* and a dozen faces turn to stare at me. "Well lookee here, there's a stranger in town." Two huge TV's dominate the bar. One is showing baseball. It's a bit like cricket but with

stupid round bats. On the other is American football which is a bit like rugby except they wear crash helmets and have smaller balls.

This is farmers, truckers, and logger's country. The patrons swear and wear torn checked armless shirts revealing hairy muscled arms. And that's just the women. My cup of tea is served with two plastic drinking straws in it and I must request cutlery. "If you mean silverware, it's over there!" tuts Ashley, this year's winner of the towns' customer service prize.

I feel like a character in a *Bart Simpson* cartoon and I'm drinking in *Moes Bar*. "Can someone check the washroom for a Hugh Jass?" Duh. Despite its apparent shallow mediocrity, I'm about to get to know some of the most beautifully eccentric and inspiring characters I have ever met.

Anneka's Uncle Bill Frazier, a seventies something Qigong teacher, acupuncturist, professor of all things esoteric and second-hand Persian carpet dealer is my most affable host. He reminds me of Professor Dumbledore in Harry Potter with his white rumpled hair and beard.

Bill has been practising a specific variation of an internal practice known as *Qigong* for forty years and has become a well-loved teacher to a loyal group of young students. He practices for three hours a day and exercises a strict daily routine including meditation and resting in his hot tub. This combined with his daily diet of brown rice, yoghurt, popsicles and gin clearly attribute to his good health and vitality.

He invites me to sit in on one of his lectures and soon we are transported, as though on a magic carpet ride, back in time through Chinese dynasties. We learn the secrets of the *'Armour of the Golden Bell,'* a specialised technique to develop Chi to such a level that it is said that the warriors were even impervious to the bullets of their Western foes. Sadly, this claim was proven to be untrue during the 'Boxer Revolution.' He is a wise and humorous teacher and I can see why his students adore him. He reminds me a lot of my friend Ken, and I discover that they met in the early '70s at a nearby intentional community called *The Two Rivers Farm*.

From my room balcony, I can hear the familiar sounds of scolding blackbirds and the chattering of sparrows and starlings. But there are new creatures also. Azure backed blue jays shriek through the laurel trees which are festooned with tiny finches and other birds unknown to me.

At night I can hear the coyote howl and yelp like jackals. There are also foxes, raccoons, gofer, and tiny ground squirrels with antennae tails pointing skyward. I have lots of roommates in the form of box elder beetles. But they are friendly and don't bite.

Just 50 yards from my room, the train line crosses the main road. The entire house shakes when the freight and passenger trains roar past; their horns blaring like the seven trumpets of Babylon. I love that sound. During the first night, they wake me up every time they pass. After three nights I only hear the one which goes past when it's time to wake up.

Mike Byrnes bought the derelict town granary in Aurora in 1999. He had a smaller shop in nearby Portland but acquired items faster than he could sell them. "I just needed a bigger place to store everything." he says.

When you walk into this place it is mind-blowing. Every inch of space is crammed with salvaged and restored vintage items. Hundreds of brass door knockers, metal signs from bygone days, antique furniture, farming equipment and shiny old cash registers which cost a fortune. "Who does the dusting?" I ask. "It's a family business," he laughs, "and we all take our turn." People keep replacing old things with new and he is quick to snap up the old stuff and save it for a later day. He's going to need a bigger store soon.

I take a stroll through the town and down a wood-lined track. There are unusual wooden artworks along the path. Tree roots are carved into beautiful scenes of deer, salmon and first nation symbols. Wooden angels hang from the trees and full-sized Buddha's guide the way. It's like an art installation but it is clearly permanent. However, the ivy and mosses are slowly reclaiming them as they decay back to the soil from where they originated.

Jim appears on his tractor. He is the wood sculptor. We make acquaintance and he shows me around his 'work' place. "I was a woodworker making tables and functional furniture but my time at the Farm gave me the confidence to discover my inner artist. I carved my first Buddha years ago and have been making them ever since. The wood guides me in what it wants to express."

His garden is not only beautiful but functional. "I grow most things we eat here," he says. I'll cook your dinner while you look around." There are lots of colourful Salvias planted in his garden and they are buzzing with hummingbirds. I am in awe as these tiny beauties zoom by like miniature helicopters. There must be hundreds here.

"These little fellas have a tough time in life." he says. "They get eaten by owls and other birds and many of them die when they migrate south to Mexico and South America. It feels good to give them a little help."

We share our love of birds and soon we are tucking into a delicious vegetable stew cooked on his barbecue. Jim seems as though he is really stoned and living in a dream world. But he is not. "I practice meditation for three hours every day," he tells me. "Tibetan Buddhism is my chosen path. I first learned about this at the Farm. Everything is connected and nothing really matters except what we are experiencing right now. You just gotta do what you love."

Afterwards, Jim walks me back up the track. "Here," he says. "Have this squash, it's delicious and these pineapple tomatoes are outrageous." Chilies, peppers, eggplants, and kale follow. "There's plenty here for all of us." he says. With arms full of vegetables, I head for home.

All these people including my friend Ken met in the Seventies at The Two Rivers Farm. It was set up by a follower of *Gurdjieff*, a mystic, philosopher, and spiritual teacher. He taught that most humans live their lives in a state of hypnotic 'waking sleep', but that it's possible to awaken to a higher state of unified consciousness and achieve full human potential through a technique which he called *'The Work.'*

I am curious to find out more about this place and how it so profoundly affected these wonderfully eccentric individuals. Mike meets me at *The White Rabbit Cafe* and gives me a lift over to The Farm where I walk around the fields of apples, walnuts, and hazelnuts. Oregon grows 4% of the world's supply of hazelnuts and most of these are bought by *Ferraro Roche* and converted into gold.

I am walking past the small Waldorf School when one of the teachers waves at me and we talk. She introduces me to Carl the principal. "You need to come back here and help us set up a LETS (Local Exchange Trading System)" he says. "Come on, I'll walk you over to meet Margaret, Ken's ex-wife and mum to Anneka."

I'm soon sitting drinking proper English tea and connecting the dots of the people I have met from the present back into the past. It's quite incredible to me that occasionally certain individuals appear in this world who affects us so deeply that they create a legacy which continues well into the future. Their ideas take root in the minds of others and live on through them, influencing future generations and shaping the world in which we now live. *Gurdjieff* was certainly one of those.

The three characters I have described, share some things in common (apart from all being over seventy years young and much younger at heart). Firstly, they are completely dedicated to their own 'Work' whatever that is, regardless of social norms and its' need for them to conform.

Secondly, they are all actively passing on the gift they have discovered within themselves to others. And last but not least, they are doing this with humility and kindness, patience and understanding.

I am looking deep into the pond in Jim's garden. Caddis fly larvae are crawling along the bottom. They are basically tiny maggots with arms, little sacks of skin with a tube in the middle. A mouth at one end and an anus at the other.

They carefully collect tiny particles of stone and glass to create a beautiful protective crust of jewelled body armour. Each one is unique and magnificent in its own way.

Are we humans so very different?

"We are stardust, we are golden
We are billion-year-old carbon
And we got to get ourselves back to the garden."

Crosby, Stills & Nash

Bianca and The Giant Redwoods...

October, Days 26-31: 8,690 miles

As I drop down to land in *San Francisco*, I look down and see wind and kite surfers skimming over the sea. I can also see the Golden Gate Bridge in the distance and that's what I hope to be crossing over tomorrow. I'm renting a car to do a wide sweep of the coast and countryside around the bay in search of the giant sequoias, the largest trees in the world.

Anneka's' friends Amber, Johann and their cute dog Frankie, kindly pick me up from the airport and give me a sofa for the night. In appreciation, I offer to buy dinner in the local pub down by the beach. The band is playing *Stevie Ray Vaughan "Riviera Paradise"* as I tuck into prawns the size of my thumbs.

The next day we go to the car rental company. I am feeling very anxious about this. I have never driven on the wrong side of the road from the passenger seat before and I am not familiar with this crazy road system. I have reserved a nice small manual Rav 4 with four-wheel drive for off-road driving. However, they tell me that they have all gone and, instead they are giving me a Subaru 3.5i. It's a powerful automatic and it's the size of a small boat.

There are more switches on the steering wheel than the *Starship Enterprise* and I haven't a clue what they all do. It comes with all the mod cons though - Concession Fee x 11%, State Tax x 9%, CA Tourism Commission $4/day, Insurance $18/day, Sat Nav $8/day etc. The final bill is double the headline rate and I feel conned and

unhappy. This is not what I wanted.

There's no handbrake, just a silly button. I hate this car already and I'm really anxious now. I can't even get it into drive mode and Johann explains that I must depress the footbrake before I do so. Jeez! Help! "We'll convoy you to the expressway and then just follow the signs for the *Golden Gate Bridge*. Stay with the traffic and follow the Sat Nav. You'll be fine," he says, but I notice that he is biting his lip.

We move off slowly and I follow carefully. I have no sense of the size of this vehicle and the lanes in the City are narrow with lots of road works. I don't understand most of the road signs anyway, so I just concentrate on keeping up with the car in front. Soon my friends take their exit and I am slingshot into three lanes of traffic heading north and over the Golden Gate Bridge. Gulp! There are lots of birds of prey circling in the sky. Or are they vultures? Either way, I hope I don't end up as their next roadkill.

I just have to remember to steer straight, only use my right foot for gas on the right, look to the left, go with the flow, and follow the signs. But which lane is the inside lane? Drivers overtake and undertake me on both sides and the lanes seem really narrow, especially sandwiched between two huge trucks. Yikes! I stay in the middle and soon we merge with another three lanes going in the same direction. Yes, that's six lanes, on each side! Highway 101 is wider than the length of my High Street back home. And still, the cars bunch up and get jammed.

I decide to exit and take the coastal road instead. It's a 'normal' road with just one lane each way. "I am rerouting you to the shoreline highway, take next right." The car says. People don't overtake on these roads; everyone just drives at 5 mph above the speed limit and goes with the flow. At junctions and crossroads, there are no roundabouts. Every car must stop and the person who got to the line first has right of way.

You can also go through red lights to turn right if there is no traffic on that lane. It's simple and seems to work well. I didn't see any cop cars or accidents, it's mostly radar-controlled or policed by aircraft. These roads are silky smooth with few potholes. The traffic signs are clear and simple. And they have a clever way of indenting the edges of the surface. So, when I stray over them, the vibrations tingle right up my base chakra in a not entirely unpleasant way.

My hands are sweating, and my shoulders ache tight. But I start to relax. Through winding roads and beautiful coastal scenery, we glide. This car handles really well, and the automatic gearbox is really quite good. I'm getting a feel for this machine. It's even got air conditioning which is cool. Eventually, I stop and read the manual. This is a talking car - yes you heard me correctly. "The door is a jar." she informs me. That will be handy in a traffic jam.

The talking sat nav soothes me with reassuring instructions though. "In a quarter of a mile take the second junction on the right along *Del Monty Avenue*." She seems to know exactly where she is going, and she is usually right. She is always calm, and she even reroutes me when I go astray. And she has a sweet and lovely voice. Indeed, she is the very best travelling companion and I name her Bianca because she is bright and white. I like this car.

She has a LOUD 4 door stereo system with blueteeth connecting to the music library on my phone. "Bianca, play The Eagles, Hotel California, Loud. "Yes of course," she replies obediently.

"On a dark desert highway, cool wind in my hair,
Warm smell of colitas, rising up through the air."

I am staying for just one night with *Ivy Hunter*, her dog and two cats in her lovely AirBnB cabin. In a gypsy styled room in *Gypsy Hollow* deep in the woods. The house sits on a steep hill and from the balcony; I am looking straight into the forest with a 50' drop below me. It's like being in a treehouse.

I am in search of the big trees, the giant sequoia of the *Sierra Nevada Mountains.* Ivy knows her trees and loves to trek and forage. She gives me great advice on where to head and I decide to drive east across the mountains to the desert beyond. Then I will return through *Yosemite National Park to Sonora* where I am staying for two nights. After that, I might head back to the coast south of San Francisco in a big circle, stopping by *Monterey* to see the whales.

It's a 900-mile road trip over six nights covering a lot of different ground and roads. It's great to have the freedom to just go where I'm drawn. This car has enough space for a queen-sized bed in the back and I haven't booked anywhere to stay for tonight. In *Santa Rosa*, I find a thrift shop and for less than $10 I leave with a *'Snoopy Dog'* circular pillow and a thick *'Paddington Bear'* sleeping bag - clean and fresh as new.

We drive for ten hours through flat farming country, past huge expanses of apple orchards, hops, and cornfields. This is also California wine country and there are miles of neatly trimmed vineyards. The roads are straight and seem to go on forever. In the distance, the gently rolling hills look as though they are covered in soft suede. We are purring along at an easy 60 mph and we haven't seen another car for ages.

It's time to see what Bianca is hiding under her pretty white bonnet. I floor the pedal; she drops two gears and growls as she lunges forward like a beast unleashed. My head is pushed back on the headrest and my fingers tighten on the wheel as she climbs effortlessly through 70, 80, 90 mph. The red dial eases through 100 and she feels safe and firm on the road. 110, 120 mph.

The clock goes all the way up to 150 mph, but I chicken out at 130 mph. My new personal land speed record. "Wow Bianca, you have hidden talents, I love you." "I don't know that destination." she replies. Man and machine meld together into cyborg romance. Yes, I am in love with a car.

Sometimes not getting what you want is the best thing that can happen.

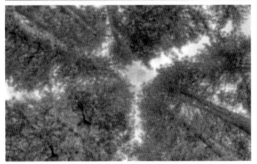

In the rear-view mirror, I watch as the sun seems to inflate in a last gasp of golden bright, turning the fields and hills into a fiery landscape. It gets dark and we drive on together through the night. When I get too tired, we pull into a gas station in the middle of nowhere. They sell everything here; hot food, coffee, liquor, groceries, and there is a washroom with showers for the truckers.

I ask Tony where the nearest civilisation is and if there are any campsites nearby where I could sleep in my car. She laughs "This is it, fella. The nearest town is 90 miles away. But you can sleep in the staff car lot round the back and have a hot shower in the morning. We are open all night if you need anything."

It's dark at 8 pm so Bianca and I find a quiet corner in the car park and soon we are snuggled down together for a surprisingly good sleep. "Will I lockup and shut down or would you like to ride some more?" she asks. Ooh, Bianca!

I'm wide awake at 4 am. It's dark and cold and there's not a breath of wind outside. After a quick shower and a pint of coffee to go, I am also good to go. Coffee cups are bigger than pint glasses over here.

The roads are empty, and I have just four hours if I want to make it to the top of the mountain to see the heart of the sunrise. Soon we are climbing through dark winding roads cutting deep into the forest,

This must be *Stanislaus National Forest* and there is nobody about. No houses and no streetlights either. Bianca glides around the sweeping bends like a barn owl in flight. As silent as a lover's whisper.

A road sign tells me that we are at Elevation 4,000.' That's as high as Ben Nevis. 5,000' and the sound system is playing all my favourite tunes. 6,000' and Sly is singing, "I want to take you higher." 7,000' and still we climb. 8,000' the headlights pick out the silhouettes of beautiful trees on either side as we weave our way up the mountain. At 9,000' the white granite rocks take on a strange blue luminescence. The tree bark turns pink and red as though someone has dusted the trees with chalk. It's probably some fluorescent red lichen says my scientific brain.

A deer is standing at the side of the road. Still, just watching with bright eyes, her ears long and alert. I pull over, stop, and get out of the car. This place seems strangely familiar. The weathered rocks, the ancient gnarled trees, the sage grasses, the smells. Is this another deja vu or a past life memory? Maybe I'm just remembering some old *John Wayne* movie.

I wind down the windows, turn the music up loud and switch off the lights. My eyes get used to the darkness and the stars turn into bright crystals. It's pitch dark with no one around me for maybe 30 miles or more. The air is dry and thin and it's minus 10 degrees. I gasp like a fish out of water, steam rising on my out-breath. There are mountain lions up here, rattlesnakes and bears. It's pitch black but I step outside.

The big dipper is fully dipped, its panhandle pointing straight down. Orion is high and at an angle that I have never seen before. The Milky Way spirals silver and deep violet. It is silent and SO magnificent. I am filled with gratitude for everything, past and present. For everyone who has ever known me, both friend and foe, and for every event, both good and bad, that led me to this incredible experience, right here, right now.

I feel so alone and infinitely small in this vast space and I seem to shrink and disappear. The car stereo plays *Adagio by Safri Duo* which fills the void and the soaring strings echo across the canyon. The music builds and I am overwhelmed. As the sun rises, my heart expands like a warm balloon and saltwater flows from my eyes. This must be what Joy feels like.

Soon, the darkness turns to pale blue. I count eight aircraft high above. They slice the sky like silver paper cuts. The sun comes up, its blood orange light slowly flowing down from the mountain tops like golden honey. The desert smells of sage, pinyon pine and juniper berries. It's a new day and it's so good to be alive in this beautiful world.

I drive back west across the mountains through Yosemite National Park. It's famed for its giant, ancient sequoia trees, and for *Tunnel View*, the iconic vista of towering *Bridal Veil Fall*, the granite cliffs of *El Capitan* and *Half Dome*. The air is so clean here and every twist on the

road reveals a stunning new vista.

We finally make it to our next stop in *Sonora*. We have driven 500 miles in 24 hours but have yet to see a single sequoia. I am staying with Dianne in her beautiful garden sanctuary complete with pool and hot tub. Dianne is a professional astrologer and health therapist, and this is the perfect place to recover and unwind. She also gives me lots of good travel tips and sends me on my way to *Calaveras.*

This forest is full of huge trees, Douglas fir, Spruce and Pines but nothing prepares you for your first sighting of the Giant Sequoia. They glow golden in this light towering so high in the sky like solemn cathedrals. Other trees are dwarfed in comparison.

The early white settlers who discovered them cut down the largest one to make a ten-pin bowling alley. It was over 3,000 years old, 25' wide across the base and weighed 2,600 tons. Thankfully, these trees are now cherished and well protected. Majesty is too great a word to be used for a mere mortal monarch. These Giants are the true Majestic Ones.

Occasionally two trees growing close together will simply merge into one, cooperating and sharing the light from above and the nutrients from the soil below. I find a quiet place at the foot of one of them. Its bark is like the fur of a scraggy brown bear and it feels surprisingly soft and smells of old carpet.

There is still the scent of smoke from last year's forest fires which destroyed so many trees. In silence, the birds soon reappear from their watching places. Red-crested woodpeckers drum noisily on the dead tree stumps. Tree creepers creep around the trunks of the smaller trees and a charm of goldfinches flutter in the bushes.

Every so often, there is a crash and a huge pinecone, even bigger than my big head, falls from high. The seeds within will feed the deer, chipmunks, and squirrels. Some of them will be buried and forgotten and grow into the giants of the future. They could be fully mature by 5,000 AD. Even these seemingly immortal beings will die eventually. There are several lying on the ground, slowly decaying like the carcasses of giant whales.

I feel refreshed and reinvigorated and head for home. I am told that the Humpback whales are feeding in the bay. "Bianca, put some flowers in your hair, we are going to *San Francisco*."

Oh, and play *The Byrds - I wasn't born to follow.*

"No, I'd rather go and journey
Where the diamond crescent's glowing
And run across the valley
Beneath the sacred mountain
And wander through the forest
Where the trees have leaves of prisms
And break the light in colours
That no one knows the names of."

The Byrds

Whale watching in Monterey...

October, Days 31-32: 8,803 miles

Monterey Pop was held in the summer of 1967, at the fairgrounds in *Monterey*, California, down the coast from San Francisco. It was pivotal in rock's evolution as a force in the entertainment business and the culture at large. It served as the blueprint for the explosion of rock festivals that culminated in Woodstock with its crowds of face-painted hippies and slogan of 'make love not war.'

Monterey defined the look, spirit, and sound of 'The Summer of Love.' Janis Joplin was discovered here, and Jimi Hendrix famously tried to set fire to his guitar. Those tie-dye hippies are still around but they are using Zimmer frames now. There's still a lovely, mellow, and relaxed vibe here though.

This is a nice sized beach town with a population of less than 30,000. Everything is a short walk or drive away from my *Thunderbird* motel and the rugged coastline is a great spot for watching whales, dolphins, sea lions, pelicans, sea otter and people.

At this time of the year, the great whales migrate north from the Bay of Mexico and feed in the rich waters off the Californian coast. The best way to see them is by boat so I head up to *Moss Landing* to book my trip. I am soon aboard 'The Sanctuary' chugging out of the harbour with a dozen other enthusiastic whale watchers.

The sea lions compete for the best jetties to warm themselves in the morning sun. They bark noisily as we pass. One of the world's biggest populations of sea otters lives here and they lie on their backs opening clams as they watch us cruise by. Hundreds of black cormorants guard the harbour walls like sentinels.

Jodie is our knowledgeable marine biologist and tour guide. Unfortunately, she has a voice like Minnie mouse on laughing gas, so I move away from the tannoy to the back of the boat. There's less chance of sea sickness here. We are told to look out for flocks of birds and sea lions. They follow the whales to pick off the anchovies which the whales coral into huge shoals before lunging up from below with mouths agape.

There is some activity in the distance, and we track four huge humpbacks that are the central stars in a feeding frenzy. Big packs of sea lions swim together to help surround the tiny fish and the birds swoop down to pick off the scraps. We get so close that the whales swim under our boat. They are twice the size of this vessel and I'm hoping they don't breach too close. These creatures can grow up to 50' in length and weigh up to 30 tons. Their pectoral fins are up to 10' long and they are famous for acrobatics.

There are gasps on board as they power out of the water together, swallowing thousands of anchovies with each gulp. There are misty rainbows above their blowholes as they come up for air and spout. I smell the rainbow breath of a whale and it smells of.... fish.

As if on cue, one of them slaps the water with its fin. Jodie tells us that this is thought to be a sign of agitation. Another whale powers up from the depths and leaps completely clear of the water. It makes a massive splash and the bow waves rock the boat. I'm glad I'm holding on tight.

I meet *Christopher Blue* in the park. He is a homeless blues harp player and his life possessions are neatly bundled up on his pushbike and trailer. I offer him my pillow and sleeping bag which he accepts gratefully.

"Thanks man, it's getting cold at nights." He tells me that he has played with *Eric Clapton*. He certainly looks the part with his cowboy hat and black leathers but I'm not so sure. Now he cycles around town doing gigs for food and cash. He sings me some crackled blues. *Crossroads Blues by Robert Johnson*. He's surprisingly good and the ducks join in on the chorus.

The next day Bianca and I take our last trip together to San Francisco where I'm spending a few nights in another AirBnB. I'm really going to miss this car. It has been a most wonderful relationship. I started off hating her and quickly grew to love her. She has been a calm and reliable companion, keeping me safe for over 900 miles. We have shared a wonder-filled time together. But all good things must come to an end to make space and time for new good things. Bye, bye, Bianca.

I'm back on foot in the sunshine city of San Francisco with another million of us, being human. *Eddie Brickell* is playing at *The Fillmore* so I'm heading downtown.

"All across the nation
such a strange vibration
People in motion
There's a whole generation
With a new explanation
People in motion
People in motion."

Scott McKenzie

Rockin' the Fillmore...

October, Days 37-41: 9,452 miles

San Francisco is on a peninsula and can be accessed by four bridges including the famous *Golden Gate Bridge* at the north side. I am staying in *Oakland*, one of the posher areas. The Bay Area Rapid Transit or BART for short, runs right past my home in Rockridge to the airport and to all other major city destinations. I'm told that it was originally known as the Francisco Area Rapid Transit, but FART wasn't too cool.

It's a short stroll from *Rockridge Station* to my Air B&B home where I am sharing a house with 4 young software engineers. This is a mad but happy city. The pedestrian alert at the traffic lights even makes a cuckoo noise when it's safe to cross. There are eccentric characters and ageing hippies everywhere.

Everyone seems to know or want to know someone famous. I meet *Joni Mitchell's* ex-brother in law on the street. He said he was a retired lawyer. "Did you say, liar?" I ask. He shrugs his shoulders, "The same thing." he replies "But I got paid well and half the lies I told were true."

I meet Leon, a cool Afro Caribbean slide guitar player in *The Saloon*, Friscos oldest bar. It's just a small seedy room with a dozen bar stools and a drum kit but it's a blues bar with an atmosphere as thick as the cigar smoke wafting in from the street outside. It looks like it hasn't changed much in 158 years. Alvin Lee of the band 'Ten Years After' is playing 'Going Home' on the

jukebox. It sounds as though the music hasn't changed for 50 years.

Jo, the ageing bartender shuffles around behind the tiny bar. She started working here when she was 50 and is celebrating her 30th anniversary on Halloween night. She is too weak to open the screw tops, so I get a job. Soon, and much to the other customers' amusement, I am wobbling on top of a barstool trying to hang her Halloween decorations.

The last big earthquake happened here in 1989 and 67 people perished. This street was on fire, but the firefighters rushed to save this building before any others. "There was a brothel upstairs back then," laughs Jo. "I guess they didn't want to lose that!"

I'm told that *Edie Brickel and the New Bohemians* are playing at The Fillmore tonight. "Get your ticket at the door," says Leon. "The website doubles the price."

I arrive early and get talking to the stage crew outside. "Is that Edie's bus?" I ask, pointing to a huge shiny space shuttle bus sitting outside. "Has it got a swimming pool inside?" I jest.

The door man is a large black guy, bigger than the stage door he is guarding. He looks like *Mr T* and he has the scariest, meanest face I have ever seen. He could turn milk to butter with just one glower. "The best live album in the world was recorded here," I proclaim. "Oh really, and what would that be then?" he asks in his drawling accent. "*Humble Pie* of course '*Rockin the*

Fillmore' and I bet they didn't have a bus like that back in those days." Mr T finally cracks and shows one of the happiest, bubbly faces I have ever seen. "You have two amazing faces." I tell him. "Mr Mean Ass and Mr Happy as."

I am 'high fived' by the brothers and soon I am rubbing shoulders with the sound man, Eric. "This is probably the only live venue in America that still uses old school analogue amplifiers," he says proudly. "We maintain high standards and we like to keep things as they have always been. Are you any good at packing down cables?" he asks. "I know my phonos from my XLR's," I say. "Great, we're short of hands so your now part of the stage crew for tonight. Wear this badge, take the stage door and I'll see you inside." Woohoo.

Eric shows me around and takes me to the famous Fillmore Poster Room. All my guitar and rock heroes have played here and the iconic posters for each gig are mounted on the wall of fame. I am in awe. The careers of the *Grateful Dead, the Jefferson Airplane, Santana, Quicksilver Messenger Service, Big Brother and the Holding Company, Moby Grape, the Butterfield Blues Band,* and countless others were launched from this very stage.

Everybody who became somebody in Rock World has appeared here: *Jimi Hendrix, Otis Redding, Cream, Howlin' Wolf, Captain Beefheart, Muddy Waters, The Who.*

More recently, *Primus, Chris Isaak, Michelle Shocked, The Afghan Whigs & Redd Kross, Queen Latifah and Solsonics, Gin Blossoms, Jimmie Dale Gilmore and Marshall Crenshaw, D'Cuckoo and Pele Juju, Sir Douglas Quintet and The Hellecasters, Brian Setzer Orchestra, Mother Hips, Ali Farka Toure and Ben Harper, Huey Lewis and the News, NRBQ, Blues Traveller and Soul Hat, They Might Be Giants and Frente!, Counting Crows, Thinking Fellers and Union Local #282.*

The most appearances award goes *to Tom Petty and the Heartbreakers*, who have played a total of 27 times. Los Lobos brings down the house annually in December. *Willie Nelson* and Lucinda Williams both have a soft spot for The Fillmore. *Radiohead, The Cure, Sonic Youth, Prince, The White Stripes, Dave Chappelle* and even *Tom Jones* have graced the stage many times.

"We are the same.
There is no difference anywhere in the world.
People are people.
They laugh, cry, feel and love.
Music is the common denomination that brings us all together.
It cuts through all boundaries and goes straight to the soul."

Willie Nelson.

Edie Brickel is married to *Paul Simon*. I've always liked her, and she always surrounds herself with great musicians. They walk on stage like they are walking into your front lounge. Her adoring fans crowd the dance floor under the famous ten candelabras which hang from high. My feet stick to the beer trodden carpet and I am transported back in

time to my student union days.

The band plays their new set and many of their oldies including my own favourite, *What I Am*. The 7-piece band is sensational. The lead guitar player, *Kenny Withrow*, jumps into my league table of top 10 living rock guitarists. Most of them are dead already and it's getting harder to replace them.

I am standing at the urinal and thinking "I wonder who has stood in this exact same spot having a pee just like me." Eric pops in. "There you are, the band will do two encores and then I'll meet you on stage to help pack it down." Later, I stand on the stage at The Fillmore and coil Edie Brickels' microphone cable.

Now, I never thought I would ever say that!

*"I'm not aware of too many things,
I know what I know if you know what I mean,
Philosophy is a walk on slippery rocks,
Religion is a light in the fog.
I'm not aware of too many things,
I know what I know if you know what I mean."*

Edie Brickel and the New Bohemians

Life's a Beach in San Clemente...

October, Days 37-41: 9,452 miles

My plane arrives late and, as I pick up my bag from the baggage reclaim, I turn around at the exact same moment that Donna walks in to meet me, her arms waving enthusiastically. I first met Donna and Paul when they stayed for just one night with me as guests on AirBnB. From the very moment we met, it was like seeing close friends again. Synchronicity is a hallmark of our relationship. We all feel it.

If California is the Golden State, then *San Clemente* is liquid gold Spanish style. It is known as the 'Spanish City by the Sea' and is built around small verdant hills overlooking the ocean. This forms natural, human-scaled communities in direct contrast to the massive graph paper cities of the flat plains.

Donna Bond is a successful spiritual life coach and counsellor and Paul, her surfer husband is an extraordinarily talented artist. They are both riding the crest of their waves and they are one of the shiniest couples I have ever met. Two cool cats called Rumi and Mystic also live here.

Their house is stunning, perched high on a hill overlooking the tree-lined gardens in the valley below. Two gryphons guard the back-garden wall amongst the palm trees. There's an outside bar, barbecue area and a hot tub.

The garden is beautiful. Sculptures of angels, faeries and Buddhas peep from the shrubbery and wind chimes sing with the tinkling water in the garden fountains. Large hawks patrol the boundaries and there are hummingbirds here too. They dart down for a closer view like old friends.

I'm just five weeks into my year-long journey and my body and spirit need rejuvenation. Donna arranges for Lindsey, her neighbour, to give me a professional massage. Lying on a massage bed in this beautiful garden, I soon feel the lumps and bumps in my muscles being skillfully eased back into place. Afterwards, I lie in the hot tub with the powerful water jets finishing off the job. And then I sleep.

It's just five minutes to *Capistrano Beach* and I am soon watching Paul walk out into the sea with his surfboard for his daily wave therapy. It's sunny and hot and apart from a few dozen surfers, joggers, dog walkers and lifeguards, we have the 20-mile long beach pretty much to ourselves.

Tonight, Donna is conducting her workshop 'Partnering with Your Authentic Self.' We learn the difference between our separate or 'ego selves' and our shared or 'unified Self.' It's a powerful and clear message presented well and with total clarity and conviction. Afterwards, the group partake in mutual eye gazing to practice being open and being truly seen by each other. Some of us are moved to tears as we seem to recognise and really see each other for the first time.

It's a new concept for Humberto. He has spent most of his life bodybuilding and serving in the military. It's a breakthrough moment for him as he now realises that he has created his tough-guy personality because he felt so scared and vulnerable. He is blown away and cries like a baby reborn. The path to our connected soul is through our eyes. It's a real eye-opener.

The 'Oceanside Pirates' are playing the 'Escondido Werewolves' in the final of the School American Football league. I join Paul's family to support his grandson Braden who is playing. The sweet junior cheerleaders do cartwheels and chant with their pom-poms flying. On the pitch, the young boys fight it out. Gender roles are programmed from an early age in this society.

In the spectator stand the proud parents shout and stamp their feet. It's brutal. A lifetime diet of chips, meat and cheese have resulted in most of them being far too overweight to do what they are compelling their children to now do. Some of these parents can't even get themselves up the stairs. After the game, we enjoy a healthy brunch.

Tonight, we walk up the hill overlooking the neighbourhood. The vegetation is brittle dry due to the lack of rain this year. There is coyote poo on the path. The climb is worth it as we share a beautiful sunset over the Californian Sea.

Paul connects me with friends and family in Mexico, Costa Rica, Bali, and India. I know that I am going to appreciate this further on down the road. I am going to miss these guys and feel so grateful for this friendship. I am now re-newed, re-nourished, re-vitalised and ready for the next chapter.

Carlos Santana is playing an 'intimate concert' in *Las Vegas* on Halloween. He has been one of my greatest musical influences and heroes ever since I first heard him fifty years ago. It's just an hour from here so I just must go.

I have a feeling that I am moving from the sublime to the ridiculous.

"Have you ever been south of Monterey ?
Barrancas carve the coastline,
And the chaparral flows to the sea,
'Neath waves of golden sunshine.."

The Beachboys

Carlos Santana plays Vegas on Halloween...

October, Days 42-44: 10,264 miles

I am flying into *Las Vegas* at night. Down below the City looks like a giant microchip surrounded by the dark Nevada desert. Orange streetlights outline the main grid pattern and multitudes of tiny white lights reveal the streets and houses inside. Red and white car lights flow through the grids like data streams.

Even from up here you can see the famous *'Vegas Strip.'* The four-mile-long boulevard which is home to the huge Disney World style hotels and casinos. I can see a huge illuminated Ferris wheel and a beam of white light rising straight up from the centre high into the night sky. Even I should find it hard to get lost here with this beacon.

As soon as you step out of the plane and into the airport there are lines of slot machines. This city was built with Mob money and gambling profits is still the primary fuel. It's now home to over 2 million people and more than a few billionaires. The hotels are expensive, so I am staying in a less glamorous AirBnB with a lovely Vietnamese family just 15 minutes from the 'Strip.'

This City is nuts. It's the most expensive four-mile strip in the world. An acre of land starts at £30 million (enough for four normal houses) and that's just for the barren desert land - the cost to build and furnish the average hotel room is over £1 million. This is paid for by over 50 million visitors generating an annual income of over $50 billion. One-third of that is from the Casinos. There are a few people getting crazy rich and 49,999,990 going crazy and getting poorer.

I am in the *Mandalay Bay Hotel*. Well, I say hotel. This place is massive. With over 3,200 rooms and apartments, it's bigger than the town I come from. And it has an 1,800 seat concert hall, a casino, a shark reef, an 11-acre artificial beach, health spa, golf course, 5 bars and nightclubs, 16 restaurants, a convention centre, and a wedding chapel! Nuts! There are over 20 of these hotel resorts on the 'Strip.'

Next door is the *Luxor Hotel* which is designed to an ancient Egyptian theme. It features a black glass pyramid (which is the source of the light beacon) and a replica of Cleopatra's Needle next to the half-size Sphinx. Further down the street, there is *Caesars Palace*, a hotel designed like New York with its own Statue of Liberty. *Circus Circus* has its own circus inside.

And then there's *Paris* and *Venice*, *MGM Studios* and *Planet Hollywood*. No expense has been spared in trying to recreate the real thing. The palm trees are imported from Mexico at a cost of $10,000 each and there are thousands of them. The Trump tower downtown looks cheap and impotent compared to these other mega-resorts.

The casino floor is acres of bright flashing slot machines and folk get free drinks if they are playing them. As I don't gamble, I must pay £12 for a large

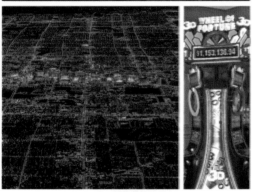

G&T. It's enough to make you want to start gambling just to try and get your money back.

I talk with Margaret in the Casino. She recognises my accent because she left *Inverness, Scotland* where she was born, 30 years ago. She and her husband are here from *Philadelphia* and are here conventing at the Annual Convention for... Nuts and Bolts Manufacturers. Really!

She tells me that there's a special Casino upstairs for folk who lose a $million. They are asked to leave at once if they win it back. And the nuts do.

I feel like I have woken up inside a giant 3D cartoon. To make the setting even more surreal, it's Halloween and folk here have went to town with their very weird and expensive costumes. There are zombies, superheroes, walking skeletons, Disney characters and aliens everywhere. But it's really no joke, as this year, no one is allowed to wear a facemask. Why?

Just 12 months ago upstairs, a 64-year-old accountant and professional gambler carried out the worst mass shooting in the USA in the last 30 years. *Stephen Paddock* went up to the 31st floor, with 32 guns and opened fire at people enjoying a rock concert across the street. He fired 1,100 rounds in 35 minutes before using the last bullet on himself when the cops eventually turned up.

He killed 58 people, injured 581 and left thousands traumatised. The authorities say that they couldn't find a motive. Of course, having easy access to automatic weapons and losing his money and soul to gambling wasn't considered. But hey, shares in gun manufacturers rocketed because of this incident. The victims couldn't even sue the hotel as this was considered to be the responsibility of 'Homeland Security' which can't legally be held liable.

As a result, this year they have really cracked down on security by.... banning masks! There was no security at the entrances anywhere, no bag checks and few police to be seen. I could easily have nipped down to *Wal-Mart*, bought some guns, hidden them in my suitcase and just walked in. Just nuts. To my mind, the spirit of Mammon is worshipped here, and it seems to be thriving.

Anyway, I am here to see the man responsible for my desire to play the guitar and my lifelong love affair with Latin music. The legendary *Carlos Santana*. Soon I am standing within yards of my hero and watching his fingers weave and bend their magic on the fretboard of his golden Gibson guitar.

At 71 years young he hasn't changed a bit since his famous debut at *Woodstock* in 1967. He plays all the most famous songs from his astonishing 24 albums including *'Soul Sacrifice,' 'Black Magic Woman,' 'Samba Pa Ti,'* and many of his new tracks including *'Smooth'*, which he most certainly is. He also appears actively healthy and happier than any septuagenarian I know.

Everyone here simply loves this man and not just for his supreme guitar wizardry. He is a deeply spiritual altruistic person and a political activist. He promotes love and kindness and an end to national borders. It's also great to hear a Mexican in Las Vegas calling out *President Trump* for his silly wall idea. I am so mesmerised that I don't dare move from my spot at the front of the stage to claim my free drink at the bar.

His band is sensational and the depth of their love and connection is palpable. There are not one but three of the best drummers and percussionists I have ever seen. One of those, his wife *Cindy Blackman Santana* has the energy of a whirlwind throughout the entire three-hour set.

I feel so lucky and blessed to have finally seen one of my heroes, and for a moment, our eyes meet in a big rapturous smile. Indeed, I am feeling so lucky that I am tempted to put my last $100 on red. Instead, I call *Mr Uber* to get me out of here. It's just too nutty for me.

This town never sleeps, but I must get up early in the morning to head to *Mexico* where my soul brother was born.

"I'm Leaving Las Vegas
Lights so bright Palm sweat,
Blackjack on a Saturday night
Leaving Las Vegas
Leaving for good, for good
I'm leaving Las Vegas
And I won't be back
No, I won't be back
Not this time."

Sheryl Crow

Mexico City on the Day of the Dead...

November, Days 45-48: 13,019 miles

I arrive in *Mexico City* on the *'Day of the Dead'*. It's the cheapest and easiest stopover on my way to *Cancun* on the eastern Caribbean coast of Mexico. The Hotel Playa International is close to the airport and the price of £9 seemed too good to be true. It was.

My taxi is only just hanging onto its wheels as we drive at night over bumpy and broken roads. Out of the window I see squalor. Garbage bags are piled up on street corners supplying food for stray dogs and birds. The houses and shops in this part of town are dirty, decaying and decorated with graffiti.

Working girls line the streets as cars drive slowly by and stop to discuss terms of trade. I have already learned that things always look worse at night and so it's always better to arrive in daylight whenever possible.

Jose hands me my room keys and TV remote control from the seedy hotel office. In the dirty window, there is beer and condoms for sale. This could be a good indication of the clientele here. On the corner outside, a bunch of youths are creating a street party with a loud PA system.

My fourth-floor tiny room smells of carbolic but at least the sheets are clean. There is just one plug socket for the TV. I check the channels. Sixty-six are in Spanish and the last three, in English, are porn channels with the same storyline. So, I use the socket to recharge my laptop and phone, stuff in my earplugs and try and get some sleep on the hard pillows and plastic under-sheet.

The next morning, I check out and wander around. Outside the hotel door is a shrine for a young man, who at the age of 26, was killed in a knife attack.

The Day of the Dead is unlike Halloween. It's a distinctly Mexican tradition which dates back some 3,000 years and it's a celebration of the lives of those who have passed on. There are macabre smiling skulls in every shop window and on street corners. Colourful parades and street parties take place over the three-day holiday period. Folk here believe that it's important to show their ancestors and dead family members how much they are still loved.

It's grimy here in this part of town. Vendors cook burritos on makeshift street barbecues and the shop keepers use microphones to hustle customers inside the open front shops. There are rows of small shops selling second-hand mobile phones, ripped DVDs, and cheap clothes.

It's hard to make eye contact with anyone let alone share a smile. So, I give my happy eyes and smiles to the little kids who still know how to reflect them and connect. Many of these folks have stunted growth and appear to have rickets. I believe that this is caused by Vitamin D deficiency which surprises me in this sunny country. Despite the great climate, it's hard to find healthy food here. Fried or barbecued meat with beans and rice is the staple diet. Or crisps or sweets. Oh, for a healthy fruit smoothie.

Suddenly there is a commotion. A cyclist races the wrong way up a one-way street. He is hotly pursued by shouting pedestrians. The lady traffic cops blow their whistles and a dozen armed cops on motorbikes, cars and vans appear from nowhere and give chase.

Five minutes later I am standing with a crowd of spectators watching as the young guy is cuffed and bundled into the back of a van. His rucksack is emptied onto the street and dozens of mobile phones spill out. I have been warned to avoid the cops here, so I hold on tightly to my iPhone and phone a cab to take me back to the relative safety of the airport.

Cancun is a Mexican city on the *Yucatan* peninsula bordering the Caribbean Sea. I find an AirBnB house for just £16 per night and it is beautiful and full of light. I awaken to the sound of lots of birds, none of which I recognise. The garden is filled with palms and tropical plants and a swimming pool to cool off in. Geckos and tiny lizards dart through the grass as I walk. They nod their heads at me from their safe vantage points.

It's hot and humid and I am grateful for the air conditioning in my room. Smells seem to be amplified in this climate. The sweet fragrances of flowering shrubs like the Mexican frangipani smell like vanilla. In contrast, human smells are sour and acrid as the heat dries the sewer systems underground. People here are much more open and friendly and there are fewer cops to be seen. Could it be that beautiful natural environments help us to feel safer and more connected?

Maye and Albert own the house. Albert is a talented woodworker and the house and garden have some great sculptures and furniture which he has made. I meet Ryan, a young A.I. programmer and professional poker player who is also staying here. He is travelling around the world, trying to show that a nomadic lifestyle, remotely working via the internet, is a viable way of life.

We both agree that the new peer to peer platforms such as AirBnB, Uber, Facebook, and apps like Google Translate and Google Maps are helping humanity to connect and share resources and knowledge in new ways. I for one would be lost without them. All we need now is a peer to peer currency bypassing the money lenders and the banks.

The beaches have the softest caramel sand and my feet feel like they are walking through warm sugar. I gaze across the turquoise sea towards *Cuba*, my next destination. Just beyond that are the Bahamas. But first I intend to explore this coastline region as far south as Belize. I am looking forward to finding out more about the Mayan people who live here and the ancient pyramids which remain.

But right now, it's tequila time.

"He wears a red bandana, plays a blues piano
"In a honky-tonk, down in Mexico
He wears a purple sash and a black moustache
In a honky-tonk, down in Mexico."

The Coasters

Quintana Roo - 7 Shades of Blue...

November, Days 49-56: 13,254 miles

I'm on a packed bus travelling south towards Belize on the east coast of Mexico in the Quintana Roo region. This is a beautiful part of the country next to the Caribbean coastline. It's hot, humid and it feels decidedly tropical. Palm trees and coconut trees line the dusty roads and the bus stops regularly so that we can use the makeshift roadside cafes and toilets.

I'm sitting next to young Alex and Ellie from Paris. They are five months into their nine-month trip travelling around the world in the opposite direction from me. Their budget is just £30 each per day including travel but they have managed so far using hostels and homemade baguettes.

They ask how I deal with being lonely and I reply that I haven't ever felt that because I'm always meeting interesting and lovely people like themselves. And I still have Facebook to stay connected with friends and family at home. I just watched the Forres fireworks show with my daughter on Facetime. I have never missed that event for the last 32 years.

I'm staying with newlyweds, Cary and Mark in a small village called Xul-ha. Most of the population of around 2,000 people live a simple life in extremely basic concrete dwellings with tin roofs. If you count the dogs, chickens, goats, and turkeys which wander around the dirt track roads, the population must be double. Mark is busy making organite and plasma generators on the kitchen table when I arrive.

The village is on the shore of a beautiful freshwater lake or 'cenote' created by the collapse of the limestone bedrock which exposes the water table below. Scientists reckon that the very first bacteria on Earth were formed here in the mineral-rich water. They now form huge coral-like communities called Stromatolites and they are over 3,500 million years old.

Throughout the night I am awakened by the sound of a million insects, a dozen dogs barking and eventually an awesome dawn chorus of loud, exotic birds squawking. There are over 1,000 species of birds in Mexico - twice as many as in Britain. My favourites are the yellow giant chickadees with their bright white eye stripes. They jump from their branches and do golden somersaults in the air as they catch flies. Large colonies of noisy parakeets streak past like they have just flown through a painter's easel. And there are rainbow marmots, orioles and of course hummingbirds. There is even a catbird. I've yet to see a Toucan but I believe I can and will.

At 8 am, Mark knocks on my door. "We are going to jump in the lake, you coming?" he says. I am still tired and groggy, but the sun is already high in the sky. This cenote is known as the lake of seven colours of blue and this morning it's the most beautiful turquoise sunshine mirror. We have the lake to ourselves and we just float in the highly alkaline freshwater. It's warm, blissful, and very therapeutic and it wakes me up.

Cary Kirastar Ellis is the co-founder of the organisation *'Global Leadership for Change'* and author of the book *'21st Century Superhuman.'*

She interviews me on the story of LETS (Local Exchange Trading Systems). Her group has over 250,000 followers so that's a lot of knowledge seeds being sprinkled around the planet. I use the opportunity to try to reach out to a sympathetic App developer to co-create my dream of GETS (A peer to peer online Global Exchange Trading System).

It would be really great to travel without all of these currency exchange charges and dodgy ATM's and I would love to be able to easily earn social currency working for friends and not to have to spend my money through the banks.

I arrive at my next destination near Bacalar in the middle of the afternoon. It's called *'The Magic Town.'* By 8 pm it's dark and balmy. I am sitting in the central Coliseum watching a Saturday night movie in the open air under the stars.

Four children take turns cycling to power the projector and sound system as a hundred of us watch the big screen for free. It's a delightful family movie about lost treasure and it's got English subtitles. It feels lovely laughing together, all of us, sitting on the earth. Little kids, young couples, old folk in wheelchairs, dogs, all together under the starry night sky. At the end of the movie, I try to give the organiser some bank money. He stuffs it back into my shirt pocket and gives me a hearty big hug instead.

Travel Tip No 7: Avoid walking under coconut trees when it's windy.

"Money, it's a crime.
Share it fairly but don't take a slice of my pie.
Money, so they say
Is the root of all evil today.
But if you ask for a raise it's no surprise
that they're giving none away, away, away."

Pink Floyd

The Tale of Tecuintlicatl...

November, Days 57-60: 13,528 miles

Alberto welcomes me at the gate of the Temazcal. "Hurry, the Shaman is about to start the ceremony," he says. I drop my bag, clothes, shoes, watch and sunglasses off at my cabin in the woods and crawl into the pitch-black stone chamber wearing only my shorts.

I am aware of 6 – 10 other people seated and standing around the glowing red fire in the centre. The firekeeper passes in a long-handled shovel containing the red-hot volcanic stones and with the door closed, we are enveloped in complete darkness.

The heat is intense and soon I am pouring with sweat. The Shaman is called Jesus and he hands me a rattle shaker made of deer antlers and then starts to beat his drum. We chant words I don't fully understand, and I shake my rattle and lose myself in the experience.

The Sweat Lodge is a place of self-purification. We literally sweat our prayers as the Spirits are called forth to help us in our personal quests. The combination of heat, darkness, burning herbs, rhythm and song can create an out of body experience. At one point I think I hear someone whispering in my ear in a strange and ancient hissing language but it's probably just the stones sizzling as water is poured over them.

For some of us, it's an intensely cathartic and healing experience. For others, the fear and the fire are too much and they leave at the next opening of the door to be reborn from this mama lodge back into the light. For me, it's a kind of homecoming and two hours later, I'm the last to leave.

Once I do, I notice that all bright lights are surrounded by huge rainbow halos. The plants are more vivid, and the night sky is spectacular. After a refreshing cold shower, we meet up in the central community area for some refreshments.

We are all smiling, radiant, and beautiful and look ten years younger. "I feel as if I have known you all for a very long time." I say. "You have, for many lifetimes," replies Jesus. "Bienvenido a casa, welcome home."

The next day I am given my Mayan name in a beautiful daytime ceremony. The Mayans believe that we each have a unique vibration or frequency which can be calculated with our place and time of birth and the name which was given to us by our parents.

I am told that this is a powerful name and when used in accordance with my life purpose, it will amplify my power of manifestation. However, if used against it or to create harm to others, it can result in my death. It's an effective karmic amplifier. My unique name is *'Tecuintlicatl'* and it stands for 'The black dog who reflects life fairly and justly.' I guess that's good qualities for a worldwide travel blogger then. Woof Woof.

Tecuintlicatl is woken up early the next morning by a cacophony of exotic bird song. This place is magical. The buildings have been designed by Eres' two children and they are out of this world. They are built of bamboo, naturally and following the sacred principles of the *'Flower of Life.'*

The forest garden is beautiful. It's Monsanto and Wi-Fi free and buzzing with life and energy. There are raised beds containing fruit, vegetables, herbs and medicines and there is also a labyrinth. On the edge of the jungle, he meets a snake, a black scorpion, and a huge blue butterfly.

Later, we drive for an hour through the jungle on bumpy tracks to a hidden Mayan treasure. The descendants of the original Mayans protect this place. The underground caves hold hidden lakes which are still protected and revered as sacred places. The energy of the dark and the light meet here. The trees above the ground send down their roots in search of the water of life. They fall through the open spaces below and are mineralised by the calcium-rich alkaline water forming organic shapes of limestone.

Stalactites and stalagmites form strange shapes which constantly change in this dancing light. The catfish here are blind but have other senses which allow them to thrive. Swifts and bees nest in the ceiling of the caverns and they hum and skirl as they fly around us in the darkness. After exploring deep into the caves, we disrobe and jump into the dark, cool water. Water stores energy and memories and, as we swim, our voices echo as the past and the present seem to merge.

The Temples of *Tulum* and *Cobo* still remain as part of this once very advanced civilisation. The city of Cobo alone was home to over 1.5 million residents. The Mayans created two symbols to represent all numbers. These were simply a circle and a line. A circle had a value of one unit and a line of five. So, the number eight for example, would be a line with three dots. The number 27 would be five lines and two dots. This was the first known binary code which is now used by all modern-day computers.

These people also invented a circular calendar of amazing accuracy and complexity. The full cycle mapped an 'Age' of 5125 years which started again in our year of 2012. This was the start of this new *'Age of Aquarius'* and not the end of the world, as some fatalists had wrongly suggested.

The Harris Hawk skirts the cenote searching for small fish in the shallows. Tecuintlicatl gazes in awe and free of thought he inflates and fills up with Love of All that Is.

He imagines what it feels like to have the wind brush past his feathers, his wingtips stretched and spread-eagled like long fingers caressing the ether. Through his mind's eye, he leans and turns to soar effortlessly on a thermal vortex of warm air up into the sky.

Soon he is looking down to see the earth and the beautiful blue water reflecting the Light from the Golden Sun. Lighter than air now, he spirals to become One with the Sky. When the air thins, he focuses on a point far below and tucks in his wings to simply fall in a steep dive back to mother earth.

It is only when he gets close to the ground that he becomes aware of the shadow he casts. He sees the shadow of a man lying on the ground looking up at a bird.

Back down to Earth I reflect on my most amazing week so far. I was anxious about visiting Mexico as I had heard so many frightening stories. However, my experience was clearly the exact opposite. This is a stunningly beautiful and mysterious part of our world. Natural Magic is still alive here.

Travel Tip No 8: It's essential to learn six words in any foreign language. These are 'Yes,' 'No,' 'Please,' 'Thank you,' 'Beer' and 'Toilet.' It's also particularly important to know when to use 'yes' and when to use 'no.'

"Time keeps on slipping, slipping, slipping into the future
I want to fly like an eagle, to the sea
Fly like an eagle
Let my spirit carry me."

Steve Miller

The Colours of Cuba...

November, Days 81-68: 14,068 miles

It's a bumpy landing and the passengers burst into spontaneous applause when we touch down. The first things I notice about Cuba are that the airport isn't quite as clean as others I have been to. It's hot.

The airport officials are mostly attractive young women with sexy short green uniforms and fishnet patterned stockings. It's really hot. I step out of the airport and for a moment it seems that I have walked into a vintage car rally or a 50's film set. There are dozens of brightly coloured classic American cars used as taxis. It's....really cool.

Four things, all first experienced in my teens, attract me to Cuba. *Ernest Hemingway's* classic *book 'The Old Man and the Sea'* was written here. It was the first novel I read which began my love affair with books and so I became a reader. There's a bronze statue of him in *The Floridita* - the pub where he wrote the story. He looks familiar.

Like many teenagers in the early seventies, I had a red and black poster of *Che Guevara* on my bedroom wall. I became a Socialist and still like to wear a red bandanna when no one is looking.

The first time I heard Cuban Jazz by *The Buenos Vista Social Club*, I was hooked and learned to play the guitaro. And, last but not least, the first alcoholic drink I enjoyed was rum and coke. *Havana Rum* is cheaper than water here. So, if I were to stay here for more than a week, I would probably become an alcoholic too.

Driving in from the airport, I am struck by the level of decay. The cars are held together by string and ingenuity and they belch black exhaust smoke everywhere. There are holes in the street bigger than cars. It's a bumpy and smelly journey.

Inside Havana, it looks like a war zone. The buildings are often just empty shells and are falling down. Leon, my driver tells me that every three days, parts of them fall into the streets below, sometimes killing people. Occasionally, complete buildings simply topple over.

But there is also a strange beauty here in the aesthetic Spanish architecture. Pastel paint brightens up the facades and creates a city full of colour, texture, and character. Cubans are a strong and resilient people and they have learned how to make the best of scant resources. In the faces of the people, it's a happy place and Cuba scores surprisingly high in the world happiness league table.

OK, here's a very brief history of this fascinating island. In 1492, *Christopher Columbus* invades the country and claims it for the Spanish Royal family. They fell the hardwoods to make their superior Spanish warships with which they invade the South Americas. Havana harbour proves to be an ideal location for berthing their expanding fleet and from which to trade gold and other precious minerals. The Spanish grow exceptionally rich from their plunder. Within the next two decades, the Spanish Empire wipes out most of the indigenous population and, in turn, transport upwards

of 30,000 slaves from Africa to work vast plantations of cash crops, most notably sugar cane.

Numerous slave rebellions arise during the early 19th century; in 1868, Cuban landowners join in, launching the first war for independence. The second, in 1898, subsequently sparks the Spanish American War and US influence on the island. For the next half-century, Cuba is America's tropical playground. And then a series of dictators, culminating in the reign of Fugencio Batista in the 1950s, leads to one more revolution and a 50-year halt in friendly relations with the USA.

The *Fidel Castro* era is fraught with tensions between the US and Cuba, but by 2013 those tensions begin to thaw. The US embassy reopens in Havana, and trade and travel restrictions are loosened. Today the island once again welcomes Americans to her shores. Tourism is now Cuba's major income resource which may explain why we are welcomed and treated so well.

This history also explains why racial and sexual differences are not even an issue here. Everyone in every skin shade gets on very well. The women carry themselves with real pride and dignity. They don't try and look like Hollywood stars and just let it all hang out in simple fashion, proudly bulging in T-shirts and tight pants, whatever their shape or age. It's sexy but not sexual if you know what I mean. If anything, the women have the upper hand. They have had to learn to be strong, resourceful survivors. There seems to be real racial and sexual equality here and it's very refreshing.

There are two Cubas. One is for the tourists and one for the locals. They even have their own currencies, economies, rules, and laws. The Tourist CUC (Cuban Convertible) is tied to the American Dollar. This is a wise strategy which prevents international financial exploitation and abuse by global money traders. The locals use 'CUPS' or Cuban Pesos.

The State wage is equivalent to just £300 per month. Education, health care and accommodation are free for everyone. There is no private option. A neighbourhood doctor is available to everyone 24/7. I saw no homelessness or serious drug and alcohol abuse. (Drugs are strictly illegal here and crime is low). There is a real sense of social solidarity. 'We may not have the best standards but at least we are all in this together.'

This place is full of paradoxes and I love it already. My AirBnB couldn't be more central, just a few hundred yards from the Capital Government Centre which looks like The White House in Washington. Like other major public buildings, it is going through major restoration work.

Slowly but surely this country is rebuilding its sense of identity and pride. This time without the help of its empire-building neighbours. The scale of the task is overwhelming though.

When I walk into my guest house, I meet two Glaswegians, Kerry and Richard. They have arrived prepared with pockets full of chocolates which win over the hearts of the restaurant and bar staff we meet. Chocolate is a prized rarity here. As are so many things we might take for granted. Shampoo, soap, perfume, car parts, trainers.

Later that night Richard pops his head in my door. "Hey big man, there's a party next door, grab some beers from your room fridge, let's go." Richard is sporting his Celtic coloured green *DJ Che* shirt and hands me a red Aberdeen coloured shirt with the motif *Che You Jimmy*.

We pop around the corner and there are loud beats blasting through the air as dozens of Afro Cubans dirty dance in the dirty street. We are the only white guys here but we (and our beer) are welcomed with open arms. I am soon introduced to the delights of twerking with large bottomed Afro-Cuban girls.

At 2 am the police arrive, and the party is brought to an abrupt close. Scots? Wha's like us? Cubans are. They too really know how to have a good time. I guess without material distractions they have learned to make the best of what is free in life. Great music, free parties, dancing, love, laughter, fun and happiness. This is the polar opposite of my experience in Las Vegas. Could it be that the less material, the more spiritual and vice versa?

Technology is not this country's strength. The internet is notoriously slow if it works at all. And so many sites are banned to prevent money draining out to the likes of Macdonald's or other foreign interests. Indeed, global corporations just don't exist here at all. It's local all the way. The upside is that you don't have to worry about getting the best deal on your taxi fare or tour. Everything is state-run and fairly priced at the same amount. It works surprisingly well for visitors.

Carmine and Hector, my AirBnB hosts represent the newly emerging private class. They are sharing their income with their taxi driver, their cleaner and their English-speaking tour guide, Janet. Everyone mucks in and everyone is grateful for our presence and presents.

The next day I ask Janet if she will take me for a 3-hour walk around the city so that I can acquaint myself with the area. We are soon strolling past the posh tourist hotels on the square, through the avenues of local street artists displaying their work and down to the fortified harbour. She speaks excellent English and is very knowledgeable about the history of her country.

Suddenly two young blue shirted military cops approach us. The brown-shirted police officers protect the people, the blue ones the State. They start asking her lots of questions and completely ignore me. "I am so sorry Stewart, but can you find your own way back? They are arresting me. Don't worry, this is what they do here to the locals. Please ask Carmine to come and rescue me please."

Two hours later, she returns safely and tells her story. She was suspected of prostitution with a tourist, that's me! She was eventually set free. I give Janet $20 and thank her for a great tour and for not having sex with me. Everyone laughs.

We are walking around a fantasy village on the outskirts of town and everything is covered in the brightest and most intricate mosaics. In 1975, Cuban artist *Jose Fuster* decided to brighten up his humble dwelling in colourful mosaic. Once he was done there, he asked his neighbours if he could decorate their homes and businesses as well. A few accepted his offer and the tile creations grew.

Over the course of a decade, doctors' offices, bus stops, fountains, benches, gateways, and more were enveloped by Fuster's whimsical imagination. Today, his artwork coats the neighbourhood in a rainbow of strange, enchanting fantasies. And the tourist dollars are flooding into his friends and neighbours.

The grimy dirt and air pollution finally get to me and I decide to see what it's like in the countryside. I take a day tour to a beautiful valley called *Vinales*. Our minibus hurtles along the dual carriageway which it is hoped will one day run along the entire length of the island. They started building it 40 years ago and it's only halfway there.

From the bus window I see the weirdest assortment of modes of transport; Beaten up transport lorries, shiny tourist busses, rickshaw bicycles, tuk-tuks, people on horseback, ox-drawn farm carts. If it rolls it's here. On the road, hundreds of folk stand by the roadside flashing cash in the hope of gas sharing a lift. Farmworkers hang from open-topped trucks pulled by antique tractors.

Two hours later we arrive in Vinales and it is spectacularly beautiful. We take a boat through underground caves, visit a small family run organic tobacco farm. I taste my first nicotine-free hand-rolled Cuban cigar, dipped in honey. It's smooth and it's not unusual to see Cuban women smoking them in the streets. We visit a mountainside cleaned and painted by an artist in tribute to the original native people who once lived here. I even meet a cow whisperer who puts his cow to sleep in his lap and wakes it up with a magic word.

The Casa Carmine guests have become a tight-knit family group and we decide to end our last night here in style. Soon we are watching some of the original performers of the Buenos Vista Social Club in a great show. The movie screen behind the stage shows footage of them in the '50s. It's very poignant as they perform now in front of their younger versions. The quality and passion of the music haven't changed a bit and soon they have us up dancing on the stage. They serve rum by the bottle here.

Cuba seems to be split into two paradoxical realities. Here the old meets the new. The City meets the countryside. Socialism meets capitalism. Poverty meets abundance. Through it all, the friendliness and the resilience of the Cuban people shine through. Viva Cuba.

"Havana, ooh na-na (ay, ay)
Half of my heart is in Havana, ooh-na-na (ay, ay)
He took me back to East Atlanta, na-na-na (uh-huh)
Oh, but my heart is in Havana (ay)
My heart is in Havana (ay) Havana, ooh na-na."

Camila Cabello

Bogota, Colombia and the big comedown...

November, Days 69-71: 15,445 miles

I am guessing that by now you must be thinking that this travelling malarkey is one continuous kaleidoscope of fun and good times. However, I promised you at the start that I would report honestly on my travels. So, here's the down that follows all those ups. This is the story of how one silly mishap led to a chain of events which so nearly turned out to be a catastrophe.

Things started to go wrong before I left Havana. A few days earlier, the first rains had fallen in the city. Months of dried sewage and filth in the archaic plumbing systems started to ripen and the whole house came down with the sniffles. And it wasn't just because I was leaving. That combined with the exhaust fumes in the city seemed to go straight to my head and I started to feel very unwell.

On my last night out with friends, I lost my phone. We did a lot of dancing and a fair bit of medicinal drinking too so I guess it may have fallen out of my pocket. I didn't miss it until I awoke the next day and by then it was too late. My flight leaves for Bogota in 3 hours - my intended stepping-stone to the beautiful coastal town of *Cartagena.*

It's not possible to book an AirBnB in a foreign country inside of Cuba so I could only do this when I arrived at my next destination in Colombia. All immigration authorities need proof of a residence before they will let you into the country and I just didn't have one yet. The grumpy official wasn't too impressed

and without my Google translate app, I wasn't particularly good at explaining myself.

Half an hour later, I finally manage to connect to the free airport Wi-Fi with my laptop and quickly book the closest place I can find near to the airport. I manage just in the nick of time as her patience runs out and I'm facing the prospect of not being allowed into Colombia and being sent back to Cuba with no way to phone ahead or to make arrangements.

I convert my remaining Cuban currency at the airport. I now have 300,000 Colombian Pesos to my name and feel like a rich man. But it's only worth around £75. I find an ATM machine but without my mobile phone, the bank system can't verify my ID and won't deliver. Oops.

My head hurts, I'm dog tired and I got the shivers. It's 8 pm at night and dark outside the airport. No one here speaks English and my AirBnB host isn't answering my online messages to give me directions. Without Google Maps I am at the mercy of the dodgy taxi driver. And he knows it.

We drive through dirty streets and he tries to drop me off in the middle of nowhere but I'm not having that in this dodgy neighbourhood. I tell him that he is not getting paid until I am at an open door. He seems to understand and manages to call someone at the residence for directions. Phew. He charges me double for the effort and I can't even argue with him. I have just £50 left.

Bogota, Colombia is a massive city of over 9 million people. That's bigger than the entire population of my country back home. At over 9,150 feet above sea level, it's also one of the highest. Altitude sickness starts around 8,000 feet. I must stop halfway up the stairs to get my breath. I feel dizzy and ready to faint. Not good. I'm also hungover and haven't eaten all day which can't help.

At least I have a warm bed for one night. I'll sort things out in the morning when I'm feeling better. Things always look better in daylight after a good night's sleep, right? Not this time.

The seedy pub across the street plays loud music until 3 am. Even with my earplugs in, it's noisy. I find some clean water in the house; mix in some oregano drops and down a couple of Panadols. I wake the next morning with wet sheets from the night sweats. My head is pounding, every bone aches and it's hard to think clearly.

There's no way I can fly out of here even assuming I can sort out my bank to buy a ticket. So, I agree with my host to stay another night for cash. That buys me some time. I wander out to look for a pharmacy and a food shop. I don't recognise any of the brands, so I buy myself a bottle of natural lemon juice, some garlic, and some honey.

The shops and cafes here are desperate. Salted crisps, sugary white bread and pastries. I hover around a cafe and when someone buys something which looks kind of edible, I go in and point at the dish and then at myself. It works and I'm soon eating some kind of avocado, tomato, egg and creamy mash.

I'm down to my last £10 and sit at my laptop alone all day, self-medicating and trying to sort out my bank account. It's not at all easy. With this thing called two-step verification, the bank security systems are sending the codes to my lost phone so I can't prove my id! I realise that only six numbers are separating me from being just another old guy in a heartless city, cashless, homeless, and hungry. This is turning into a nightmare.

My only consolation is that I am still connected through Facebook to my friends and family and that is my only support and lifeline. At worst I can call for a rescue mission or a money transfer somehow. I feel so weak and helpless, alone, and vulnerable and I can't, for now, see a way out.

At times like these, I have learned that the thing to do is get back to basics and get myself right first. Body and Mind. Stop, breathe, drink water and lemon juice with garlic and honey, sleep and wait. I am still here. Maybe tomorrow something will change. I just want to be back home in my own warm bed around friendly faces and the people I love. Eventually, I fall asleep imagining that's where I am.

I awaken with a new idea. My friend is house-sitting for me. If she can find my bank dongle device, we can reactivate my bank account. We Facetime and eventually she finds it in one of my drawers. Between us, we manage to reactivate the password numbers. I head back out to the ATM in the shopping mall, two miles away.

Everyone here seems to have a dog and they are not the pretty ones. Bullmastiffs with grizzly faces and powerful jaws, thankfully most of them are muzzled and most are on leads. The streets are dirty with garbage everywhere. There's a guy wandering down the street with his hand inside his pants. Is he doing what I think he is doing? Oh, God! On the path is a dying rat, its little shiny eye looking up at me. I know how it feels.

I finally get to the bank and with fingers crossed punch in the numbers. The ATM finally pays out. What a relief it is to have cash in my pocket again. Now I can buy a replacement iPhone, medicine, food, and a ticket out of here.

My Uber is working again so it's easy to get a cheap, trusted taxi. However, transferring my online accounts to my new phone proves to be a frustratingly slow and complex process. I will need a new Sim card in Peru. It's going to take over a week before my Id's are confirmed so that I can restore all my apps, calendars, maps and contacts.

For now, I'm grateful that I have a basic functioning phone with a camera and I'm starting to feel better. I remind myself that on this circle spiral of life every high has a low. It seems that the deeper and darker I can dig, the higher and lighter I can fly. There's life and a few more blogs in this old dog yet.

So, it's upwards and onwards now to the mountains of Peru.

"When things go wrong as they sometimes will,
When the road you're trudging seems all uphill,
When the funds are low, and the debts are high
And you want to smile, but you have to sigh,
When care is pressing you down a bit,
Rest if you must, but don't you quit."

John Greenleaf Whittier

Onwards and upwards to Peru...

November, Days 72-79: 17,951 miles

It's a huge relief to be finally flying out of Colombia. The dramatic Andes mountain range is down below and, at almost 23,000 feet high, it seems that we are skimming the white snow-covered tops. They extend from north to south through seven South American countries: *Venezuela, Colombia, Ecuador, Peru, Bolivia, Chile, and Argentina.*

I'll be following them down through Peru and then to Chile. As the sun sets, they change from dark chocolate brown to rust, crimson and scarlet. They are spectacular in this light.

My flight is late as we arrive in Lima, the largest city and political capital of Peru. I have missed my transit to Cusco. I am given a free taxi ride and overnight stay with a delicious dinner and breakfast in a posh hotel 30 minutes from the airport.

It feels nice to be sleeping in crisp cotton sheets in a silent room and to have a good shower for a change. I'm up at 3.15 am to head back to the airport to catch the first flight to Cusco. Yawn.

Even at this time of the morning, this place is buzzing with activity. The taxi driver weaves in and out of the traffic lanes at high speed, tooting as he goes. Above the road, huge video screens scream the latest 'must-have' high tech products. Along the roadside, people sleep in shanty style tents and corrugated iron shelters. I'm glad I'm not spending more time here.

I am descending into the *Cusco* valley watching the terracotta rooftops which contrast beautifully with the green fields and mountains. This airport is so different from Colombia. People are smiling and the taxi drivers are friendly. Soon I am in my AirBnB on the outskirts of Cusco and head straight to bed.

When I wake up, I go out for a walk around the neighbourhood. I'm in the poorer part of town. The streets are lined with people selling everything you can imagine including every kind of fruit and vegetables. (There are over 2,000 varieties of potato here.) Also, chocolate covered corn sticks, snacks, live chickens and dead chicken bits, meat, razor blades, shampoo.

It seems that everyone here is selling something or other. I am told that there are no state benefits here and the people must sell or barter to survive. The Peruvian people are small but so incredibly strong. The women carry everything wrapped up in their colourful back shawls including babies and puppies! They are literally walking mobile shops.

The 'Mamitas' or older women wear distinctive high brimmed hats and sit at the roadsides trading their wares. It seems that there is a lot of hardship here but there is also life, colour, and vibrancy.

The next morning, I meet up with Naya and Tobias for an alternative tour around the town. We instantly connect and become friends and start the day with an invigorating drink in the local smoothie bar. I choose

pineapple, mango, banana, and ginger, all made fresh with local produce. It's delicious and wakes me up.

We walk around the historic part of town through narrow cobbled streets and stop at Nayas friends' shop. I just can't resist buying a beautiful handmade alpaca rainbow poncho, even though it might not fit in my backpack. Great price though.

Cusco is the historic capital of Peru and, at one time, the entire Inca territory which spread throughout this continent. It's known as Puma City because it was designed in accordance with the shape of this sacred animal. Once the Spaniards arrived, the population of twelve million indigenous people was decimated to just one million, largely due to murder and disease.

Now the City is home to many Catholic churches, but I don't think they will survive as long as the original ancient temples which were built to last. On the hills which surround the City of 400,000 inhabitants stand three symbols, all vying for connection.

On one is the original crown centre of the Incas. On another, dozens of radio television and 3G masts. And on another is a cold marble depiction of a white Jesus. I jest to my friends that it would be a great statement if someone would make him a giant rainbow poncho to help him look a bit more comfortable in his local surroundings. They love this idea.

Later we drive into the country to visit the sacred site known as 'The Temple of the Moon.' The snow-covered peak of Mount Q'umirqucha glows white in the south. We walk with dogs and horses to the ruins which are still used today for sacred ceremonies. I throw my poncho on the grass next to the altar and after a ritual cleansing and blessing, we enjoy a lovely picnic together.

A local farmer appears and tells us that he is the ancestral custodian of this place. He shows me where to find the special herbs used for health and for pleasing the spirits who reside here. We leave these along with our flowers and cocoa leaves charged with our good intentions in the door of the structure.

San Pedro Market is where the locals' shop. It's about the size of Tesco back in my hometown in Scotland but at least five hundred people are self-employed in here. Outside, there are street musicians and the air is filled with music and the sounds of life. There is a young blind man playing the most impressive 16 string electric guitar. And of course, there are panpipes. There are always panpipes.

To walk through this market is a deluge on all my senses. The arts, crafts and textiles are of the highest handmade quality and the colours are rich and vibrant using traditional local dyes. My eyes feast on the vivid neon colours.

There are rows and rows of stalls selling the most fragrant and beautiful local flowers and herbs for every ailment. The smell is sweet and makes me feel happy. The food section is overwhelming. Stalls offer every kind of fruit and vegetable imaginable including pulses,

potatoes, maize, cheese, nuts, and local honey.

I experience new tastes and flavours, so healthy and always locally produced. There are fish and meats of every kind, but the smell of dead meat is a bit offal. Cows' noses are a delicacy here as is guinea pig. Nothing is wasted and little is imported or processed.

My AirBnB room is clean and well-appointed, and my host couldn't be friendlier, but the location isn't the best. I am next to the main dual carriageway and it's a bit of an uphill hike to the centre of town. I decide to spend the second half of my eight days here in another more centrally located place.

Soon, I am next door to the town police station and just 100 yards from *Plaza de Armas*. It couldn't be safer or more central. This is the tourist zone and it soon proves to be a completely different kind of experience. From this vantage point, Cusco is such a beautiful City. It's surrounded by verdant green mountains. At night, the houses and streetlights on the nearby hills twinkle like stars.

At an altitude of over 11,000 feet, it's hard to breathe with so little oxygen in the air. *John Peel* died here when he was 65, of a heart attack, and I can understand why.

I have had enough of living a bohemian lifestyle these last few weeks. I'm under budget and decide to spare no expense in getting my health optimised before I tackle *Machu Pichu* and *Rainbow Mountain*.

I am tucking into the best 12 oz fillet steak served on a sizzling hot volcanic stone and cooked to perfection with tasty sauces. It's accompanied by local potatoes and the most delicious avocado salad and of course a half bottle of the best Chilean Red to wash it down. It's pure quality and at only £25, a bit of a bargain.

Over the next few days, I embark on a health regime starting with a cup of cocoa leaf tea, lots of water, 20 mins meditation, 30 minutes yoga followed by a healthy fresh fruit smoothie and a really good breakfast. In the afternoon I get the best therapeutic sports massage I have ever endured in a health sauna spa. My massage therapist is professional and masterful.

I walk around the town all day talking to folk. In the evening I dine well in the local Peruvian restaurants and there are so many to choose from. There are always great vegetarian and vegan restaurants options. My health and strength quickly restore. I meet lots of fellow nomads and backpackers of every nationality; Chile, Argentina, Venezuela, Germany, Italy, Japan, North America and of course Australia.

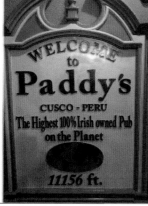

The next morning, I walk down the street. There are hundreds of military personnel on the square and I am thinking that war must have started. However, it's only the annual show of strength by the police, military, and public servants. Separate groups chant their battle cries as they march around the square accompanied by a military brass band (without panpipes). There are guns and shiny boots everywhere, but few residents have turned out to show their support.

You can't take two steps here without someone trying to sell you something. "Nice Restaurant Amigo?" "Relaxing massage senior?" "Nice shawl for your wife?" "Look at my paintings." "Shoeshine?" "'Pretty llama?" "Taxi?" It can get tiresome repeating "Non-Gracias," . I remind myself that these people are just trying to survive and if they don't sell, their children don't eat.

After a few days walking the same streets, the same faces get to know me and I smile, chat with them, and hand out chocolate kisses. It seems that they all know *Braveheart* and *William Wallace*. They are soon saying 'Hello Escoces amigo' and stop the hassle.

My health and strength are back and I'm ready now to tackle the climb to *Machu Pichu* and once I recover from that, the *Rainbow Mountain* at 17,100' above sea level.

Will I survive?

"I'd rather be a forest than a street
Yes, I would if I could, I surely would
I'd rather feel the earth beneath my feet
Yes, I would if I only could, I surely would."

Simon & Garfunkel

The Sacred Valley, Machupicchu and Rainbow Mountain...

December, Days 80-82: 18,135 miles

Years ago, my sister sent me an amazing photograph of a mountain in Peru known as *'Rainbow Mountain.'* As soon as I saw it, I just knew I had to go there.

That and seeing *Machupicchu* for myself, are the main reasons I have come to Peru. It's on every world travellers' bucket list and it's one of the wonders of this wonderful world.

I've had to get myself in shape for both climbs as the altitude is no joke. I decide to do a tour of *The Sacred Valley*. I get the bus to a little village called *Pisac* just 30 minutes from Cusco and stop off for breakfast.

Afterwards, I am sitting in a street doorway waiting for my next bus and three delightful young girls dressed in their native costumes sit down and join me. They are carrying two cute little lambs and have a pet baby Alpaca. "Can I take a photo?" one of them pleads. She can't be more than ten years old and she is showing me how to use the features of my new iPhone, including live feed and slo-mo.

It's a sign of the times when kids in a remote part of a 'third world' country know technology better than me. What fun we have. Even the alpaca seems to be amused.

The bus takes me up the mountain to the *Ruins of Pisac* which are a taste of what's to follow. The view down to the green valley floor below is beautiful. At the entrance of the ruins, dozens of local people have their handmade crafts laid out on the ground. The tourist dollar is their main source of income here and I'm both disappointed and relieved that I can't buy anything as I have to travel light.

The Inca civilisation was as advanced as the Aztecs who were based in Mexico. The Sun of God was the deity they worshipped, and the currency of Peru is still called the 'Sol'. Gold was believed to be the blood of the Sun with spiritual qualities which enhance fertility, health, and a smooth transit to the afterlife.

They created incredible towns based on detailed astronomy and the cycles of the seasons. A highly refined agriculture system was key to its success. The terraced retaining walls follow the contours of the mountains. These were backfilled with earth on top of sand on top of small rocks on top of large rocks. This stored heat and provided effective drainage.

The scale of these structures is formidable, especially when you consider that the soil was carried up thousands of feet from the valley floor below. These were exceptionally strong and organised people. Scientists still can't agree on how the buildings were built without using concrete and how the huge five-sided stone blocks were moved here and shaped to fit together so precisely.

Further on I visit the township of *Ollantaytambo*. Across the valley, hundreds of feet high are storage chambers carved into the face of the mountain. There are also lots of holes in the rock face where the dead

were buried in fetal position along with gold and silver to help pay their way to the sun god and the moon goddess in the next life. These were later pillaged by Spanish gold raiders who robbed the dead. How the Incas managed to carve these chambers into the sheer mountainside so high up is beyond my understanding.

At *Ollantaytambo* station, I take the Peru Rail *'Vista Train'* to the town of *Aguas Calientes* which is better known as Machupicchu. I'll be staying the night here in a hostel before heading up the mountain.

It's a delightfully slow two-hour ride in a beautiful train with a semi glass roof. The views as we follow the river are astonishing. Looking up I see huge sheer mountains towering above me into the blue cloudless sky above. I am served the best cup of coffee with milk that I have had for months, along with a perfect thick slice of moist carrot cake.

Machupicchu is a small town on the valley floor below the ancient site known as The Citadel. It's entirely dedicated to tourism. The hilly cobbled streets are full of restaurants, cafes, pubs, tourist shops, hotels, and hostels. A thousand people a day visit this site and most of them are young backpackers from all over the world.

There is also a natural hot springs spa and that's where I head to when I arrive. It has been a long day with lots of walking and climbing and the idea of soaking in hot mineral springs is too good to miss. It's only £2 for locals, £5 for Peruvians and £10 for foreigners like me. Fair enough.

The next morning I'm up at 5 am to catch the first batch of busses up to the top. The bus winds its way snake-like up the narrow rough track. It's a sheer drop to the valley below and the hairpin bends don't add much to my comfort levels. However, we arrive intact at the car park.

There's a hotel at the top owned by the wife of an ex-president and it costs $1000 per night to stay there. We are so high that the morning clouds drift well below us and yet the mountain tops still tower above. This really feels like the realm of the Gods and it's easy to see why the Incas revered this place. It was the home of the elite back in the day - the priests, scientists, astronomers, and professional class.

There are around 150 dwellings, temples, altars, and a sundial as well as a huge terraced agricultural area. The Spaniards never found this place when they plundered Cusco and destroyed the rest of the civilisation. Little wonder. However, without the support of the capital, the residents died of malnutrition and disease. It was then lost in time to the jungle.

In 1911 an American treasure hunter called *Hiram Bingham* discovered it. He set the jungle on fire to expose the ruins and went off with most of the gold and treasure. Since then it has been carefully restored but the treasure has never been recovered.

Two days later I am up at 3 am to head up Rainbow Mountain.

The bus driver is crazy, and he doesn't slow down around corners. The poor Volkswagen minibus almost leaves the ground as we hurtle up the bumpy mountain track for a grueling three hours. I tell myself that he has done this lots of times and try and sleep but it's impossible.

We arrive at the car park at the base of the mountain at 6 am and it's a beautiful day with sunny blue skies. Just perfect. At 17,060 feet above sea level, breathing is difficult. I can only walk about five steps before stopping to catch my breath. I am like a fish out of water. A dozen deep breaths and I'm ready for another few steps.

I realise with some horror that I am one of the oldest people here. Most of the others are more than half my age and they are struggling too. I'm a lifelong smoker with a heart condition. This is hard going but if I'm going to die today, I can't think of a better place to do it.

I finally make it to a place where the local farmers offer horse rides up part of the track. I jump at the chance and soon I'm strapped on and saddled up. There are dozens of horses being led up the track by tiny men and women.

I feel like *Clint Eastwood* with my poncho on. Staying on is easy when my horse is walking but then my horseman decides to start running up the narrow mountain track! The horse breaks into a canter and soon I am bumping up and down trying hard to work with the rhythm and not fall off.

The last 1,000 feet is on foot and it seems to take forever. The scenery is also breath-taking, and I just have to take it slow, one step at a time. I chew cocoa leaves and eat fruit and nut chocolate which seems to help.

There's a huge white glacier at one side of the valley. It's been melting for years and will soon disappear entirely. The landscape is out of this world. Neon green plants grow on mostly red iron oxide sand.

I finally make it to the top and see for the first time the famous rainbow vista. I am not disappointed. Blue cobalt, yellow sulphur and red iron oxide stripes paint the sides of the summit. At the top, there is a local farmer with two alpacas. I give them a cuddle and one of them kisses me on the cheek.

A kiss I will never forget.

Travel Tip No 9: Don't try and take selfies when you're on a horse.

"Somewhere, over the rainbow, way up high
And the dreams that you dreamed of once in a lullaby.
Somewhere over the rainbow bluebirds fly
And the dreams that you dreamed of really do come true."

Harold Arlen with lyrics by Yip Harburg

It's Hot in Chile...

December, Days 83-85: 20,865 miles

It's 30 degrees on a sunny Sunday in *Santiago*. Santa songs are playing in the supermarket and the shoppers are swinging to Sinatra. That's alliteration for you.

I grab some water and snacks and head out towards Plaza Brazil. I've been told that it's the funky artistic part of this massive City of over seven million inhabitants. Chile is the wealthiest country in South America according to GDP per person. It's twice that of Peru. This is due to copper mining which represents nearly 60% of its exports.

It's only half that of the UK but the roads are clean and well maintained. The city green spaces have their sprinklers on and there is employment, prosperity, and progress here. People seem happily content. I see no homeless, no beggars, no hustlers, no honking on the freeway and it's surprisingly cosmopolitan and feels strangely European.

The sound of Scottish traditional music grabs my ears and I find the source to be a Viking Restaurant and Pub. The walls are covered with artefacts of bone, wood, and metal. A waiter appears wearing full Viking battle armour. When he discovers that I'm from Scotland, he raises his big fist for a Viking handshake and shouts 'Escocia' while trying to give me a hug. It's like hugging a Dalek with all that armour on and a bit uncomfortable but he is friendly, horns and all.

It's the football final with Chile who is up against their old rivals, Argentina. The match is being held in Madrid. The stadium is full which must be a nice little earner for the Spanish authorities and air companies. Every pub here is packed around the big screen televisions. Whoops, cheers and groans are heard across the streets.

I order a pint and a tabla of savoury tapas for my brunch. The plate comes stuffed with olives, cheeses, meats and pickled vegetables and it's enough to feed four people. I've had my fill and pass the plate to the folk sitting on my left and minutes later there's another pint sitting in front of me. "Gracias." says Roberto. "Cheers." I respond.

He is from Chile and is here with his Argentinean girlfriend Pilar to watch the game. It goes down to penalties and Argentina steals it. People here cheer the game as opposed to the individual sides. Good ball play is applauded whichever side has control. Of course, there are some sad faces when Chile loses but everyone seems genuinely happy that it was a great game of football.

As I have discovered elsewhere on my travels, people just love us Scots. I ask Roberto why that is. "You are a brave people," he says. "I have seen *'Braveheart'* and *'Trainspotting.'* You guys are strong but kind despite years of suppression. You are also fighting back against your Royal masters in your pursuit for independence. We admire that here and wish we could do the same one day. Maybe you will show us the way?" "No, it's your accent," says Pilar. *"Billy Connolly* and *Shaun Connery*, very sexy!"

The next day I am travelling by bus through the fertile wine region. Santiago sits inside a huge ring road and it is circular by design. The City lies nestled between the magnificent Andes and the Coastal mountains. Soon we arrive at the coastal town of *Valparaiso.*

The sea air is cool and refreshing and the beaches are beautifully quiet. Pelicans fly in formation above the turquoise waves. The stubby palm trees have trunks which look like giant pineapples.

Valparaiso gets busy in the holiday season which starts in a few days when the population of this town increases tenfold. My timing is perfect. This town is built on the steep hillsides overlooking the ocean. Here they don't jail graffiti artists. The authorities seek out the most talented ones and commission them to paint beautiful murals on the grey concrete. The result is a riot of colour on every corner.

The houses themselves are painted in simple pastel colours and I follow the rainbow around the picturesque streets. Tourists like me love this and we bring our spades and bucket-loads of cash into this beach town.

It has been nearly three months since I left my home in Scotland, but it feels like a year. I have crammed in so much over that short time and travelled through both North and South America. I realise that I have just scraped the surface of these two great continents. The contrast between them is striking.

Our Royal ancestors must have agreed to divide the spoils five hundred years ago to build their respective Empires. The British Royals took the North and their Spanish cousins, the South. The Portuguese went east.

Despite the divisive news on people's televisions, I have experienced true racial integration and tolerance in the streets of South America. However, it has taken over five hundred years for this peace to mature. Everywhere I have been so far, I have met very kind and friendly people. I think that the biggest inequality which remains to resolve is the fair distribution of wealth, but that's another story.

"Take a pinch of white man
Wrap him up in black skin
Add a touch of blue blood
And a little bitty bit of Red Indian boy
Oh, like a Curly Latin kinkies
Oh Lordy, Lordy, mixed with yellow Chinkees,
Yeah you know you lump it all together
And you got a recipe for a get along scene
Oh, what a beautiful dream
If it could only come true, you know, you know
What we need is a great big melting pot
Big enough to take the world and all its got
And keep it stirring for five hundred years or more
And turn out coffee-coloured people by the score."

Blue Mink

New Zealand (South Island) with Penguins...

December, Days 85-89: 30,043 miles

It's a long overnight flight from Chile to New Zealand as we fly over 6,000 miles of sea and Antarctic Ice flows.

At *Wellington Airport* there are two huge life-like golden eagles hanging from the ceiling. One even has a full-size Gandalf sitting on its neck. I wish I could get up on the other one.

It is easy to see why *Peter Jackson* chose New Zealand for most of his locations in *Lord of the Rings*. I'm taking a few days to explore part of the South Island and heading to *Golden Bay* at its northern tip.

I rent a budget car at the airport and I'm delighted when I discover that it's a *Toyota* electric hybrid. I have dreamed of driving one of these for a long time. With only 2,000 miles on the clock, she is almost brand new.

She is a shiny ice white colour like the car I rented in San Francisco but smaller. I name her Baby Bianca in her honor. She has a loud blue tooth stereo system, an onboard GPS computer, and she talks to me in the same calm sultry tones as her big sister. With power steering, ABS brakes, wide wheels, and traction control, she zips around these windy gravel mountain tracks and hugs the tight bends like a Scalextric toy.

This is the perfect car for these roads and driving her is thrilling. The only downsides are she is as quiet as a mouse and she knows when I am speeding. "Stewart, please obey the local traffic regulations." That gets a bit

tiring when you hear it a hundred times. It's like having your mum on board. Mr Toyota is a very clever man but there should be a way to gag the nag.

We wind our way up and over the Takaka Hill which at 2,500 feet is a steep mountain where I come from. These mountains are made of marble and limestone and they create the most beautiful sand on the beaches below.

At the top, I am lost in the clouds but as we descend, the full expanse of the beautiful Golden Bay area presents itself. Cinnamon coloured sandy beaches stretch for miles along an aquamarine green and turquoise sea. Huge tree ferns cover the mountainsides. The valley floor is flat, lush green farmland sprinkled with little white sheep. Wow! Soon I am parked up at my yurt where I will be staying for a few days near a little village beach town called *Pohara*.

I wake to the sound of a bubbling brook, sparrows chattering and the familiar sounds of song thrushes, chaffinches, blackbirds, and sheep. It's just like home except there is a strange bird call which comes from the much-loved Tui bird. It's like a blackbird but it has what looks like cotton buds on its chest and it whistles wonderful, whacky loony tunes.

My hosts, Steve and his wife, moved from *Guernsey* nineteen years ago and bought the six chalets. Since then they have transformed the whole area into a charming eco-centre. Streams have been diverted into freshwater ponds and into the plumbing system. There

are bridges, a pizza oven, a yoga workshop, a massage room, a yurt, and a big hippy bus. Golden Bay is full of wonderful characters like Steve, old school hippies enjoying nature and the good life.

The small town of *Takaka* is just five miles away and the high street is lined with whole food shops, veggie cafes, fish and chip shops and art studios. There are lots of hostels and campsites with camper vans full of young dread-locked freedom fighters and girls wearing shorts and walking boots.

On Steve's recommendation, I head up to the nearby *Wainui Waterfall* in one of the protected National Parks. It feels great to be back in the calm green jungle. There are no snakes or biting insects here apart from the sand-flies which are like giant midges on steroids. And there are no native four-legged mammals. There are however giant snails as big as your fist and with six thousand teeth, eat giant earthworms as thick as your thumb.

At last, it feels like I am in a foreign country. Huge nikau palms, rata trees and tree ferns line the path and the sounds of unknown songbirds call from the bushes. The path leads me up a toothpaste clear river across a bouncy swing bridge towards the source of the sound of rushing water; a crystal cascading waterfall bursting with light sparticles.

I sit on a massive granite boulder as the mist swirls around the moss-green rocks and water. It's so peaceful, refreshing, and lovely to be here alone with the sights, sounds and smells of nature. Green, stone faces peer out from the rocks and change with the sunlight and the shadows. A beautiful tiny bird known as the fantail appears and spreads its white tail feathers before leaping a perfect cartwheel into the air in the hope of attracting a mate.

The next day I explore the beaches which Golden Bay is famous for. Just when everything seems too familiar, I come across something quite unexpected and bizarre. There are road signs alerting me that penguins are crossing! Yes, p-p-proper little p-p-penguins and they are b-b-blue! The beaches are beautiful and deserted and the water is warm enough to just float away.

At the most northern point of South Island is *Wharariki Beach and Farewell Point.* The Maoris believed that this was the place where their spirits left the island when they died. It's very windy up here and I have to hold on tight as I scramble up the steep hills above the cliffs. If I'm not careful I could soon be joining them.

Looking down I see how generations of sheep have terraformed this land. From up here, it looks like a gently manicured golf course. The sheep have grazed on most of the local exotic vegetation leaving the familiar grasses, clover, buttercups, and daisies to thrive. Lovely meadows now exist where there was once wild marsh and woodland. This could be the Yorkshire Dales if it weren't for the Tolkien styled lumpy hills and the sunshine.

Walking through the wind-shaped juniper and gorse groves miles from anyone else feels good. My mind releases all thoughts of 'the

world' and I too disappear as I attune to the marvelous landscape with its twists and turns. The grasses tickle my legs and I start to notice the tiny details; miniature blue moths and golden butterflies flit through the buttercups. Ladybirds crawl to the ends of grass tips and launch themselves whirring into space. A beautiful universe exists in just a square foot of meadow.

I hear the song of chaffinch, yellowhammer, and skylark. I am halfway around the planet, some 11,000 miles from home, yet it's all too strangely familiar. I descend the steep path across a stream and onto the remote beach at Whararaki, I see two Sooty Oystercatchers. They are like our own except that they are jet black with fluorescent orange beaks and feet with sharp claws. I try to get up close and friendly for a photo when all hell breaks loose. They go mental and start shrieking as they fly straight at my face.

Their bills are like sharp orange knitting needles and I am soon tumbling backwards into the sand, arms flailing. Like bats out of hell, they don't give up. I scramble to safety and realise that I must have dropped my new sunglasses near their nest.

I arm myself with my selfie stick extended like a sword and my backpack as a shield and head back into battle. They come straight at me again, one at my face and one at the back of my head. I see my glasses and grab them before running as fast as I can with the demon birds in hot pursuit.

That was exciting and my heart is pounding. On the beach, I spot a large baby seal lazing on the sand. It looks so cute as I approach for a photo. Suddenly it makes a feeble floppy lunge at me and growls a set of huge razor-sharp teeth. Its mum must have nipples like thimbles.

I am beginning to think that Darwin may have had his head stuck up his Galapagos. And Noah was really the story of Nora from Brora. I think she filled fishing boats with sheep, birds, local flora, and fauna including cabbage white butterflies and bumblebees and shipped them all over here.

Sheep, birds, plants, and insects here seem to be 80% Scottish. Perhaps the stronger and more resilient Scottish genes then quickly took over, displacing the locals. A bit like what we did with the Maoris who now represent only 15% of the population.

"All that is gold does not glitter,
Not all those who wander are lost;
The old that is strong does not wither,
Deep roots are not reached by the frost.
From the ashes, a fire shall be woken,
Light from the shadows shall spring;
Renewed shall be blade that was broken,
The crownless again shall be King."

The Return of the King.

New Zealand (North Island) with Hobbits...

December, Days 93-99: 30,729 miles

An old friend, Warren kindly collects me from the airport and after a couple of hours of much-needed sleep he whisks me off to band practice.

Samba Ao Vento is a great bunch of drummers, dancers and percussionists in New Zealand and I have just one rehearsal to prepare for their Festive Gig held in a huge arena in *Palmerston North*. It's a very professional setup, big stage, great sound and light system, TV cameras and a happy and appreciative audience of 500 - 800 folk. We go down well, and it feels great to be back on stage banging my drum with such a great bunch of musicians.

Of course, the after-gig parties are always the best and we get to do the whole thing all over again at a great garden party with folk from all over the world including Chile and Mexico where I've just come from.

Warren and his partner Sandra, live in a lovely rustic colonial country house with a huge garden including two pigs, two cats and of course a bunch of sheep. Their garden includes oak, fir and gean trees, hydrangeas, English roses, gorse, and broom.

House sparrows chirp and swallows dip to catch their breakfast on the wing. There are also song thrush, blackbirds, wren, chaffinch, yellowhammer, and even black-headed gulls. The lawn is full of clover and bumblebees. If it weren't for the eucalyptus trees and the few palms and exotic grasses, this could be anywhere in sunny Scotland (on a good day).

The next morning, I am awakened by a shake and tremor. That was one of our many earthquakes says Warren. "Sometimes the whole house shakes and there are many active volcanoes here which occasionally blow." Phew! I'm glad we don't get those in Scotland!

I have been invited to a *'marae'* by a local Maori family for a *'hangi.'* It's a great honor for me to meet the real locals. A marae is a Maori tribal or family community gathering place. A hangi is a traditional method of cooking food in a pit under the ground.

The guys greet me with the traditional *'hongi'*, heads and noses touch as we 'see' and welcome each other. The food has been cooking and steaming on beds of cabbage leaves all day under a big mound of soil. The soil is dug away revealing metal baskets of chickens, pork, beef, potatoes, and other root vegetables. It's enough food to feed an army and the whole lMaori community soon arrive to share the feast.

This is a family affair and it's a real privilege to be part of this. Afterwards, we party, play music, drink, and socialise into the early hours. The community space includes a large dormitory where everyone sleeps on comfortable floor mattresses and no one needs to drink and drive. I discover that Maoris party hard and snore loudly, so we wake early and head for home.

Warren is a generous host and he is keen to show me more of this island. We have a wonderful time in *Wellington,* the cosmopolitan capital of this country. It's a youthful, fun, and arty place with great pubs and

restaurants. Then we take a road trip north to *Taupo*, a lovely town built around a huge submerged volcano.

We stay in a motel called *'Twin Peaks'*, coincidentally one of my favourite TV series of the nineties. In the morning we soak in a nearby mountain stream with hot spring water flowing down waterfalls at over 40 degrees. It's a fantastic way to blow away the cobwebs.

We then head to *Hobbiton*. I failed most of my exams in 5th year at school due to my addiction to one of the greatest fantasy books ever written. It was 1,158 pages long and I had no time left for studying boring stuff. *'Lord of the Rings'* and 'The Hobbit' have more recently gained global popularity due to the movies. But for me, Tolkien, their author, is still the master of 'other worlds.'

To be walking around the film set makes me feel so happy, innocent, and childlike again, facing the seemingly dark and foreboding future. My alter ego could be *Bilbo Baggins* and my favourite scene is where he chases after *Gandalf* and jumps over the gate in the meadow shouting "I'm going on an adventure." Isn't it amazing how ideas formed in our early years can manifest for real further on down the road? I guess we just follow who and what we love and connect with. Destiny then pulls us forward.

Christmas is all about connection. We send cards to folk we haven't seen for years. We get in touch. We eat, drink, and get merry. And that is exactly what I am doing here. Sandra cooks not one, but three delicious Christmas dinners. We demolish the wine rack and we are very merry indeed. I receive so much love and feel spoilt, just like Christmas past. We didn't watch the Queen's message but instead, I have a message for you ...

If Brexit bankrupts Britain and we don't have the confidence to vote for a fresh start and stand on our own feet. If you are young enough to start again and feel adventurous, consider moving here. Keep your record clean and get the necessary qualifications. This place is like home but with opportunity, hope and pleasant weather. Your parents and friends will miss you, but your kids, grandkids and new friends will thank you. It's only 11,000 miles around the corner and for less than 10p per mile, it's a bargain. Start saving just £1 a day now and you could be here in 3 years.

This is an incredibly beautiful world we all share. Get out and experience the people, things, and places you love while you still can. It's changing so fast now. Everything and everyone you now love, you will lose one day. But this I have learned - That love will always continue and return to you in a different form.

It's hot and balmy on Christmas Day and Warren is getting the barbecue ready. I hear the pop of the first bottle of strawberry fizzy wine so it's time to go.

"And in the end.
The love you take
Is equal to the love you make."

John Lennon and Paul McCartney

Fireworks in Sydney, Australia...

January, Days 100-107: 32,068 miles

If New Zealand is like Scotland, then *Sydney* is like England. Even the street names are English. I am staying in Kings Cross, near to *Oxford Street, Bayswater Road* and *Liverpool Street*. *Hyde Park* is a popular central place to hang out under the oak trees. The streets are lined with cafes selling English breakfasts and there are Pommies everywhere.

Kings Cross was renamed from Queens Cross which is ironic because it was the home of the LGBT movement in Australia in the Seventies. It's now full of wealthy-looking, silver-haired queens who now camp out in the great street cafes and restaurants. Muscled, toned, and tanned Adonis type young men parade and jog along the pavements with nothing on but tattoos, shorts, and expensive trainers. And their shorts seem far too tight to be either respectable or comfortable.

My AirBnB is near a quiet neighbourhood conveniently close to the city centre and which managed to hold on to its local Aborigine name. *Woolloomooloo* means 'baby kangaroo.' I decide to use the *Hop-on, Hop-Off* transport network to bounce around the town and get my bearings. It's a wonderful way to see the sights.

I am told that when the first invaders came here from Britain and saw Skippy for the first time, one of them asked a native what it was. The Aborigine answered "Kangaroo" which translates to "I don't know what you mean." And the name just stuck. It seems that the locals still have difficulties communicating with their 'more sophisticated' rulers.

It's often said that convicts initially populated Australia. What we are not told is that many of these convicts were convicted for the most trivial crimes, for example, chopping down the landlord's tree or not paying the rent. The British Royal masters and their legislatures then bundled them on to ships partly as ballast and to become unpaid slaves to their aristocratic friends. The commonwealth was not for commoners.

I hop off at Sydney *Opera House* which looks like some upturned white seashells. It's smaller than I imagined but beautiful, nevertheless. I then hop on a ferry which takes me around the bay area with its many beaches, yachts, and pleasure boats. This is a huge city which grew around this beautiful natural harbour. It's one of the deepest in the world.

Outside of the modern and sterile commercial centre of usual global corporate brands, it has kept its 'small town' feel with local shops and restaurants. Sydney is really lots of villages all strung together. The people are friendly, know their neighbours and support their local communities.

The first currency used here was rum. It was used not only to pay the sailors but also the first road builders and city planners. No wonder the streets aren't straight. It's 38 degrees here today and too hot to walk in the open sun. But there are lots of green spaces in this city to sit in the shade and it feels light and open.

The top deck of the bus is blistering hot so I hop downstairs for the air conditioning.

The next day the weather forecast is even hotter, so I head for *Bondi Beach*. That's where the rich and famous are said to hang out including *Kylie Minogue*. It's huge, hot, and packed with beach babes, boobs, beach balls and beach bums of all nationalities. Thankfully though, nude bathing was stopped a few years back.

I find a space to spread my towel and soon merge into the mass of oiled and basted sun-seekers. The water is freezing and the contrast between that and the heat of the sun is a bit of a shock to the system. The waves are big enough to surf and long lines of people are deluged when the big waves crash to shore. There are lifeguards everywhere keeping an eye out for the sharks and the shark food.

It's mostly tourists here. I hear British, Americans, Indians, Germans, French, Italians, Polish, and Chinese. I guess the Aussies are much too sensible to be cooked on the beach like this. I imagine that they are all at home with their feet in the fridge and their hands on a cold beer around the barbie or are watching last year's cricket on the telly.

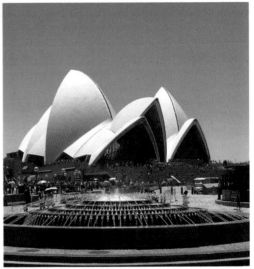

I make sure that I lash on the sunscreen in my attempt to turn my skin colour from milky to 'milky tea.' The wind picks up and soon I am covered in sticky sand which is the best sunscreen of all. Things start to get really hot when the couple sitting just yards away from me get a little too amorous. And I thought 'Sex on the Beach' was the name of a cocktail! Of course, I avert my eyes but can't help having a wee sideways peek through my sunglasses now and again.

Suddenly a rogue wave hits the beach soaking a mile of sunbathers and dampening my neighbours' passions. To the sounds of shrieks and wails, everyone is trying to rescue their soaked beach towels, phones, and bric-a brac. Thousands of bottles, plastic spades and buckets are sucked into the sea while hundreds of people frantically chase after them. It's hilarious to watch but it's also just another small contribution to our ocean's plastic pollution. I didn't see Kylie.

My bedroom overlooks the back garden in a quiet neighbourhood. However, at dusk, it gets much noisier with strange and unusual birds. There are lots of big Australian magpies which make the most wonderful sounds. The much smaller and aggressive minor birds chase them away. But the noisiest of all is a huge white-crested cockatoo which screeches like a cat with its tail on fire. There are also beautiful rainbow lorikeet parrots and yes, kookaburras sit in the old gum trees.

Just before dark, the sky is filled with huge black flying foxes. They are really megabats with three-foot wingspans and heads as big as a fox. They silently swoop into the garden and hang out in the banana trees. Spooky. There's a spider carcass in the woodshed as big as a small hand and lots of strange creepy crawlies here too. Most of them bite. Scary.

Sydney

This time last year, it was cold, wet, and windy in Scotland and I decided to spend my Hogmanay at home with Jack Daniels and a movie. I was sad, bored, and alone and I can't remember midnight or indeed, the end of the movie. I didn't hug anyone.

Next day I made a checklist of things that I still love, places I would still love to see and activities I would still love to experience. It was a lengthy list without many things. That was really the start of this journey. Sometimes we can't see the light until it gets dark.

Sydney was on that list because I love people, parties, and fireworks. Every Hogmanay, millions of us come here to connect, to celebrate life, to express hope for the future and to enjoy one of the most spectacular fireworks displays in the world. A billion of us watched it on television last year.

It's Hogmanay and a freak storm hangs over the City. The birds in the garden go quiet as massive thunderclouds billow above me and then Mother Nature starts her own show. Huge lightning forks flash high in the sky followed by the loudest thunder I have ever heard. The house shakes and then is deluged in a downpour which keeps up all afternoon. People are sleeping in the public parks to get the best view of the fireworks. They must be getting soaked. Mother Nature shows her strength and it's the best free show in town.

I have a ticket for a trendy New Year's beach party at *Watson's Bay*. Soon I am jostling with the young and beautiful to try and get a drink at the bar. I pay £10 for a plastic bottle of Heineken and spill most of it trying to get back to the dance floor.

The countdown begins and, at zero, the place erupts into mayhem. There's a better view from the beach out front and it really is spectacular and on a grand scale. I watch in awe as a million pounds of synchronised pyrotechnics per minute erupt into the skies above.

The roads are gridlocked all the way back home on the 2-hour bus ride. The banter is good with those of us who are still soberish and awake. Outside, the streets are lined with young revelers walking barefoot into the new dawn and a hopeful future. Firstly, they will have to find their shoes and lose their hangovers though.

In the last 15 weeks, I have travelled over 32,000 miles in 21 flights, 18 buses, 8 trains and 12 days by car. I have slept in 34 beds including the car. Tomorrow I pick up my hippy campervan for a road trip to visit my friend Sharon on the Gold Coast before flying to reunite with my friend in Perth.

I wish you all the very best for the year ahead but especially good health and good fun. I hope you all live your dreams in twenty nineteen.

"Raise your glass and we'll have a cheer
For us all who are gathered here.
And a happy new year to all that is living
To all that is gentle, kind and forgiving
Raise your glass and we'll have a cheer
My dear acquaintance, a happy new year."

Pink Martini

Surf and Turf on Australia's East Coast...

January, Days 108-116: 33,098 miles

I hire a colourful hippy camper van for a week-long road trip up the East Coast from Sydney. It has the words 'Let Go' on the bonnet.

It develops a fault and is replaced by a black sleek machine which looks more like a funeral car. It's not what I want but it turns out to be exactly what I need to rough camp discreetly in the public car parks and forests on this part of my journey.

I name her 'Black Betty' and we zigzag up the coast to Brisbane, alternating between the hot beaches and the cool rain forests. A kind of surf and turf road trip. She has everything I need including air conditioning, a great stereo, a comfortable bed and even a kitchen sink.

A few hours North West of Sydney is *Katoomba National Park*, home of the *Blue Mountains*. These are blanketed with eucalyptus trees and the oil from them refracts the light into the blue end of the visible spectrum. The mountains really do appear blue.

I find a free campsite at the top of one and park up in the trees. There are around eighty young folk here tonight; wild campers, backpackers, trekkers, and climbers. At night we gather around campfires to share travellers' tips and stories. When it gets dark, the cicadas start to sing. How these small beetles can make so much noise is incredible.

My campsite neighbours are a happy young couple from Canada. Mark and Avril flew to Sydney and bought a cheap camper van on the internet. They are now spending three months driving around mountains and climbing them with ropes strapped to each other. At the end of their holiday, they intend to sell the van and are hopeful that they will get their money back. That's the way to do it.

Black Betty has one-way darkened glass, but it still feels weird getting ready for bed and seeing the people outside. By 10 pm the campsite is silent, and I decide to get up before dawn to see the sunrise over an amazing local natural feature known as *'Echo Point.'*

It's 5 am and bleary-eyed I arrive at the viewing place. I look down in amazement to see milky white clouds flowing below. The surrounding mountains are silhouetted dark against the morning sky. It's dreamlike. Parrots screech in the canopy far below me, their shrieks echoing off the canyon walls..

The sun breaks through its scarlet shroud to appear behind the 'three sisters.' These are an unusual rock formation which rise up high into the sky. The clouds then slowly change colour from white to yellow, to orange and then to scarlet before softening into pastel tones of blue and yellow. Finally, the dark mountain silhouettes change to shades of green fading to blue at the horizon far away.

The *North Pacific Highway* is a good road with lots of road works and strict speed limits, but it gets a bit boring after a while. I look for a beach south of *Newcastle* to camp up for the night. Most of them are privately owned or are next to commercial caravan sites. Eventually, though I discover *Redhead Beach* next to a public car park and find a space under the trees. I heat up my chicken noodle soup, spread some sandwiches, pop a bottle of red, and sit on the sand to watch the sunset over the sea. It's glorious but sadly, there are no redheads in sight.

At 6 am the car park is full again and I awake surrounded by early morning dog walkers, joggers, and surfers. Australians get up and get going early to avoid the mid-day heat. And so, do I. First stopping at a beach town called *Port Nelson* to climb *Tomaree Mountain* for a better view of the landscape. It's a steep ascent through the forest in this sweltering heat.

A kookaburra flies over my head with a gecko still wriggling in its beak. I hear the excited call of its chicks as it feeds it to one of its young. At the top, I am rewarded by a soothing cool breeze and a magnificent view over the *Karuah River* estuary with its beaches and islands and the Tasmania Sea beyond.

I stop for the night in *Port MacQuarrie* at the mouth of the *Hastings River.* I have now developed an eye for good parking places. It's probably not entirely legal but the best public car parks are often near to good public facilities. The public toilets here are exceptionally clean and there are picnic tables behind my car. There is even an outside shower and the beach is just a stone throw away.

Beaches are great for surfers, swimmers, joggers, and dog walkers. If you are not into any of those pastimes, then it's just sun, sand, sea, waves, wind, and sky. The coastal towns I have seen so far are also home to booming yachting and boating communities.

At *Coff's Harbour*, the large rocks used to shore up the harbour defences have been painted by people with personalized messages. Mostly births, marriages and deaths or hatches, matches, and dispatches. It's very poignant and thought-provoking and it certainly brightens up the area. Near where I am parked there are people dancing with poi fire sticks. They are accompanied by a group of djembe drummers and I am invited into the circle.

A cute baby girl, who can't be more than 18 months old, crawls towards me. I find a small drum and hand it to her. Soon she is keeping rhythm with both hands and she can't even walk yet.

Across the street, the funfair winds down for the night and it's quiet and peaceful when everyone leaves. I have the night beach to myself with only the sound of the ocean surf to gently lull me to sleep.

For some reason, big things seem to attract people and Australian businesses know how to exploit this. Across the country, there are dozens of 'Big Things' and there is even a Big Things road tour for folk who want to tick them off their big bucket lists. There is a 40-foot golden guitar, a 50-foot lobster, a 50-foot tall Koala bear which weighs

12 tons, a 50-foot aboriginal hunter who weighs only eight tons, oh, and cricket stumps big enough to walk through. Today I am here to marvel at 'The Big Banana.' It's big, yellow, made of plastic and people are queuing up to take a selfie. Today sadly, I am one of them.

The *Dorrigo Rainforest* is a bird watchers paradise. There are over 800 bird species in Australia - and 11,000 in the entire world. The birds here have great names such as; Lewin's Honeyeater, Golden Whistler, Grey Fantail, Australian Brush Turkey, Satin Bowerbird, Topknot Pigeon, Wompoo Fruit-Dove, White-browed scrub wren, Brown Thornbill, Eastern Yellow Robin, Red-browed Finch and Grey Goshawk.

The forest walk starts from high up and leads steeply down to the rain forest floor. At the bottom, there are two beautiful waterfalls. I then must climb back up another steep path to get back to the beginning. It's an eight-mile trek but the forest is cool, mysterious, and inviting with fascinating glimpses of wild nature.

As I walk down, large whirring beetles fly around me, like tiny drones checking me out. Under the matted canopy, the sun becomes furtive. It sneaks down through the tangle of treetops, ferns, orchids, and lichens. On the ground, the forest smells of seduction, fermentation, and death. Huge vines climb around their hosts like serpents seeking the sunlight.

The forest ranger told me that he has seen large snakes knocking possums from the trees and swallowing them whole. Gulp!

Down, down, deeper, and down I go, and the sounds of bird song intensify. I mimic them and some come closer to investigate. Across the path, I spot a four foot long shiny black snake with a scarlet belly. It slithers back under the shrubs, but I look nervously upwards for signs of falling possums. Later, I discover that it's called a 'shiny black and scarlet snake' and it is venomous.

My final surf town is the infamous *Byron Bay*. Inspired by the Woodstock festival in 1969, a group of people organised a hippy festival in the nearby town of Nimbin in 1972. That festival set the scene for the entire alternative movement in Australia. The surf waves in Byron Bay are two miles long and it's now a magnet for surfers and hippy backpackers. The hippies got high and invested in real estate and property prices are now sky high too.

It's a great small town full of juice bars, burger joints, Mexican takeaways, surf shops and cool themed bars. It's known as the rainbow town and at night, the rainbow people converge on a grassed area near the beach to watch the sunset and listen to the talented buskers. At dusk, hundreds of chattering rainbow lorikeets arrive to find their roost above us in the trees.

There is an old guy asleep on the grass and his few belongings are blowing in the wind. I bend down to rescue them and slip them under his begging hat. A couple of nomads passing by thank me for being kind to their friend and invite me to join them.

A wise person once told me to always try and befriend the old grannies in strange countries. Why?

Because they are survivors and the dodgy kids are probably their grandchildren. I sit on a bench next to an old Aborigine woman and I call her *'Princess'*. 'My name is Diana' she tells me, 'but I am no princess', she cackles with a toothless grin. "Buy me a bottle of sherry?" she then asks.

There are four distinctive tribes on this beach tonight. Firstly, there are the young and beautiful kids, tanned and tattooed and looking cool while taking endless selfies. Then there are the silent disco group.

Two young guys are travelling around Australia with a VW camper converted to a DJ camper. For $5, you rent a set of L.E.D. headphones and chose your favourite music channel. The headphones change colour to show what music you are dancing to. The beach is full of folk with bright lights on their heads, dancing in the dark to different tunes. It's like a surreal silent movie.

The group I am in I call the 'local nomads'. There are 150 homeless folk here who sleep on the beach. Many of them have mental health issues and alcohol dependencies but the older survivors are some of the kindest and wisest souls I have ever met.

The final group is the evangelistic young Christians. They have set up a stage to perform Jesus songs and they are handing out free pancakes while offering free spiritual healing to anyone who wants to join them. We gratefully accept the pancakes but decline the invitation to be saved.

I overnight park nearby, and in the morning head to the talking toilet. I press a green button on the door and the stainless-steel door slides open. "Welcome to Exoloo, I am a self-cleaning toilet, please take a seat." I prefer to stand but do as I'm told. "You have 10 minutes before the doors open," it announces. Jazz music then plays through the speakers. I am Mr Bean trying to poo to the sound of *'The Girl from Ipanema',* It's surreal.

After only a few minutes, the voice announces, "I have not detected any motion for several minutes." Jeez is there a camera inside the bowl watching my bum? "Please make a motion or move your arms or the doors will open in 30 seconds." ... Shit!

So here I am, shorts at my ankles waving my arms frantically around to an invisible camera when, you guessed it, the door opens wide and I am exposed to the entire beach area. The face of the guy waiting to get in is a picture. "Struth mate, that's not what you want to see first thing in the bloody morning!" I manage to waddle to the door to press the close button and then the toilet self-flushes and steam laced with smelly disinfectant hits me from all angles.

Coughing, I try to wash the detergent from my face and hands. There's a smart shiny stainless-steel sink in the wall. It automatically dispenses, soap, hot water, and hot air. I lean in to wash my face and a

big blob of sticky soap lands on the top of my head. I wash off the bubbles and then the hot air blows them all over my face. The doors open and I manage to escape the tortureloo. I am now clean and disinfected but smell like a toilet so it's back in the sea for me.

Later, I pass a painted shopfront which says, "More animals, fewer robots." I must agree.

Near to Byron Bay, there is an interesting place called *The Crystal Castle*. It boasts some of the largest geodes and crystals in the world. There is even a huge hollow stone big enough to lie inside surrounded by thousands of violet amethysts. There are beautiful peace gardens, bamboo groves, a labyrinth and Buddha statues everywhere. It's £20 for admission but for an extra £20 you get to meditate in the crystal cave. New Age is Old Business.

I drive up to *Brisbane* to return Black Betty and then catch a train back down to *The Gold Coast* to spend two nights with my friend Sharon. We first met a couple of years ago when she stayed with me as an AirBnB guest. We share many interests including bio-geometry, energy healing and nature.

If anyone is in any doubt at the effectiveness of this work, they only have to sit in Sharon's garden. Birds and animals are more sensitive to energy, electricity and Wi-Fi and they are almost tame here. Water dragons which are two-foot-long lizards pop their heads out of the shrubs and walk like puppets on strings towards us. Crows, magpie birds, minor birds and others fly in to sit next to us just meters away. I have a lovely two nights in a comfortable bed and enjoy the first proper bath in a long time. On the way to the airport, I catch my first glimpse of kangaroos.

Fully refreshed, I book the long 3,000 mile flight to *Perth* on the other side of this huge continent to continue my journey.

Travel Tip No 10: In tropical countries with strange creepy crawlies, always carry a torch. Especially before using an outside toilet.

Travel Tip No 11: Use sunscreen.

Travel Tip No 12: If you leave your shoes or clothes outside, always check for spiders and scorpions before putting them back on.

"May the long-time sun shine upon you
All love surround you
And the pure light within you guide your way on."

Paul Joseph (Nimbin Festival 1972)

Australia's Wild West...

January, Days 117-130: 36,998 miles

I fly nearly 3,000 miles across Australia from the East Coast to the West. It's a brief stopover in Perth followed by a short flight to *Albany* to meet my friend Skip.

We plan to spend a week glamping in remote *Bremer Bay* before travelling north another 800 miles into the hot red heart of this huge continent. Here I am about to meet some of the most eccentric, independent, and toughest people on earth enduring very hostile environments in pursuit of their dreams.

Fremantle is a small suburb of Perth and I am staying here in a great AirBnB for just two nights. I couldn't have found a better host. Glenn is an *Alexander Technique* practitioner and teacher. He is about my age in similar circumstances and we share similar interests, so I feel instantly at home. He gives me great local tips on what to do in my brief time here.

It's a short walk to the harbour and into the centre of town. There is a fantastic indoor market here with stallholders selling a wide range of local foods, arts, crafts, and homemade products. Outside, street entertainers thrill the assembled crowd with magic tricks, juggling and wicked irreverent Aussie humour.

I have found Australians to be generally a very friendly and easy-going bunch. The West coast folk seem even more friendly than those in the East and strangers smile at me and say "How ya going, mate?"

There are two massive fish and chip shops here serving seafood straight from the harbour. I am in the *Kailis Fish Market Cafe* with another hundred customers and I am being served by Janice who used to work in the chip shop in *Anstruther, Scotland*. Two pieces of fish, huge battered prawns, scallops, squid rings and chips double fried to crispy perfection. With dollops of homemade tartar sauce and a mug of tea for just £10, it's the best fish and chips I have ever tasted.

I meet Skip in Albany and after stocking up at the local supermarket we drive 112 miles to Bremer Bay on the south coast.

This is a remote and small rural community of only 250 people. There are two pubs though. Access roads have been built into the peninsula and the bushland carved into blocks for sale. My friend has bought one of around eight acres with magnificent views over two of the five nearby beaches. There are now two small caravans on-site with a rainwater collection tank and an outside dry toilet. Electricity to charge the fridge, L.E.D. lights and our laptops is via a solar panel. Most folk here live entirely 'off the grid.'

Gavin and Jayne are our closest neighbours and they have been developing their lot for around seven years. First, they cleared a small part of the land and laid gravel roads and building pads. Then they built a small office and a huge metal 'shed' before starting to build their house from mostly recycled wood, steel, and modern materials. They have now planted up their garden with fruit trees and vegetables and brew their

own alcohol. They hope to be living well off the grid within the year. Gavin's port, rum and beer are excellent. Hic! Their dream is nearing completion, but others have yet to begin.

Workers here usually stop work when the temperature reaches 35 deg Celsius. It's 44 degrees Celsius or 112 degrees Fahrenheit today. The sand is too hot to walk on and the soles of my sandals and the tarred roads are melting. There's nothing to do but stay inside or get into the sea, drink lots, and sweat it out. My washing dries, hot to the touch in just twenty minutes in the shade.

The creeks and lakes have all dried up leaving vast areas of white dry salt. The news reports of hundreds of wild horses dying of thirst and informs us that this is the hottest month ever recorded. There are many bush fires here often started by lightning. Everything is so dry that the fires quickly spread through the oil-rich shrubs and gum trees which explode in the heat.

After a week of sun and sea, we strike camp and load up the caravan to tow it north to Kalgoorlie, a journey of nearly 500 miles through red arid desert and black burnt bush. The Nisan Patrol 4WD vehicle struggles with the weight and the heat. Soon the heating gauge is showing dangerously high levels. We can't risk getting stranded out here miles from anywhere, so we slow down, switch off the air conditioning and switch on the heater to try and cool the engine. Burning hot air blasts through the vents and I have to stick my head out of the open window to try and cool down. It's 44 degrees out there and it must be over 60 in here.

We drink lots of water and keep going like two eggs being slowly poached. Suicidal kangaroos jump across the road. If they can survive this heat wearing a fur coat surely, we can too. Every hour or two we pass a petrol station, park in the blistering shade, and seek respite in the air-conditioned shop. Ice cream never felt so good.

The Western Australian gold rush began in 1893 in *Kalgoorlie*, when *Paddy Hannan* found gold in the area. Today, Kalgoorlie-Boulder is one of the most important mining areas in the world, with several large mining operations located in and around the town, including the huge 'Super Pit' which is one of the largest man-made holes on our planet. There is around 200,000 tons of excavated gold in the world now and this pit produced over 26 tons of it last year. A staggering 600,000 tons of earth is removed and processed for each ton of gold.

This place feels like the Wild West, but the horses have been replaced with monster trucks and off-road vehicles. The roads are wide and small shops line the main street. The towns' clock tower is sheathed in gold leaf and shines like a beacon. The hotel bars feature 'skimpies' - bar girls wearing skimpy bikinis. People have to be tough here to endure the grueling work, the remoteness and the fierce heat and it has made them strong, independent, and resilient.

We head out into the bush with an elderly couple who are now in their eighties and have been searching for gold for the last forty years.

The largest nugget they have found is worth $40,000. My metal detector beeps loudly, and I scrape the hot red earth with my pickaxe only to discover some rusty old wire and metal. However, one of us finds a tiny piece lying on the surface weighing around four grams and worth around £100 at today's prices.

The streets here are lined with gold. Finding it is the problem, and over the years, thousands of miners and prospectors have lost their lives searching for it. A few have made their fortunes.

It's hot work and afterwards, we pop into *the Broad Arrow Tavern* for a pint. It's in the middle of nowhere and yet the entire pub, including the toilets and the ceilings, are covered with visitors' names and messages dating back many decades. Virginia from *Tasmania* has been running this bar for years and she seems tougher than some of the locals.

Australia Day is the official national day of Australia. Celebrated annually on 26 January, it marks the anniversary of the 1788 arrival of the First Fleet of British ships at Port Jackson, New South Wales, and the raising of the flag of 'Great Britain' which claimed the continent as its own. It's a public holiday with fireworks in the park. Afterwards, most folk head to the pubs but the aboriginals stay outside on the streets blagging cigarettes, their preferred currency.

There is a real clash of worlds and cultures here more polarised than anywhere else I have visited so far. As recently as 1972, the aboriginals were classified as 'Flora and Fauna' with no human rights and they were not protected by the constitution.

It's estimated that between 1883 and 1969 more than 6,200 children were taken by Government agencies and the church from their families in New South Wales alone. They were treated like slaves and severely punished if they were found to be talking in their own language. They are now known as the 'Stolen Generations.'

In 2008, the Australian prime minister apologised. Although things are now changing here, centuries of mistreatment have resulted in today's divisions, crime and social problems. It seems that there is now no 'quick fix.'

I bid Skip farewell and catch the train at Kalgoorlie Station to travel back west to Perth. It's a seven-hour journey before I head north to *Bali, Indonesia*.

Travel Tip No 13: It's vital to stay hydrated in hot countries. You can easily monitor this by observing the colour of your pee. Clear is clear, drink more water if it's yellow or orange, red and you're dead. Women may find this technique a bit trickier.

"All babies together, everyone a seed
Half of us are satisfied, half of us in need
Love's bountiful in us, tarnished by our greed
When will there be a harvest for the world."

The Isley Brothers.

Bali Highs...

February, Days 131-141: 38,657 miles

1-2-3 and Wheeeeee. I am pushed off the landing pad and launched into space, swinging high above the jungle. I have just sampled ten small cups of Bali coffee including one made from the poo of a civet cat. It's a rush and I am as high as a proverbial kite. The ropes are tied to two tall palm trees and I'm hoping that my flight instructor is as good at tying knots as he is at the gentle art of persuasion.

The airport at *Bali* smells of lilies and everyone seems to be smiling here. Shiny eyed smiles and white teeth contrasting with flawless coffee coloured skins. I felt a strange excitement about these islands of Indonesia when I planned my year-long journey around the world, and I am soon to discover why.

The taxi drives me for 40 minutes to my hotel and never gets out of second gear. The streets are dusty and incredibly narrow, traffic is head to tail and we are surrounded on all sides by hundreds of mopeds or *'gojeks'* as they are known here. They overtake on both sides, darting through tiny spaces between the cars and even mount the pavements. I see a family of four on one bike carrying a table and no one is wearing a crash helmet. It seems crazy and chaotic. Beep Beep.

We drive through *Kata*, notorious for its dodgy nightclubs and all-night bars. In 2002 a car bomb exploded here next to an Irish bar killing 202 people. It was blamed on *Osama bin Laden*.

Denpasar is further on and is less gaudy. My hotel is on the beach further north far away from the bright neon lights. For just £40 a night I am treated to 5-star luxury. It's the quiet season just after the Australian Christmas holidays and just before the Chinese New Year so there are four staff to each guest. This place is immaculate. I am upgraded to the Princes Suite for free.

Later, the hotel manager explained that he thought my surname *'Noble'* was my title and decided to make a favourable impression. He certainly did, and laughing, I told him that his British Knighthood was in the post. *The Grand Balisana Suites* has everything; beautifully manicured gardens, pool, bars, restaurant, spa and massage centre, its own small Hindu Temple, and a private beach. The fishponds are alive with huge bright orange coy carp which follow me as I walk by.

I decide to pamper myself to fully recover from my Australian outback experience. I feel like a millionaire as 1 million rupees is worth around £50 which is roughly three weeks wages for the hotel workers. It's easy to be generous here and a £5 (100,000 R) tip is received with huge heartfelt appreciation and even more big broad smiles.

On people's recommendations, I head north and inland to the town of *Ubud*. It was made famous in the movie *'Eat, Pray, Love.'* It's also known for its arts and crafts scene, 'new age' yoga retreats and great restaurants.

Bali was conquered for the sixth time by the Dutch in 1902. Following international outrage at their harsh and brutal actions, control of the island was restored to the local people where it has since gained international status as one of the friendliest tourist destinations in the world. Most local people here speak English now.

There are scores of vegan, vegetarian and raw food restaurants. The food is locally grown and deliciously healthy. Bali is multi-religious including Protestant, Catholic, Islam, Confucianism, but Hindu is the main one. There are Hindu temples everywhere and most shops and businesses create beautiful daily offerings which are placed on their doorsteps.

This is a country which demonstrates religious tolerance and the common denominator is simply Happiness. There are few signs of alcohol problems (except from the western tourists) and Indonesia like most Asian countries is drug-free. The local news recently featured a man who was caught growing a marijuana plant and he is now serving 10 years in jail. The death penalty is still in force in Malaysia. As a result, the streets are much safer here than in the west and 90% of people are smiling wherever I go.

Down the road is the world-famous *Sacred Monkey Forest Sanctuary.* There are over 740 long-tailed Balinese monkeys here and they are protected and treated like royalty. There are signs everywhere warning the tourists not to touch or feed them as they have sharp one-inch teeth and will bite if they feel threatened.

Everyone wants a selfie with a monkey, and I watch in disbelief as a young Chinese woman encourages one to jump on her shoulder so that her husband can take a photo. He didn't catch the moment when the monkey sunk its teeth into her breast though. Ouch! I bet that hurt. One monkey jumps in front of me to look at its reflection in my iPhone and then I get the best monkey selfie ever. It takes one to know one. We are relatives after all, relatively speaking.

For just £40 I book a day tour with my friend Sempi. He drives me in his car for 10 hours around the local waterfalls and temples and I get to experience this place through the eyes of a local. At 6 am and before the heat and humidity get too much, we head for some secret and sacred waterfalls.

We then drive to the famous rice terraces where eco-tourism is replacing rice growing. Why break your back while ankle-deep in rice fields when you can make more money pushing tourists on swings? Before I too am launched into space, I sample ten local Balinese coffees. I can't remember when I last felt so high.

The most expensive coffee in the world is made from beans which have been eaten by the civet cat. When the Dutch enslaved the locals to grow their coffee plantations, the workers were not allowed to take any of the valuable produce. However, the wild cats helped themselves and left their poo outside the fields. The slaves discovered that by carefully washing them and dry roasting them, they became even fuller of flavour. Now it's the most expensive and sought-after coffee in the world. When life deals you shit, it can sometimes turn into a bowl of cherries.

We enjoy a light lunch of fresh mango juice, Nasi Goreng, and freshly fried banana fritters. It's delicious and costs just £1. The farms here often have restaurants which use their own produce. Some of them even offer cooking classes. It's a better way to assure quality than in the West.

Afterwards, we go to *Pura Tirta Empul*, the Holy Water Temple. Here Hindus purify themselves in the many sacred fountains. It's a local public holiday and everyone is happy and dressed up in their favourite rainbow colours. I am one of the few tourists and it seems that everyone wants to take a selfie with me. Happiness is infectious and free, but the young folk don't seem to be as enthusiastic.

I quickly fall in love with this place. It's the happiest and most diverse place I have yet visited. My planned four-day visit quickly extends into two weeks and I stay in four great local B&B's costing less than £15/night including breakfast and swimming pool.

The ATM swallows my bank card and yet again I find myself with no cash. My host kindly lends me a million rupees (£50) on Trust and shares his family dinner with me until I can arrange for the card to be returned from the bank. It's a real lifeline.

I promised myself in New Zealand that I would get my first tattoo. Today is that day. I designed the shape of the flower of life on my computer and then coloured it in with the colours of the rainbow. It's deeply significant to me and represents the inter-connectedness of all. That's what I have been experiencing on this journey in so many ways. Three hours later and it's done. No pain, no blood and a perfect representation of my design is now permanently etched on my shoulder. At the very least, it should make body identification easier if one of my planes crash or I get eaten by a giant lizard.

My next stop is *Komodo Island* where I want to see the Komodo Dragons. These are huge prehistoric lizards which, I am told, eat buffalo whole. I meet the lovely Tety who lives in the nearby Island of Flores.

She once ran a boat tour business taking tourists to visit their ancestors and she is happy to offer me logistical advice and accommodation. We agree to meet over dinner, and I decide to push the boat out. *Trip Advisor* tells me that *'Swept Away'* is one of the best restaurants in Ubud.

My driver collects us, and we drive through lush countryside to a resplendent 5-star hotel surrounded by rice terraces. We are greeted by our personal butler who leads us to a golf buggy. Then we are driven down through the most beautiful manicured gardens to our private table by the river. It's a real rock star entrance.

A thousand candles sparkle around us and we are treated to the most lavish and delicious six-course dinner I have ever experienced. They have even personalised the menus and, on my request, have

created the word 'Adventure' with rose petals on the floor. We are both swept away by the setting, the romantic ambience, and the friendliest staff. The rain starts and the river rises rapidly but we don't even notice.

As two adventurous Virgos just 10 years apart, we quickly realise that we have a lot in common and we seem to be completely in sync with each other's life experiences and values. We are very clear and honest mirrors for each other and agree to meet again to arrange my visit to see the Dragons.

Will I be eaten alive? Does this Fire Dragon lady breath fire? Things are certainly starting to get hot on this wonderful adventure.

Travel Tip No 15: Not all ATM's automatically dispense your card with your cash. Always press the button 'No further transactions.'

*"Bali Ha'i may call you.
Any night, any day
In your heart, you'll hear it call you
Come away, come away
Bali Ha'i will whisper on the wind of the sea
Here am I your special island,
Come to me, Come to me."*

Alfred Apaka

Flores and the Komodo Dragons...

February: Days 142 - 148.   39,414 miles.

Stepping off the boat at *Komodo Island* is like stepping into a scene from *Jurassic Park*. You can smell death and reptile poo. It's the size of cowpats and its spread all over the beach. A small herd of deer is huddled together for safety. The giant Komodo Dragons have been seen ripping them apart and eating them whole. I am hoping they are not hungry today. I am also hoping that someone in my group can't run quite as fast as me.

Getting to Komodo Island involves a short flight from Bali to the island of *Flores* and then an overnight boat trip to visit the beautiful small islands nearby. There are over 17,000 islands in Indonesia, and I am only visiting a few of them. I am staying with my guide, translator, photographer, and companion in her *Joglo* in the pretty harbour town of *Labuan Bajo*. Tety rebuilt this traditional Javanese wooden house which is usually reserved for aristocrats in honour of her home in Java. We quickly become good friends.

Flores is also known by its less attractive name of *East Nusa Tenggara*. It's much more basic than Bali. The roads are often just dirt tracks with huge potholes. We travel around with Gojeks. Almost everyone with a bike is happy to taxi us anywhere for less than £1. *Wawan* drives me into town at night for dinner, the chain pops off his bike and we grind to an abrupt halt. Luckily, we didn't fly over the handlebars onto the busy road. Most

people here have scars from bike accidents. Tonight at least, I am not one of them.

On the harbourfront, the street food vendors set up their stalls. Freshly caught fish are laid out and wood barbecue fires lit. We choose red snapper, fifteen huge prawns served with salad, rice and noodles and a large beer. It's delicious. The meal for two costs less than the cost of a beer back home.

At the harbour, we find a boat cruise to *Komodo Island* for just £40 including meals. It's a two-day overnight journey stopping at *Rinca Island*, *The National Komodo Park*, berthing overnight near a beautiful pink sandy beach. Next day it's *Padar Island*, snorkelling with giant Manta Rays in *Manta Ray Bay*, and finally stopping off at *Kanawa Island* before returning to Labuan Bajo.

There are twenty of us aboard *'The Mona Lisa'* including the crew, two Germans, one Swede and the rest are locals from Indonesia. We all love reggae music and soon we are dancing across the blue ocean to our first destination. Green islands rise from the turquoise blue sea around us like rock cakes sprinkled with palm trees. The colours are serene and surreal, the wind refreshingly cool on our faces.

The Komodo dragon is also known as the Komodo monitor. At up to nine feet long, it's the largest lizard in the world and can eat its own body weight in one feed. When it leaves its egg nest it quickly climbs a nearby

tree to avoid being eaten by its family members. After three years and when it's safer to travel on the ground, it eats, sleeps, and grows for up to thirty years.

Its mouth is full of forty deadly bacteria and once it bites its prey, it simply waits for it to slowly die from the venom before they all gather for a feast.

Thankfully, we are being escorted by knowledgeable local guides who know when they have last fed and when it's safe to approach them. They lead us around the island armed with long sticks. I think a shotgun would make me feel a bit safer though as these armour-clad monsters can run up to 20 km per hour. I'm not sure how fast I can run but I'm sure I would break all records if needs be. Anyway, there are some older folk in my group and they probably taste better than me.

There are buffalo skulls lying on the ground and some big bones. These lizards eat almost everything apart from the skulls and horns. We spot one sleeping under a tree. It looks huge but we are told that it's just a baby. Where's the daddy? I look around nervously. And then we see them. Their huge forked tongues flick out to taste the air, but our guide assures us that they are not hungry as they only eat every 28 days. He tells me that this one ate 21 days ago. Is that intended to reassure me, I wonder? Even I can get peckish after a big meal. Gulp. We quietly sneak behind them as the guide distracts them with his stick to take our photo.

As the sun sets, we are treated to a spectacular sunset. The sleeping arrangements on the boat are a bit too cramped for me so we decide to sleep on the prow under the stars.

The waves gently rock the boat like a cradle while the Milky Way slowly spins above us. I dream of brightly coloured fish some of which look like bananas. Rainbow coloured sea anemones carefully extend their tentacles, tentatively testing the water. Slowly they learn to feel safe, to trust, before fully opening and gently connecting with each other in the most delicate and delicious embrace.

The next morning, we wake before dawn to catch the sunrise at one of the most scenic vistas of these remarkable islands. It's a hot, steep and sweaty climb to the top of *Padar Island* but the view is outstanding.

Afterwards, we spend some time on the beach at *Kanawa Island* with its soft pink sands and brightly coloured tropical fish and coral reefs.

Later as we sail through Manta Ray Bay, I hear excited shouts as some of these huge fish are spotted swimming under our boat. They can be up to twenty-foot wide and swim like huge graceful butterflies. They have smiley faces and I'm told that they like to be touched. Hurriedly, I grab a snorkel and too hastily jump overboard.

The current here is really strong and I am quickly swept away, choking, and spluttering on the salty water which just shot up my nose. No time to get my goggles on, I just manage to get back to the boat ladder. That was embarrassing. Others take the small dingy which follow the rays before gracefully slipping into the water. I stay on board to nurse my pride.

Things are developing very fast between me and my Island girl and we are both surprised and excited. We are also feeling and acting like twenty-year-olds. Within days of our first meeting, we became very close friends, and both feel that we have known each other for a very long time.

Perhaps, because we are both Virgos, we simply understand and 'get' each other. It's also marked with so many synchronicities, coincidences, and perfect timings. Although there is only an 'L' between Forres and Flores, we are aware, however, that we come from quite different cultures and we live on opposite sides of the world.

We Virgos may be romantic, but we are also pragmatic. I invite Tety to accompany me to her home island of Java to better understand her background and to help us determine the way forward. Her face lights up and she jumps on me like a monkey and whispers in my ear 'yes, of course, baby.' Tired and glowing from our adventures we set sail into the unknown.

Travel Tip No 15: Always test the water before jumping in over your head.

"One week in we let the story begin
We're going out on our first date
You and I are thrifty, so grab all you can eat
You fill up your bag and I fill up a plate
Oh – I – oh – I – oh – I – oh - I
I'm in love with your body."

Ed Sheeran

Hot Lava in Java...

February, Days 149-155: 40,184 miles

Java is the most populated island on the planet. Over 140 million of us live here. It's also home to hundreds of volcanoes, 45 of which are still active. During my visit, *Bromo Volcano* which we had intended to climb, shot out hot clouds and lava prompting a hasty change of plans. Things are also hotting up between me and Tety, my new best friend and travelling companion.

We land in *Yogyakarta* and are immediately pounced on by the taxi drivers. Tety drives a hard bargain and the taxi driver shakes his head and walks away. Minutes later he returns with a colleague who lives near to our destination and is happy with the price of a one-way journey. An hour later we arrive at our place near *Magelang* - a beautiful wooden traditional family house set in a healthy hydroponic farm and restaurant.

We fall asleep as the singers from the nearby mosques break into song, evoking the many names of Allah to the surrounding villages. It's less harsh than church bells and sometimes they even seem to sing in tune. Muslim children learn the 99 names for Allah while still in kindergarten and, like Catholics, often use rosary beads to recount them.

Our front porch overlooks the hydroponic beds, profuse with fruit, vegetables and herbs grown without soil in water from the fishpond below. Bamboo huts surround the space, and these are full of customers at the weekend drawn by the freshest food possible. It's also an educational centre teaching this modern way to grow food efficiently.

Bertha our hostess tells me that she was previously a successful TV advertising executive. She became unhappy when she realised that financial success was leading her staff to unhealthy lifestyles. When her son tragically died, she decided to make a difference instead of trying to make money.

Now she is running this innovative social enterprise providing much-needed employment to the local villagers and inspiring others with her visionary ideas. Her eyes sparkle as she tells me that she has never felt so happy and healthy and been so empowered.

We wake at 5 am to see the sunrise over *Borobudur Temple* which is the largest Buddhist temple in the world. Our driver is hired for our 10-hour tour and agrees to take us anywhere we want for just £25. Soon we are climbing up hundreds of steps through the forest in the darkness and emerge breathless on the viewpoint just as the sun starts to rise.

Below us, the mist slowly evaporates to reveal a beautiful green vista with the massive black lava stone temple in the centre. The sun appears in golden bronze glory lighting up the faces of the spellbound spectators. An eagle flies overhead as a small plume of smoke drifts from the centre of Mount Merbabu in the distance. It's so dreamy quiet and mystical and soon I am back on a swing. It feels like I'm swinging on the moon.

Borobudur Temple is like a giant black pyramid and is dedicated to Buddha. It's also one of the Seven Wonders of the World. It's over 1,100 years old and sits solidly in beautiful gardens. We climb the steps of the nine stacked levels. The first three levels are the levels of desire, the second set are the levels of form and the final three, the levels of formlessness. On the top, there is a central dome surrounded by 72 Buddha statues hidden inside perforated stupas which look like giant upturned bells. Here I practice some yogic flying, but time and gravity prevail, and I fall back down into desire.

There are lots of school children also visiting and they excitedly ask me if I will do an interview so that they can practice their English language with a Westerner. They are so friendly, happy, and enthusiastic that it's impossible for me to refuse.

We then drive over to the *Prambanan and Sewa Temples*. These Hindu temples were built around the same time and are dedicated to the Trimurti, the expression of God as the Creator *(Brahma),* the Preserver *(Vishnu)* and the Transformer *(Shiva).* A different religion, but with temples built from the same black lava stone from the volcano.

Sewa Temple is Buddhist and is the oldest. In 2006 both temples were partly destroyed by a powerful earthquake killing more than 5,800 people and turning 135,000 houses into piles of bricks, tiles, and wood in less than a minute. Borobudur nearby was not affected. Tsunamis, earthquakes, and volcanic eruptions are mother earth's growing pains and they are felt most acutely on these islands.

The Island of Java is now mostly Islam and it is a measure of these peoples present and historical religious tolerance and respect, that all these temples still stand. Despite what we are shown on our television screens back home, the Eastern people I have met from all religions are highly respectful, incredibly open, and friendly, tolerant, and kind.

They are also very interested and curious to talk to me. The social epidemics of the West including war, murder, alcohol, drug and sexual abuse do not seem to exist here. Food and medicine are still grown locally in most places. And the children especially are so healthy, happy, vibrant, curious and positive.

It's easy for me to feel ashamed of my Christian roots and the present-day customs of the nations, societies, and people it has helped to create. I often feel that our religious leaders have now become lost in hypocrisy. Our politicians corrupted by corporate greed and power. It seems to me that we continue to suffer the worst effects of our karma.

In Yogyakarta, we rent a horse-drawn carriage to tour the town. We visit traditional batik factories, sample delicious street food and shop in the colourful street markets. It's the rainy season here and a bright flash in the sky is quickly followed by a mighty clatter. I almost jump out of my skin, but the horse doesn't miss a step. The heavens open and the streets are quickly turned into rivers.

We find our taxi driver who is asleep in his seat and head for home.

After experiencing the history and traditions of this country we head for *Bandung*, the capital of West Java. It's a University town with lots of futuristic arts and crafts centres. I book the luxury *El Hotel Royale* for a treat and we experience high living from the 18th floor. Asians love selfies and there are photo opportunities everywhere. I've heard of Chinese couples travelling to faraway destinations just for that special honeymoon photo for their digital photo albums.

We visit the *NU Art studio* featuring lots of sculptures and the biggest 3D Art Museum in the world. It's selfie paradise in a 21st Century digital reality. What is real and what is not?

Back to Earth, we drive up, up and up to *the Tangkuban Perahu Volcano*. The air smells of sulphur and the mist and clouds create an eerie atmosphere. There's just a wisp of smoke rising from the crater below. Recently the slopes were struck by a landslide and some of the traders' stalls slid down the mountain.

On the way back down, we visit the natural hot springs and are soon soaking in the toasty water, simmering nicely at 43 degrees C. I'm treated to a poolside reflexology massage by expert hands. Just £5 for 1 hour of restoration. This guy does 6 - 7 of these every day and has become expert in the process.

Finally, we visit the *Rainbow Garden* in the *Asian Floating market.* Food stalls float in small boats and we dine on satay rabbit which we thought was satay chicken. A simple error in translation. It could be worse as they eat everything here.

It's been just 21 days since Tety, and I first met. We have now shared a fascinating journey through her home country, and it has brought us even closer together.

I have learned a lot but there are always more questions.

Why do people refer to 'falling' in love when it feels like we are ascending higher? Can East meet West? Does Jesus meet Mohammad? Or is there somewhere in between or above perhaps? Time will tell.

Que sera sera.

"Que será, será
Whatever will be, will be
The future's not ours to see
Que será, será
What will be, will be."

Doris Day

Singapore Sling...

March, Days 156-167: 41,031 miles

Changi Airport in *Singapore* is reputed to be the best airport in the world. It's certainly beautifully designed and it feels like I'm stepping into some futuristic universe. Everything is sparkling clean and shiny. Highly polished marble floors lead you through the highest tech immigration and baggage collection systems effortlessly. There's tons of space and huge plasma screens display tantalising glimpses of this sophisticated and techno eco-centric City.

Singapore is a fine island City. You get fined for speeding of course or for parking in the wrong place but also for smoking in public spaces, fined for eating food or drinking on the train, fined for selling or chewing gum and bizarrely, eating a smelly Durian fruit in public results in a fine of £250. In Malaysia dealing in illegal drugs carries the death penalty. Yes, it's a fine city indeed but very safe, clean, and well behaved.

The roads are the best I've seen so far and there are construction sites everywhere. Not just the usual boring block high rise towers but glistening shards of glass and steel contrasting with organically shaped round structures of all shapes and sizes. Each uniquely different from its neighbours. This is clearly architect's heaven.

There is a high rise building here which creates its own electricity from the waste of its residents. The walls are covered in dense green plants, it recycles its own water and there are fruit and vegetables growing in the rooftop gardens under palm trees. When the fruit ripens, it's wise to wear a hard hat when you walk by.

My taxi driver Yazid, tells me that behind the facades people here are incredibly stressed and unhappy. "Everyone seems to be in debt trying to keep face, pay for their mortgage and their status cars. They work long 12-hour days so there is not much time for anything else."

I am staying on the 15th floor of a condominium called *Fernwood Towers* with Noona, a Chinese lady who lives with her tiny dog, Snowball. He steals my smelly socks and it seems to turn him on as he humps my leg at every opportunity. It must get lonely living up here.

Two thousand people live in this single block behind security walls patrolled by guards. Behind the pretty facades, the flats are protected by steel bar gates and it feels a bit like a jail.

There may be nice green spaces and walkways but there is no real sense of neighbourhood community. People seem to live in their own little safety boxes inside bigger boxes surrounded by walls, and they travel around in their shiny tin box cars to get everywhere. The public transport system is seamless and spotless and it's easy for me to get around the city using the metro and bus system with just one plastic card. It auto tracks and debits my cash for every journey.

The neighbourhood I am staying in is 40 mins from the Centre and I could be living in Hong Kong. It's full of wealthy Chinese people making their fortunes from the banking and import and export industries.

I am having dinner in the *Jumbo Seafood Restaurant* close to my room. There must be 800 Chinese people dining here tonight and I am the only white guy. There is stuff on people's plates which seems to be still alive and squirming, but my battered and deep-fried prawns are dead delicious.

Looking out across the ocean towards the setting sun, I see hundreds of vessels pointing inland against the outgoing tide. Its 33 degrees here but the sea breeze is refreshing. Air conditioning units are my new best friend and I often have to go into a shopping mall just to cool down and dry my shirt.

In contrast to the massive sterile shopping malls, Chinatown offers rich diversity and local culture. I visit the famous *Buddha Tooth Relic Temple* which claims to hold a tooth of the man himself. Down the road, I pop into the *Sakya Muni Buddha Gaya Temple* which holds a beautiful golden shrine dedicated to *Buddha Maitreya*, his future incarnation.

Thousands of beautifully carved and painted Buddha statues adorn the walls. It's enchanting and peaceful in here away from the bustle of the busy streets. I absorb the calming smells of incense before finding a nearby food-hall for lunch.

These communal cafes have dozens of small eateries offering every kind of food imaginable. You simply choose what takes your fancy and find a seat at one of the communal tables with the locals. I enjoy tasty smoked duck with noodle soup and a glass of freshly squeezed mango juice for just £3.

The Chinese shopping mall is full of thousands of small traders selling everything at cheap, cheap prices, sir. 'Stack em high and sell em low' seems to be the business model.

I've picked up another irritating cough from my air travels and pop into a Chinese medicine shop for an elixir. "You got much mucus, MUCUS?" he shouts at me loudly in the busy shop. I cough in mild embarrassment and am tempted to share my phlegm with him. "This vely good," he says as he hands me a bottle of pills. "No chemicals just nature, vely good." he smiles as he takes my cash. Later I read the instructions and discover that its main ingredient is powdered gecko. It does the trick, but I can't stop licking my eyelids now.

At night, this city really lights up. At 8 pm there's a water and laser light show outside the futuristic *Marina Bay Sands* Complex. These are three iconic skyscrapers with what looks like a giant surfboard connecting them at the top. I've booked the night cruise to get the best view and soon I'm on-board with a few dozen young Chinese people. We each get a free bottle of Singapore Sling with our admission tickets.

I watch in bemusement as one frustrated young guy can't get his ring-top open. The bottle is passed around and everyone tries various techniques, squeezing, biting, and bashing the bottle on the table. I take his biro from his pocket and just stab it through the top, much to the delight and applause from everyone. Getting booze bottles open is a Scottish art-form which most of us learn in school.

It seems like I am sailing through a sci-fi movie set. Huge buildings are lit up like giant wedding cakes all around. One looks like a golden armadillo. Giant corporate logos boast their owners' brands which are mostly banks, too big to fail or fall down hopefully. These are the new temples of our corporate world promoting the religion of materialism and money. Greed is good.

The show begins and coloured water fountains dance to the music. The music builds to a crescendo and powerful green lasers then split the sky, lighting up the passing clouds overhead. They would see this on the moon if there was anyone there. Gasps of delight and wonder are proclaimed on our boat. It seems that ooohs and aaahs are shared by every language.

Afterwards, I visit the equally impressive *Gardens by the Bay*. At night huge tree-like sculptures illuminate the park. By the man-made lakes, giant silver dragonflies seem to float mid-air amongst the fountains. No money has been spared creating this stunning glimpse of a Utopian future. It's just a shame that they replaced the real trees and dragonflies in the process.

There's a very pleasant surprise in the form of a text from my friend Tety who wants to fly over from Bali to meet me. It's only been a week since we parted company so I guess she must like me. We agree to rendezvous at the airport in Kuala Lumpur, the capital of Malaysia. However, there are two airports here and we arrive simultaneously at different ones. I had pre-booked a driver to pick us both up at 1.30 am and she makes an extended journey for us to reunite.

I've booked four nights in a classy AirBnB place. For just £40 a night we have a beautiful modern apartment with views across the City. The skyline is dominated by the 451 meters tall *Petronas Twin Towers*, a pair of glass-and-steel clad skyscrapers with Islamic motifs. Our stay allows us the use of the Sky Deck which includes a gymnasium, sky bridge walk, entertainment suites and best of all, an infinity pool and spa with stunning views.

At night, the towers look like giant illuminated rockets ready for lift-off. We are on the 35th floor and the view over our balcony to the lower swimming pools and gardens make my legs shake.

This is mostly a Muslim city with hundreds of street cafes and stalls selling Asian street food. It's hard to find a bar or restaurant which sells alcohol, but we of course persevere. Google directs us to a club with a rooftop bar called The Canopy. Smartly dressed security guards direct us to a private elevator, and we are escorted to our seats in the plush lounge bar. The towers rise up beside us as we listen to

the DJ churn out American gangster rap tunes. Around us, fashionable people smoke hookahs and sip lavish cocktails. If Al Capone were still alive, he would not be out of place here. At £20 for just two drinks, his family are clearly still alive and doing rather well.

It's hard to get around in this city without taking taxis but thankfully The *Grab App* quickly finds us the cheapest and nearest drivers. We sleep long into the morning and it's just too hot to walk outside during the day. We have everything we need in this apartment, so we don't go far.

I book another four nights in *Damansara* on the outskirts of the City hoping to be closer to the forests. Another AirBnB attracts me due to its domed roofed sky terrace and pool. It looks like my new tattoo, so I book it. However, it's located in a very commercial area and surrounded by squalid homes.

At least from our 8th-floor balcony, we can see the faces of the people below. Across the street, there are eight blocks of buildings and I estimate that there are around 2,000 people staying in the tiny flats. The ground floor has been designed to house businesses, but they are mostly unoccupied and semi-derelict. The streets are dirty here and there are few places for the few children to play.

I haven't been too impressed by Malaysia. What I have seen are mostly massive infrastructure projects and construction sites. Like most large cities, the centres boast spectacular showpiece buildings but further from town there seems to be both spiritual and material poverty. Perhaps because of this country's strict rules and regulations and its focus on Western-styled and funded commercial development, the people here don't seem to be happy.

Despite that, we have a great fun time together creating many happy memories. And for the second time, we say our goodbyes at the airport to head on to our respective countries. I book my ticket to *Saigon* in *Vietnam* and Tety flies back across the Java Sea to the Island of Bali.

"We are the new Kings
Sailing our seas of diamonds and gold
We are the new Kings
Seldom seen, elsewhere and unknown
We are the new Kings
Buying up London from Monaco
We do as we please
While you do as you're told.
We're too big to fail
We're too big to fail."

Marillion

Sick in Saigon...

March, Days 168-176: 42,039 miles

Saigon, now known as *Ho Chi Min City*, is not for the feint-hearted. I need nerves of steel just to cross the street and, as I was soon to discover, a very strong stomach.

This city played a pivotal role in the Vietnam War and is now a place where East meets West, an interface in the Yin-Yang of global supply and demand. There are 30 million people in this part of the country and 7 million mopeds. The pavements are lined with them. Everywhere.

They are tightly parked in front of the shops and I have to clamber over them just to get inside. The traffic is organic and crossing the busy roads becomes an act of faith. There seems to be one simple rule here. Don't hit the person or the vehicle in front of you. Anything and everything else goes.

I watch a man with only stumps for legs cross over on his bum. My turn then. I step into the face of oncoming traffic and stride purposefully across the street, arms waving. Hundreds of bikes, cars, lorries, and buses then slow down or stop as I cross. Others weave past missing me by inches. I need eyes on the back of my head and also on each side to try and maneuver between the vehicles safely. This place is mental. The smell of the dry sewers and the garbage lined streets is sickening.

I'm staying in the Downtown area in a little street called *Bui Vien* and thankfully I don't have to walk far for everything I need. There are dozens of small local restaurants and cafes catering for every taste including snakehead soup and battered frog curry. Convenience store, laundry, pharmacy, taxis, massage spas and tour operators are all within yards of my hotel door. What's not available in the shops walks or cycles past 24/7.

This city never sleeps. Around the corner is *Walking Street*. It's a pedestrian area. I get stuck in a people jam and shuffle inch by inch with the masses going nowhere slowly, keeping my hands firmly on my pockets.

Everything is for sale here one way or another. Sex, drugs and rock 'n roll, sunglasses, weird fruit and vegetables, eggs, live chickens, cuttlefish, souvenirs, lottery tickets, bags of meat. I notice that there are few dogs here so decide to avoid buying those.

Every street corner is occupied by someone cooking up something or another. Pretty girls with golden dresses walk past in groups. They offer suitable suitors packets of cigarettes with a price list of additional services on offer. Wherever there is demand there is supply. My neck gets sore from shaking my head and saying, *'Kong Cam On"* (no thank you).

Old potbellied westerners slouch on roadside bar tables behind rows of empty beer bottles. Pretty young Asian women, young enough to be their grand

daughters sit dutifully by their sides. I pass a young woman sleeping on a blanket on the pavement, two babies no more than six months old lie beside her. An empty bowl carries the message. 'Help me.' I'm told that orphaned babies are loaned out to beggars to increase the income for their pimps. It beggars belief. And it's both shocking and heart-wrenching.

Only 2% of the population are employed here and the average wage is around £25 a week. There is no benefit system, so people have had to become extremely enterprising and work long hours to survive.

From 11 pm till 4 am the local bars pump out loud dance music. Laser lights flash around this part of town, lighting up the white walls of the high-rise buildings. I'm glad I brought my blindfold and earplugs.

I wake at 4 am with the most horrendous gut cramps. It feels like my intestines are being tied in knots. I double up in pain as waves of spasms engulf me. I'm soon at 8/10 of my known pain threshold and it's frightening. At 10/10 I could blackout and I'm alone in this hotel room. Those deep-fried prawns I had for dinner were delicious, but they carried a tiny black trace of their own food source which is raw sewage. I now get anaphylactic shock ever since I first ate mussels and my immune system goes into over-drive and attacks and inflames my gut. If it gets into my bloodstream, I know I'm in big trouble.

I've booked a tour and at 7.30 am. I lurch across the street to cancel. Lee, the tour booth salesperson takes one look at me. "I so sorry," she says. "You look so bad, so white. I know this is seafood poisoning. My whole family in the hospital for five days last year. Yes, I lost 5 Kg and I still not right!" She kindly takes me to the pharmacy on the corner and translates for me. I leave with a bag of medicines and retire to my room to ride it out. Lee checks in on me in the evening to see if I need a doctor. It takes four very long days and nights before I can venture far from my toilet and another week before I can eat normally again.

The toilets in Asia usually include what I affectionately call a 'bum scoosher.' It's a simple pipe and nozzle which gets a jet of water exactly where it's needed. Why rub the stuff in with dry bleached toilet paper which blocks the drains and clogs the sewers? It's much more hygienic and eco-friendly. It's also cool and feels rather nice.

The experience makes me wiser. I avoid the posh restaurants with their glossy menus and follow my feet down a back street. I discover a small place ran by a lovely local family. Their son is disabled but he looks happy and healthy. Shoes are lined up outside the door and there are only a few friendly locals inside. This place is clean, and the mother clearly knows how to care. I convey to her my condition with sign language and she smiles and nods with understanding.

She returns fifteen minutes later with a bowl of 'chicken porridge' - over boiled rice, finely chopped chicken, garlic, ginger and vegetables smothered in parsley and coriander and a secret ingredient which I later discovered to be a snake derivative. This is the very best food

medicine and it stays down without further pain. Mama and her kitchen become my only trusted restaurant for the next five days as my health restores and I get back to travel fitness.

Once I recover, I take a bus to the *Great Holy Sight Temple* which is an active monastery used by the *Cao Dai* sect. I find myself sitting on the bus with Saskia from *Germany*. She is solo travelling around the world in the opposite direction from me. She gives me great suggestions for travelling in Cambodia and Thailand, my next destinations. I give her tips about Indonesia and Australia which is hers. She too is coming down with the dreaded tummy bug and must get off at the next stop to return to her hotel.

The *Cao Dai Temple* is one of a thousand in Vietnam. It was finished in 1955, the year I was born, when the Cao Dai Army was formed following the Japanese occupation of Indochina. That year was also the start of the Vietnam War. Caodaists believe that all religions are ultimately the same and seek to promote tolerance throughout the world. The Lord Buddha, Jesus Christ, Muhammad, and Confucius, in addition to Joan of Arc and Julius Caesar, are all honoured at this temple. This resonates with me.

We tourists are herded like sheep around the outside of the great hall by grumpy, rude, and impatient attendants. It seems that they especially need to learn tolerance and kindness. Maybe that's why they are here. I soften my eyes and look deep into the eyes of the grumpiest one, nodding respectfully and smiling. Maybe it's my white shirt or my hair tied in a knot, but he too softens, smiles, and nods back. That's the way to do it.

I book a boat tour to the *Mekong Delta*, a vast maze of rivers, swamps and islands, home to floating markets, Khmer pagodas and villages surrounded by rice paddies. Boats are the main means of transportation. We visit *Dragon Island, Phoenix, Turtle* and *Unicorn Island* but I didn't see any of their namesakes. I did, however, see crocodiles and snakes. As I try to take a close-up of a snake in a bush it lunges forward at lightning speed and bites my iPhone. There is venom dripping all over it.

Respect snakes.

The pier is mobbed with tourists, mostly Chinese. I visit a bee farm where the honey is harvested and made into honey sweets. Everything is handmade and tables of young girls skillfully wrap each candy with rice paper and then greaseproof paper. Different colours for different flavours, chocolate, coconut, mango, strawberry, blueberry and mint.

Next, it's off to an organic fruit farm to savour the delights of homemade chocolate from the chocolate bushes. We also sample jackfruit, pineapples, pencil-sized bananas, and the smelly Durian fruit. We feed fortunate crocodiles with unfortunate catfish and I am offered a shot of snake liquor from a jar of fermenting snakes. I ask what it's good for and my guide tells me that it's especially good for

men's sexual prowess. "Better make mine a double then." I reply.

It's not too bad and the local Vietnamese musicians start to sound quite good afterwards. The rowing boats are paddled around the rivers by strong local women. I think they must have a glass of this stuff for breakfast.

The Vietnam War lasted for almost 20 years between the communist Viet Kong in the north and the U.S. backed government in the South. I visit the *Chu Chi Tunnels* which were the chosen battleground of the crafty and resourceful Viet Kong guerrilla army. They dug over 250 Km of tunnels here and despite the US army dropping an incredible 2.5 million tons of munitions including deadly cluster bombs they could not defeat them. Instead, it became a protracted cat and mouse game. Ingenuity and resilience versus money and bombs.

A deadly chemical called *'Agent Orange'* was created to defoliate the forest canopy and chemically poison the Viet Kong. That didn't work either, but it did help produce a by-product now known as glysulphate used by western farmers as a weed killer. Ironically, this poison is now known to cause Parkinson's disease and cancers in the West. It's finally being banned here 50 years later. There are 1.5 million disabled and deformed Viet Kong survivors who could have told them that a long time ago.

I drop down through a camouflaged trap door on the forest floor into a tiny gap to take me below ground. It's hot and smells of damp earth. The tunnel is a really tight squeeze and I have to crawl on hands and knees through them for just 100 meters. We see cunning booby traps containing deadly barbed metal spikes which inflicted horrendous wounds on the American soldiers.

The light of my iPhone guides me, a luxury they didn't have back then. It's a huge relief when I finally see the light at the end of the tunnel and crawl back up into daylight and fresh air. One and a half million soldiers of an average age of just nineteen years died in this war and two million civilians including children. It is estimated to have cost the American taxpayer a trillion dollars at 2011 prices.

"War, huh good God.
What is it good for?
Absolutely nothing!"

Edwin Star

An iconic photograph showing terrified naked children fleeing a chemical bomb attack finally persuaded the American public to wake up. This was the birth of a counter-reaction by a group of young people who were to become known as Hippies. They rallied behind the slogan 'Make Love, Not War.' The Woodstock Festival and our current music culture are only some of its legacies.

Travel Tip No 17: Snakes move much faster than worms.

Travel Tip No 18: Many people believe *Coca Cola* (yes, that stuff we use to clean our toilets) is also good at preventing food poisoning. 'Things go better with Coke' may be a quite literal slogan. Thankfully, gin and tonic was also created in India for the same purpose.

Travel Tip No 19: Here's my 7-step guide for food poisoning...

1. Avoid seafood and ice cubes.

2. Avoid all food if you do get the runs.

3. Drink lots and lots of water to help stay hydrated. (The Japanese sports drink called *Pocori Sweat* is excellent.)

4. Don't stray far from a toilet.

5. If you develop a fever, get a strip of antibiotics from a pharmacy shop. (Amoxylyn is available in Asia without a prescription). Suck carbon lozenges. Ibuprofen helps with gut inflammation and pain. Imodium helps with diarrhea but in my view, it's best to just flush it out.

6. When it eventually 'passes', drink probiotics, yoghurt or kefir to regrow your healthy gut bacteria.

7. Eat bland foods initially (The BRAT diet is Bananas, Rice, Applesauce, and Toast).

*"All those who remember the war
They won't forget what they've seen
Destruction of men in their prime
Whose average was nineteen
Ni-ni-ni nineteen."*

Paul Hardcastle

Cambodia is Kampuchea...

March, Days 179-192: 42,667 miles

I discover too late that I could have taken the bus from my hotel door in Saigon straight to *Sihanoukville* on the coast of Cambodia. The immigration office in Vietnam insisted on seeing my exit ticket before they would let me in. So, I felt pressurised to book that flight too soon.

It's always a fine balance between forward planning and just winging it as you go. It would have been a quarter of the price and taken half the time by overnight bus, but I would also have missed out on a most bizarre journey.

The immigration process for tourists here is the most bureaucratic and expensive I have yet experienced. I fall in line with my documents only to be told that I need two colour passport photos but there is no photo booth to be found. I get back in another queue and offer up instead a photocopy of my passport and, after a long wait with some sour-faced uniformities, I am told to go to the back of the next long line.

At this counter, I hand over $30 and then I'm directed to the back of the next long line to collect my passport with the necessary little rubber stamp. The whole shuffling process takes about 90 minutes and I realise that I have now missed my pre-paid bus out of *Phnom Penh*.

The taxi driver informs me of another bus heading to Sihanouk and drops me off in the middle of a muddy pavement with a simple wooden table and a few plastic chairs. This apparently is the bus office. Everything is written in the local Khmer language which just looks like Tolkien runes to me. I buy a ticket and wait patiently.

An hour later I am bundled into a tuk-tuk and taken to a packed old rickety bus. There is only one seat left at the very back where the engine noise and diesel fumes are strongest. It's also next to the toilet cupboard which smells even worse. It's hot and the windows won't open. There is no air conditioning or Wi-Fi and every pothole catapults me into the air.

I settle down for the eight-hour journey and watch the outside world pass by my dirty window. The road verges and waterways are lined with garbage, plastic bags, and bottles. They are ripped apart by dogs and vermin and blow over the fields. It's the worst I've ever seen, and it hides the brown soil and what is left of the dying brown grass.

Young people returning from school are herded onto open-topped lorries like cattle trucks. They stand squashed and holding on tight like sardines in an open tin can. Despite the squalor, they return my smiles and wave back at me. It helps to pass the time and lifts my spirit. I have been told that Sihanouk lies on the south-west coast of Cambodia near to tropical islands with palm-lined beaches. Just what I need after my city Saigon experience.

The bus finally drops me off in the middle of the town and I discover that it has been turned into the most massive construction site. All around me are multi-story hotels and huge neon-lit casinos. The skyline is filled with tall orange cranes and the roadsides are strewn with construction vehicles, pipes, cables, and even more litter.

This is development on a massive scale. It's happening around the clock and the workers sleep in the open concrete shells as they rise up from the ground. The air is filled with the smell of diesel fumes and eye-watering dust and dirt. The steady thump of pile drivers, generators, drills, grinders, and cement mixers is deafening.

There are no pavements and it's impossible to walk here on the busy and dangerous roads. I grab a tuk-tuk which is basically a motorbike with a fancy chariot towed behind it. With the help of Google maps, I manage to direct the driver to my destination at the end of a very long and bumpy track full of potholes, muddy brown puddles, and more garbage.

Thankfully, my guest house is a tiny oasis of serenity and calm in the surrounding madness. It's at the end of the road on the mouth of a river where it flows into the sea. Gerald and Kerstin moved from Germany four years ago and fell in love with this small piece of land. They then designed and built Spayhiti Guest House - including 10 guest rooms, a swimming pool, their own luxury accommodation, and a lovely restaurant overlooking the river estuary.

"Back then this was a naturally beautiful and unspoiled place" explained Gerald. "It attracted beach lovers, travellers and hippies wishing to visit the nearby islands for the full moon parties. And then this Government decided to deal with the Chinese and turn this into the new Macau - currently the Chinese gambling capital of the world. They are halfway through building a new high-speed train line from China through South East Asia and the big money has already arrived to exploit the expected invasion of rich Chinese people."

"Everything you see here over two storeys high has been built in the last two years and it's changing the landscape and displacing the local people and their culture. The so-called *Peoples Cooperative Party* is neglecting health, education, and environment for this new dream. Many of the biggest private developments are owned by ex-government officials and everyone knows where the money comes from."

"Why does this country use the American dollar along with its own currency while trading with China?" I ask. "Cambodia has had a very ugly history and it has always played both sides of the game for the benefit of its officials and at the cost of its people," Gerald replies. "I have already been offered four times the price I paid for this place and the offers just keep going up. But I have built Spayhiti to fulfil my own lifelong dream and that's priceless. Maybe we will cash in when I retire in ten years' time and go back home to Germany.

"But won't they just level this place and build another Chinese palace?" I ask. "Nothing lasts forever, my friend," he replies. "We can

only do our best to be happy now. Now, what do you want for breakfast?"

The next day I walk over the footbridge and follow a narrow forest track to the beaches further north from here. Its 37 degrees in the shade and the coconuts are cooking in the heat. It's still beautifully basic with few people around and no concrete buildings or shops in sight. I stay to watch a glorious sunset and then realise that I must walk a long way back in the dark and through that forest.

I'm glad I brought my torch as the forest is black as night and there is no moon to guide me. I also haven't had time to check what dangers may lurk in here. Halfway through I hear a large pack of dogs running up behind me growling and barking in a very unfriendly way. They are probably freaked out by my torch. I grab a big stick and keep on walking not daring to look back. They soon fall behind but I am off track now and lost in the forest undergrowth.

An old poem comes into my mind...

What do you do when you are lost in the forest?
Stand still.
The trees above and branches beside you are not lost.
Wherever you are is called 'here.'
The forest knows where you are, and you must treat it as a powerful stranger.
Listen.
The forest breathes.
It whispers, "you may leave this place at any time and return saying 'here'.
Stand still.
The forest knows where you are.
Stand still.
You must let the forest find you.

So, I switch off my torch and stand still. My eyes soon adjust to the darkness and I can see more clearly without the dancing shadows and my projected fearful imaginings. The adrenaline rush subsides and my heart-beat returns to calm. I'm still here. I listen. Behind the sound of a million unseen insects, I hear the distant waves as they crash against the rocky shoreline. The sea sounds like she too is breathing. "Shhhhh, come heeeer," she whispers repeatedly.

I push through the thick undergrowth in that direction knowing that I can then follow the shoreline back to my hotel. As I walk slowly, I beat my stick hard on the ground to alert any snakes and other night denizens of my presence and I eventually find myself safely at the edge of the sea. There is no one else around, no path and no beach. Just lots of huge craggy rocks and the tide is coming in. But I can see the lights of my hotel in the far distance.

I climb and clamber over the slippery rocks one very careful step at a time. My torch creates thrilling shadows. Is that a snake or a branch? Is that a scorpion or a crab? I watch how my mind reacts to different thoughts. When it gets too much I stop, stand still, listen and

breathe until the fear dissolves before moving forward. Soon I am back safely in my room with its familiar things and surroundings.

That primal adventure only lasted for 40 minutes but it felt like an eternity. An entirely different reality. All of my senses were heightened, and I somehow felt more alive. I'm relieved and grateful that I still am.

I take the ferry to *Koh Rong* and *Koh Rong Sanloem Islands*. I'm sitting next to Mark from *Colorado*. He is the same age as me and he has been travelling the world since he was a teenager. He has visited every country and every region, and he is a walking encyclopedia of knowledge about everywhere on our planet. We soon discover that we both learned to meditate in 1974, got married and divorced in the same years and have the same taste in beer and blues. It's always good to meet 'another myself.'

It's an overnight bus journey to *Siem Reap* in the North. I travel there feet first on a very narrow top bunk. For only £20 I also get a free blanket, a bottle of water and a plastic bag to put my shoes in as I board the bus. I get as comfortable as I can, push in my earplugs and put on my blindfold. Ten bumpy hours later we arrive as the sun rises above the rice fields. I grab a quick coffee from a street vendor and then Hun, my hotel driver arrives to welcome me and take me to my next home.

Siem Reap is a small resort town which is the gateway to the ruins of Angkor, the seat of the Khmer kingdom from the 9th - 15th centuries. More recently, it was featured in the 2001 movie *'Tomb Raider'* which made *Angelina Jolis* character *Lara Croft*, every man's dream girl, including me.

I meet fellow solo traveller Kaitlin from *Denver* at the local ATM machine. At 28 years of age, she realised that there must be more to life than selling air conditioning units. So, she chucked her job and came travelling for three months. She too is going in the opposite direction from me, so we trade best locations and travellers' tips. We agree to team up to share the tuk-tuk costs, to stay safe and to share our photos.

The temples of *Angkor Watt* are astonishing. It's one of the largest religious monuments in the world spanning over 162 hectares (imagine 162 football pitches side by side). Originally constructed as a Hindu temple dedicated to the god Vishnu for the Khmer Empire, it was gradually transformed into a Buddhist temple towards the end of the 12th century.

The massive stone structures are similar to the Mayan temples of Peru. Huge, uneven stone blocks lock together without mortar. They are carved with the most intricate designs. The happy faces seem to change their expressions as the sun moves across them from East to West. Over time, nature has reclaimed her place and now giant trees grow through the stonework in a curiously complementary way.

The delicate carvings might also reveal the purpose of the various temples. Some tell the stories of the various Hindu deities. The

largest temple includes many ancient bathing pools and the carvings on the walls are very sexually explicit and even make me blush. Perhaps this was one of the original spas and health centres where wealthy citizens took their pleasure or were nursed back to health and virility? I was soon to discover their modern-day equivalent in the massage parlors and 'KTV' establishments in town.

On the way back from our day tour, Kaitlin notices a beautiful golden wedding invitation lying on the seat. Sinat, our tuk-tuk driver tells us that his colleague is having his wedding celebration that night and he kindly asks us if we would like to go. We are both excited to experience life through the eyes of the local folk, so we agree.

Ten of us are soon seated around round tables and served with six courses of delicious local Khmer food. It feels rude to ask what everything is and I'm only glad I don't recognise any crocodile meat, skewered scorpions, snakes, or spiders which are sold in the streets.

We are the only westerners here and this feels like a real honour. I can't help but notice that around 80% of the guests are young men in their twenties. There are only a few women and children and I am by far the oldest man in the room. "Most of the women are at home looking after the children," explains Sinat with a cheeky grin. "And most of us are friends of the groom who is also a tuk-tuk driver." Khmer for 'Cheers' is 'Chol Mouy' which literally means - 'let's clunk our glasses together' and that's what we all do, all night.

When someone takes a drink, they clunk the glass of everyone else and shout *'Chol Mouy'*. It means that we all drink at the same pace and with free beer in abundance we are soon dragged onto the stage strutting our stuff to the latest Khmer pop songs. It's hilarious.

These young people know how to have fun in a sweet and strangely innocent way. It's lager only and there is no room here for bitter drinkers or bad spirits. The wedding finishes at 10 pm and we are told that the groom has invited us to a local KTV bar to party on. KTV stands for Karaoke TV which is very popular in Asia and especially here. We are ushered into a private room with a huge screen and PA system.

People take their turn singing through the microphone to videos. The most popular music is what I would call melancholic pop ballads which they all seem to love. There's not one rock and roll song on the playlist. In fact, there is nothing on the playlist that we recognise at all as it's written in rune language. That's me off the hook then. Here again, the drink and food are generously supplied for free.

I recognise the male staff and owner from my hotel, the local tuk-tuk drivers and the restaurant owner where we had lunch. They are all young guys in their twenties, and it becomes clear to me that everyone is helping each other as business associates as well as friends and family. I also notice that there are more young girls here. Could these be their wives I wonder? Maybe they had organised babysitters for later on?

Things take a strange turn when an older woman walks in with a string of young women who line up against the wall. Some of the girls in the room leave and new ones are taken by the hand by some of the young men. And then it dawns on me.

This is also a brothel and it's certainly a new experience for both me and Kaitlin. It's not what I might have imagined. There is nothing sleazy or creepy about any of this. The girls seem genuinely happy to behave like sweet girlfriends and to be offered free drinks and food. Some of them are great singers. It just seems like a bunch of kids having fun. I guess that if they want to take things further there are other rooms elsewhere for that.

However, we are both feeling a bit uncomfortable about this and it's getting late. So, we hatch a plan to make our exit. I explain to Sinat that my daughter is getting tired and must get up early. "She is your daughter?" he exclaims in surprise. "I am so sorry sir, I didn't realise... I thought... of course, I will take you home straight away." One last clink of glasses with everyone in the room and we make our escape.

The streets of Siem Reap are full of massage parlors and health spas. At only £5 an hour for a variety of different massage styles, I can afford to have my body nursed back into good shape. Once you make your choice at the desk a masseur arrives to lead you to a massage couch. It all seems very respectable and safely public. I receive a relaxing oil massage from a young woman, a vigorous Thai massage from a young man and a very useless and embarrassing one from a young ladyboy.

Finally, I meet Aja, a 22-year-old young woman who really knows anatomy. She quickly finds the source of pain in my feet and legs and with great energy soothes and smooths every sinew, muscle, ligament, and meridian using a variety of techniques familiar to me. Her hands get hot quickly and I can tell that she is a natural healer.

Although she is just a slip of a girl, she uses her body weight through her thumbs, knuckles, wrists, elbows, and knees to great effect. This is one of the deepest and most thorough massages I have ever received. She is fully focused and intuitively senses just how much pressure to apply without hurting me.

Afterwards, she tells me that she has been practising for four years and learned from YouTube videos and medical books. She works from 10 am to 10 pm every day and does around six massages and therapies most days. She gets just $1 dollar for each session, with the remaining $4 going to the young guy who owns the place and takes the money. When her boss looks away, I slip her a $5 tip and her face lights up in amazement and sincere appreciation.

I return to Aja another three times during my stay. On the last day, I suggest that she also tells other wealthy foreign tourists like me the truth about this arrangement. "Just tell them that $4 goes to the boss and $1 to you but if they would like to make a donation of $5 - $10 dollars after their treatment it would help you to further your

education as a health therapist. Trust me, you are worth it. You have a natural talent and a promising career." She nods seriously and respectfully and gives me a big hug and a heartfelt smile as I leave.

At my age, it's easy to behave as a wiser elder to these young people. I now realise that it's something which has been absent in almost all their lives. It's why I have been treated with so much respect and why the culture here is so full of youthful and enterprising energy. It's also why these young folk stick together in mutually beneficial small family-like communities. It's why the AIDS epidemic is the highest in Asia and why drug misuse is so prevalent. It's why there is so much poverty here and perhaps so much litter. It's why they love singing sad songs and why they still eat insects. And it's the reason that the average age here is around 25 years old. The reason for all this is both simple and horrific.

In 1975 the government-sponsored *Khmer Rouge* army started a four-year genocide campaign to murder every adult who was on the wrong side of the war. It's estimated that over 3 million people lie buried in the Killing Fields of Cambodia or later died of disease and famine. That's 3/8th of the entire population.

Everyone alive here has dead parents, grandparents, uncles, and aunts who have been missing their whole lives. Imagine for a moment half of all the people you now know in Scotland being murdered and their bodies dumped in the fields. No adults left to care, guide or support you. How would that affect you or your children?

Many have created brilliant social enterprises to help rebuild and rehabilitate their fellow survivors. There are more victims of land mines here than anywhere else in the world. That's 40,000 people without a leg to stand on. I visit many enterprises who are teaching themselves new skills without limbs. Street musicians perform with missing arms and legs raising funds to teach others. Arts & Crafts groups teach each other how to make things out of recycled garbage.

I visit the *Phare Cambodian Circus* set up by some of the survivors. They teach circus skills to children from disadvantaged backgrounds, usually AIDS orphans. Their brilliant performances teach real stories about their history through acrobatics. All profits go back to the school to train future generations. They now support over 1200 students.

These are grassroots organisations growing themselves without government support or interference. My father had a brilliant expression. "Never forget son," he said, "It's the shit that makes the grass grow." I understand that now, but I would add that it also requires heat, air, water, and light.

On my last day in Cambodia (or Kampuchea as the locals prefer to call their country), I take a boat trip to *Tonle Sap*, the largest lake in the country, and on which there is an entire floating community. This lake rises some three meters in the rainy season and the houses around the rim are built on stilts. In the middle of the lake, people live on floating platforms. As well as houses, there are gardens, shops, farms, restaurants, mosques and even a zoo.

Everything we have on land they have on the water. Except plumbing and football pitches of course.

People catch their dinner in nets floating underneath their houses and sell or barter the remaining fish to the neighbouring farmers. The kids now paddle about in big buckets as the water has recently become too polluted to swim safely.

I watch the sunset over the lake after a nice dinner and glass of red wine on *Queen Tara*, the largest boat on the water. How privileged I am. And so lucky to be born and raised in Scotland during the twentieth century.

It's so easy to misjudge the behavior of others and so worthwhile taking the time to try to understand them. To my friends in Kampuchea, and the surviving victims of war elsewhere in our world.

You are living proof of the indomitable and enduring spirit of humanity. Thank you for being here.

Travel Tip No 20: Change any spare cash before you leave the country you are in. Or give it away to a deserving stranger who can use it.

Travel Tip No 21: Always check immigration procedures before you leave.

Travel Tip No 22: It's easier to see the light in the darkness, than the darkness in the light.

"Imagine there are no countries
It isn't hard to do
Nothing to kill or die for
And no religion too
Imagine all the people
Living life in peace
You may say I'm a dreamer
But I'm not the only one
I hope someday you'll join us
And the world will be as one."

John Lennon

Smoke and Water with Tigers in Thailand...

April, Days 193-206: 43,604 miles

Thailand is known as 'The Land of Smiles.' In *Chiang Mai*, I can't see them though, as almost everyone is wearing a face mask due to the dangerously high levels of air pollution. It's at the very least, going to result in some very interesting suntans.

I experienced the hedonistic delights of *Bangkok* and *Pattaya* some ten years ago. That's when I first fell in love with Thailand. This time I head to the Northern provinces in the hope of more rural and traditional experiences. I'm staying in the original part of Chiang Mai. It's nearly 700 years old, occupies one square mile and is surrounded by a moat. There are over 300 golden Buddhist temples here and my hotel is surrounded by them.

In the morning I wake to the sound of chanting monks and wind chimes. It inspires me to recommence my morning yoga and meditation practice which has slipped a bit on my travels. I've started to notice how the ambience and vibe of a place affect my own consciousness, awareness and resulting behaviour. I'm glad that Thailand seems to bring out the best in me.

This is perhaps the healthiest and happiest place I have visited so far. Buddhism is a practice and not a religion and the practice is so simple. The 'Four Noble Truths' are easy for me to remember. Firstly, suffering is part of being alive. Change happens and that can cause worry. Secondly, the cause of suffering is usually the result of our past or present behaviour. Our limited ego-mind will try to protect us and always thinks it knows best. Thirdly, the good news is that it's possible to end this temporary suffering by waking up from our ego selves into the truly connected mind.

And lastly, there are simple, free tools available to help us to achieve that. Meditation (unthinking), mindfulness (conscious awareness), feeling and expressing gratitude, happiness, kindness, and non-judgement will lead us in the right direction.

Our human egos then become our servant and not our master. This results in a very safe society where awakened people care for themselves and each other. They also love their work, express affection, and smile a lot. That's Happiness.

There are great massage spas and healthy restaurants everywhere here. The only health issue for me is the smoke and smog. I can't see the beautiful mountains which surround the town. Indeed, sometimes it's so bad I can't even see the bottom of the street. Chiang Mai is one of the most air polluted places on the planet at this time of the year. Only *Jerusalem* in Israel and *Shanghai* in China are worse just now.

The farmers are burning the fields to prepare the ground for the next planting season. However, in neighbouring *Myanmar*, the forests are being set alight to make space for sugar palm plantations with devastating effects. The combined smoke sinks and

flows through the valleys spreading across the entire country. Only the rainy season will disperse it but there's no sign of that anytime soon.

Wat Phra That Doi Suthep is the most famous temple in the area, perched high up in the mountain that overlooks the city. It's a golden jewel which shines so bright. When *Siddhartha Gautama*, The Lord Buddha died in 545 BC, his body was cremated, and the remaining bones were dispersed in temples around the world. One of those relics is saved here.

I have been puzzled at the multitude of places where it is claimed that one of Buddha's teeth is stored. It made me think that he must have had a mouth like a crocodile. However, a monk explains to me that fragments of bone or 'relics' are often mistranslated to 'tooth.' "Buddhism is very logical, and I also hear that re-incarnation is making a comeback," he laughs.

It's hot enough without having to climb the 309 steps to the top so I take the cable car and walk down them instead. At the foot of the steps, cute kids from the nearby Hmongs Hill Tribe are dressed in their colourful native costumes and want to take a photo with me in exchange for a donation to their school.

The team leader, six-year-old Jana, already knows the international sign language for money and rubs her finger and thumb together after our photoshoot. I visit their village of wooden huts with palm leaf roofs.

When the Thai government halted the growing of opium, the villagers were shown how to grow other commercially viable crops instead. Avocados, rubber, sugarcane, cassava, fruit, cashew nuts, corn, tobacco, cotton, coffee, cocoa, peanuts, soybeans, and medical plants are all grown here now. I couldn't help but notice a familiar five leaved marijuana plant growing in the garden. It must be for demonstration or medicinal purposes as all drug misuse is now illegal in this country with severe penalties.

I hire the lovely *Leelawadee Coco* for a few hours driving through the countryside in search of wildlife. First stop is the *Tiger Kingdom* where tiger cubs have been reared to become accustomed to human contact. The tiger trainers are very skilled and knowledgeable, and I decide to risk going into the cage with them.

I am told to empty my pockets of any clangy things like coins or phones and move very slowly and calmly from behind. That's much easier said than done when you get close to an animal four times bigger than you with teeth and claws which can rip an antelope apart.

They explain to me that these animals are not sedated or drugged, as they are in some places, but I am beginning to wish that I was. "Good luck," one of them says to me as I enter the double-gated enclosure. The other four accompany me armed with little sharp sticks.

Nelson is just four years old and he seems to be having a cat nap. "He just had his breakfast of 12 chickens, so he is now resting," I'm told. "Just lie down beside him and spoon him." Spoon him!? I can't even get my arm around his waist.

But he does feel cuddly, soft and very warm. "Look at his nuts," says the trainer. "You can touch them for good luck," he says. This feels so disrespectful, but I do as I'm told. I don't know who has the bigger balls. Just then Nelson leaks the smelliest fart and wakes up. Well, who wouldn't? It's even stronger than the acrid smell of ammonia from his pee.

I don't know if tigers feel empathy, but I am giving him my strongest best intentions and firm cuddles. "I love you, Nelson," I say inside my head. "You are magnificent. I didn't mean to touch you there. That bad man told me to do it. Please don't eat me. Eat him instead." Nelson just looks around disinterested and yawns. My head could easily fit inside that mouth and those teeth! His paws are massive, but the claws only come out if he gets upset. I refuse the suggestion to pull his tail.

A few more firm strokes and 'man pats' and I'm then introduced to his two brothers, gently and one at a time and again from the rear. It's much safer to stay away from the sharp end, they tell me. They each have distinct personalities and Rambo the naughty one, takes a swipe at the trainer and growls. The ground vibrates and I freeze till he calms down.

Next, I meet a beautiful young white tiger. "Are they all young males?" I ask. "Of course," says the trainer. "Don't you know by now that females are always more deadly than males? Once they get beyond four years old, the males become unpredictable too."

After that experience, the snake farm is a cinch. Black King cobras and jumping, spitting, slithery snakes are a breeze. I even get to play with a lovely green tree snake which thinks it's my necklace. The three feet long-bearded dragon lizard doesn't faze me at all. "I've been close to the giant Komodo Dragons you know. And I've just felt a tigers nuts!" I tell it smugly. Its sticky tongue then shoots out and kisses my nose. Respect. It's all downhill from here and the butterfly and orchid farm is really just for kids, girls and poets.

The warriors enter the ring and the crowd cheers excitedly. They look so small and young. Their rippled muscles shine and shimmer under the bright lights. Each is wearing a *mongkhon*, a type of headgear and a *prachiat*, an armband. Both are believed to provide protection during the impending battle. They are going to need it. Slowly at first, they circle and stalk each other. Their eyes lock intently to catch the first glimmer of an attack.

Like two praying mantises, they make the tiniest twitching movements to assess and measure their opponent's distance and reaction. It's like a slow and hypnotic dance. Suddenly, and at lightning speed, red shorts lash out with a straight arm punch to his

opponents' head. Blue shorts gracefully sways backwards and the blow whistles past. Instantly he responds with a knee jab to the others kidneys and a few well-aimed punches. The commentators' voice rises excitedly and the crowd cheer for more.

Muoy Thai boxing is an ancient 13th-century martial art and is now one of the most popular and dangerous sports in Thailand. There are over 100 classic moves to be mastered and the fighters start learning them as young as six years old. This is nothing like western-style boxing. The gloves are brutally small for maximum impact. As well as fists, elbows, knees, feet, and legs are also used. Each match is only five rounds of three minutes each, but few last that long. Two of the contests I watched were over in less than a minute.

The warriors get locked in a tussle and fall together through the ropes. Quickly back on their feet, they continue to circle and spar. The tension is building and sensing it, the audience rise to their feet. There seems to be real enmity between these guys, and they are certainly not pretending. Blue shorts delivers a few well-placed blows to his opponent's torso.

As they pull apart red shorts responds and with brutal force, his leg swings high and straight into the others face. Heel connects with cheekbone and blue shorts head snaps round with the impact, his sweat spinning through the air. His body goes limp and falls to the ground.

Officials rush into the ring and throw water on his face. This fight is over, and the winner helps his opponent out of the ring before taking his victory salute. The crowd are ecstatic. Those who gambled on his winning even more so. Once the water and blood are mopped up, the next two hopeful warriors enter to start all over again.

Humans are the most dangerous animal on this planet.

I timed my visit to Thailand to experience the *Songkran* or water festival. It's the start of the New Year here and it starts with a splash. It's now year 2562 since Lord Buddha was born. The Thais are way ahead of the rest of the world in so many ways. This four-day National holiday starts with a huge procession and the roads are closed to traffic.

Twenty-six precious statues of Buddha are brought out of storage and paraded around the streets. All of the 300 temples are represented, and thousands of orange-clad monks join the march along with hundreds of organisations. Dancers and musicians help to create a carnival atmosphere full of fun and merriment. It's believed to be good luck to splash the statues with water and the monks bless the crowds with holy water as they pass by.

The entire procession starts at 11 am and doesn't finish until 7 pm. Meanwhile, everyone is getting soaked. The tourists buy the latest plastic pump-action water guns. The locals still favour buckets of water or better still a high-pressure garden hose. Everyone gets soaked and there is no escape anywhere on the streets. Little kids and grannies all join in the fun.

The streets are running with water and there is not a dry shirt in sight. Street battles break out between rival groups and it's all accompanied with laughter and a polite thank you or *'Khob Khun Kup'*. There is no respite and clearly no water shortage either. The Thais don't take whisky with their water so these New Year celebrations last for days.

Open trucks patrol the streets with cheeky armed water militia soaking the pedestrians. Buckets of water fly through the air splashing the motorcyclists and even the taxi passengers. It's all done with great enthusiasm and lots of fun. I've never felt so clean.

There are lots of special events in the packed festivities program. My favourite is the *'Best Ladyboy with a Parasol riding a Bicycle Competition 2019.'* It's fiercely contested but the winner is announced to high squeals of delight, hugs, and dramatic gestures from the participants. The winner gets £500, a bike and a year's supply of pizza. It's sponsored by Coca Cola.

I'm on the bus to *Chiang Rai*, 100 miles north-east from Chiang Mai. Chiang means town so I'm travelling from Mai to Rai. It's close to the border with *Laos* and Myanmar where the river Ruak joins the mighty Mekong. This area is also known as *'The Golden Triangle'*.

This was once the world centre for opium production and was controlled by the notorious drug lord, Khun Sa. Gold was used as the currency to trade with the three neighbouring countries. One Kg of processed heroin was exchanged for one Kg of gold. The poor native hill tribes, who I was soon to meet, grew and harvested the poppies for peanuts.

It's a short longboat trip across the river to Laos. This is truly a duty-free destination, and everything is available for sale at very low prices; tobacco, jade, jewellery, poppy liquor, Viagra, snake potions, herbs. The stalls sell everything including 'Scottish' whisky at just £5 a bottle. This stuff is made near my home in Scotland and shipped all the way over here. How can it be so cheap? I have to travel light so it's easy to avoid such temptations, but the hordes of Chinese visitors snap everything up.

Back in Thailand I visit the hot springs and boil eggs in baskets in the 98-degree water. There are seats where you can enjoy them with your feet dangling in shallow stone baths. The hill tribes live in a secluded part of the forest. They were once nomads who were free to travel in this part of the world. That was before national boundaries were enforced. Persecution followed and now many of the tribes are being helped to find new ways to survive while keeping their culture and customs alive.

I meet Kwan from the Karen tribe who makes jewellery. Her father Nathapatt sells them from his stall. Most fascinating is the 'Long Necks' famous for their heavy copper neck braces which elongate their necks. Sempra had her first four bands fitted as a child and four more were added every four years. She now carries 36 bands and it's heavy now, pushing her shoulders and clavicle down and giving the

impression that she has a long and delicate neck. She says the women think it makes them more beautiful to their own tribal males. Some say that it was also created to protect them from tigers which always try and bite the neck of their prey.

Wat Rong Khun is better known as *The White Temple.* It shines and sparkles in the sunshine like an ornate wedding cake smothered with icing sugar. It's a contemporary artwork by its creator and designer, *Chalermchai Kositpipat,* a famous Thai visual artist. The landscaped grounds are full of Buddhist symbolism.

Five trees teach the rules of Buddhism; don't harm living beings, don't steal, no sexual misconduct, don't lie and don't get intoxicated. One of the trees features an unopened bottle of my national drink, Johnny Walker, surrounded by ghoulish heads hanging from the branches.

A narrow white bridge is guarded by two huge creatures that represent Death and Rahu, who decide over our fate. As we pass over in single file, I look down to see hundreds of grasping hands reaching up symbolising desire.

This area represents human suffering and hell. The bridge towards the Ubosot or 'Gate of Heaven' represents the crossing over from the cycle of death and rebirth into a state free of suffering. It also describes the way to happiness by overcoming egotistical behaviors such as pride, greed, lust, envy, gluttony, rage, and laziness.

I somehow make it over and enter the main temple which represents Heaven or Nirvana. Photography is not allowed in here and I can't tell you what lies within.

You will just have to wait and find out for your Self.

"And as we wind on down the road
Our shadows taller than our soul
There walks a lady we all know
Who shines white light and wants to show
How everything still turns to gold
And if you listen very hard
The tune will come to you at last
When all are one and one is all
To be a rock and not to roll
And she's buying the stairway to heaven"

Led Zeppelin

On the Road to Mandalay...

April, Days 207-220: 44,813 miles

In one of _Steve Jobs_ last speeches which he made before he died, he made the point to trust that you know where you are going. That only after you're there, can you then connect the dots. "You can't connect the dots looking forward; you can only connect them looking backwards."

And so, it was for me in Myanmar.

The dots to which I refer may seem at first to be random and span many generations. They include _Rudyard Kipling's 'Jungle Book', George Orwell's 'Burmese Days'_, The Swastika, Boy Scouts, Pedophiles, Brexit, and Scottish Independence.

George Orwell once said, "He who controls the past, controls the future." Bear with me while I try to join up these dots while also painting a picture of the past and present of this intriguing and complex country.

I have no doubt that my personal character and present values were, like most of us, formed when I was a teenager. My adventurous and pioneering spirit, love of nature, curiosity, self-belief, and resilience, I can largely attribute to the boy scouts. I earned lots of badges and became a chief scout winning the coveted County flag for my troop for the first time since 1937. I left when it was discovered that the scout leader was a serial pedophile and the organisation refused to take any action.

That led to me adopting a healthy mistrust of authority in all its forms. I decided instead to tune in, turn on and drop out, much to my teachers and family's disappointment. That's when I first became interested in Eastern mysticism as a way to explain the meaning of life.

Learning how to meditate gave my mind space it needed to escape the confusion of those times and it has been a most valuable tool ever since.

The British-German Royals' army went to war three times with Myanmar and eventually ruled over it as an extension to India from 1885 to 1948. They renamed it 'Burma' because it was easier to spell.

Taking full advantage of their superior military power, they plundered what they could for the realm. That included their use and abuse of the locals who were now their subjects (slaves) and deemed mere natives, "an inferior people with black faces."

In the same way that's how they treated the Scots some 150 years earlier after their redcoats decimated the clans at the _Battle of Culloden_, just 20 miles from my home. And so, the rule of the white 'Royal British Conservative Supremacist' embedded itself and has perpetuated to this day.

Mandalay was once the capital of this country and where I start my adventure.

There are over 10,000 Buddhist temples and pagodas in Myanmar. At dusk and dawn, their gleaming golden spires reach upwards reflecting the golden sun. I

climb the steps of *Mandalay Hill* to the highest temple here. The huge flat plains surrounding the *Irrawaddy River* sprawl below me with the distant mountains mostly hidden by smog from the burning fields and forests.

This beautiful temple is adorned with millions of tiny mirrors and it's a wonderful place for reflection. There are hundreds of Buddhist monks dressed in pink and I soon realise that they are both genders. The Myanmar people are small in stature. The women slim and boyish without the rounded contours of their Western cousins. With shaven heads, it's even harder to tell the difference. I have an idea that those early British colonialists may have had the same confusion.

I seem to attract a lot of attention as being the only 'tall' white guy here, and many of the locals want to take a photo of me with them. Two of the girls paint my face with *'thanakha'*, a beige sandalwood paste which protects the face from the hot sun and moisturises the skin. These people project their inner beauty naturally and don't need any other cosmetic. What they lack in stature they most surely make up for with huge hearts and happy smiles. I feel like a movie star and, I guess to their eyes, we white folk must all look the same.

Down on the streets of this huge city, it's not so idyllic. It reminds me of Colombia and Cambodia. There are few shops as we would know them. Instead, the streets are lined with grimy open stalls, offering street food, services, and bric-a-brac.

I find a small general shop, but it only sells nutrition-free food wrapped up in brightly printed cardboard boxes and plastic. The prices are incredibly low though. Whisky and rum are just £3 a bottle, and I leave with a full shopping bag of stuff for less than £5.

Outside the shop, the beggars are sitting amongst the garbage and the litter. Some with no limbs amongst old women with babies. They look up at me with desperate pleading eyes and shake bony outstretched fingers. It's hard to walk past them with a wallet full of cash.

There are no pavements here, just dusty embankments full of holes, electric wires, litter, and dog shit. People sleep rough at the roadside under corrugated iron canopies with only a blanket to keep them safe from the flies, the rats, and the cockroaches. Stray dogs run wild in packs here and one scamp takes a cheeky nibble at my back heel as I pass.

Mandalay is a strange city and it's extremely hard to get my bearings. Apart from the huge *Royal Palace* surrounded by its moat and 22-foot-high walls, there is no real centre. Everywhere seems much the same as everywhere else. I find the best restaurant in town and for just £3 I enjoy a delicious dinner including a pint of the local Myanmar beer which goes down a treat in this baking heat.

Tourists are often surprised to see the swastika on many of the temples. However, this iconic symbol of fascism was previously an ancient Hindu symbol which was used to attract and bestow good luck. *Rudyard Kipling* used the swastika on the covers of his early

books. You probably know of him because of the movie *'Jungle Book'* produced by another famous freemason, *Walt Disney*.

Anyway, Kipling was fascinated by this place while it was being colonised by the British around 1898. He wrote the poem *'The Road to Mandalay'* made famous in song by Frank Sinatra. He also represented the worst of British flag-waving imperialism with its bullying, racist bigotry, and superior world view. You may not know however that he was best chums with *Chief Scout Lord Baden Powell,* also an alleged homosexual and the founder of the Boy Scout movement.

The character of *'Akalar'* who lorded over its wolf packs and cubs was adopted from Kipling and is still part of the scouting culture. The earliest symbols for the scouting movement also included the Swastika.

Much later, the Nazis were so impressed by Powell's organisation that they formed their own version known as *'The Hitler Youth.'* It too groomed and indoctrinated young men for the military and the State. Nowadays, we call this 'radicalisation.'

It's a grueling 12-hour bus ride to *Bagan*. Twenty of us are packed tight in a twelve-seater minibus. The luggage and baskets of live chickens are strapped to the roof. There is no air conditioning and the outside heat blows in through the open windows. People just chuck their empty plastic bottles and litter out of them.

Every so often the driver spits out a gobful of betel nut juice. It's crimson red and looks like blood. Most black toothed men here chew this stuff for its cocaine-like effects. Some of the streets are clarted with it and in some places, it looks like there's been a bloody street battle.

The bus pushes its way up the mountain pass to the coast. It's mostly single track, mostly tarred, and the driver blasts his horn to deflect any vehicle in front to the side of the bumpy road so that we can pass. Halfway up the hill, there is a loud bang and a shudder as one of the suspension springs snaps.

We disembark and wait patiently by the roadside under the trees. Its 39 degrees in the shade. Some of the passengers offer me some strange but tasty fruit. I pay with a thank you and a grateful smile.

Other bus drivers stop to help and soon plastic bottles full of nuts and bolts are being decanted onto the road. An hour later it's repaired, and we squeeze back into our sweaty seats. At a roadside cafe shack, bowls of unknown foods are dished out. There are no menus and no one speaks English here so when I see something which looks edible, I simply point at it and then at my belly and give a thumbs up.

The cook grabs handfuls of warm noodles and puts them in a bowl. She then adds fishy gruel from a pot boiling on the open fire, sprinkles in some stuff which looks like crunchy fried bacon, some chilies, spring onions and coriander. I pay her the equivalent of 20p. It tastes surprisingly good until I find a tiny bird leg and claw hidden amongst

the noodles. I find the toilet but decide that it will be much more hygienic to pee under a tree instead. Looking down, I see a pile of sparrow heads and feathers. There's a barrel of warm grey water to wash my hands in.

We arrive in Bagan bus station at midnight and the bus driver kindly drives me another six miles to the door of my hotel. My room overlooks the wide *Irrawaddy River* towards stunning crimson sunsets. The fishing boats are just 100 yards away and at night I can hear the boat families talking and singing. Their voices carry across the water and merge with the sounds of the croaking frogs.

This is a happy place despite its seeming poverty. People just sing here for no other reason but for the song itself. I often hear them in the street just walking along. It's lovely and it reminds me of the time in my youth when people would whistle as they walked.

There are over 2,200 red brick temples in this small town, and I was hoping to take a dawn balloon flight to see them all, but I'm deflated by the cost. £350 for just 90 minutes will break my budget. Instead, I rent an E-bike for £5 to find some higher vantage point from one of the temples facing east towards the airport.

The first time I tried to ride a motorbike I did a backward somersault and ended up with the bike on top of me. I haven't dared try again for nearly 50 years. This bike is electric and only goes 20 km per hour flat out. I soon get the hang of it and am quietly zipping along the dark, dusty and diesel smelling roads towards a recommended outpost.

Climbing temples for a better view across the flat plain has become a backpacker's sport here. The authorities now ban people from climbing up the bell-shaped red brickwork to protect and prevent them from crumbling back into the dust.

I find a perch along with another dozen or so well informed but sleepy travellers to wait for the sunrise and the unfolding spectacle. It's so quiet, and as the sky lightens, we can make out the silhouettes of hundreds of temples all around us. It feels surreal and otherworldly as they appear through the morning mist dark against the lightening skies.

The sun rises turning the sky tangerine and the first balloons slowly rise, floating silently up into the sky. We count fourteen in total. This feels like a dream and I can only imagine what it must look like from above.

My driver, Heun, takes me to *Mount Popa*, an extinct volcano nearly 5,000 feet above sea level. On top, there is a magnificent Buddhist temple. On the roadside on the way, there are hundreds of local villagers begging with outstretched hands. People throw paper money out of the bus windows to watch them scramble dangerously amongst the traffic.

To get to the temple, I must climb 777 steps barefoot in the sweltering heat. On the way up I'm accosted by cheeky monkeys who

jump around stealing food from the pilgrims. By the time I reach the top my shirt is soaking with sweat. Freshwater and a cool breeze never felt so good and I take time to dry off before stepping back down.

On the way home, we visit a traditional local village and 15-year-old Thani proudly shows me around. "We got electricity last year so now we can stay up later," she grins. Her mum demonstrates how they collect and spin cotton to weave into blankets. She then rolls a huge cigar from corn leaves and puffs on it. A tradition passed on through the generations. Another family makes lacquered bowls and yet another carved wooden door knockers.

There are just 700 people here, yet most of the food they use is grown in the fields around the village and the water is from the well. Tourist dollars are a welcome top-up to meet their needs. The buildings are made from the wood and dried leaves of the palm trees. They also provide the sugar palm nuts from which they make herb flavoured sweets and liquor.

It's good business but sadly it's also the reason they are now burning the forests to grow more sugar palm trees. The arid brown fields are on fire as they burn the shaws in preparation for the new crops. The whole country is smothered in smoke and the pollution levels are dangerously high.

The heat, smog, smoke and dust finally get to me and I find myself spending my afternoons in the cool sanctuary of my air-conditioned room. Even the locals are saying that it's too hot. It's strange seeing umbrellas used for sun protection. I decide to head for the cooler coast and the most highly rated beach at *Ngapali.* It's remote and the only way to get there involves another 12-hour bus ride to the town of Pyay where I stop overnight in *Zingley Hotel.*

Next morning at dawn, I'm on the back of a bike to the bus station to undertake the final mammoth 16-hour bus ride. I find myself getting deeper and deeper into the local way of life. I see no other tourists or white people, and no one here speaks English.

I am so far away from my familiar world. It feels very lonely and vulnerable at times, but it forces me to reach out to connect with others in sign language and with smiles. *'Mingle abba'* (hello), *'Jayzu gay bani'* (thankyou) and *'Jayzu peu'* (please) are the only words I really need. Oh and 'Beer' of course, but that's international.

There is instead a kind of telepathic communion and the local people seem to sympathise with this ageing, strange, smiley white guy and offer me what I need. Thank goodness too for bananas and tins of cold Myanmar beer.

On the way here I am surprised when our bus must stop at two military checkpoints. We all get off the bus and have our ID's checked by stony-faced uniformed armed police. As the only obvious tourist, I am simply nodded back through the border gates. The brown-faced locals, however, must have their pink ID cards scrutinised. More research is called for to understand the reason for this.

Throughout colonial rule, the Anglo-Burmese dominated the country, causing discontent among the local ethnic communities. Rohingya Muslims allied with the British and were promised a Muslim state in return for fighting against the local Rakhine Buddhists, who were allied with the Japanese. The British finally walked away from Burma in 1948, betraying their promise and leaving the Rohingya to fend for themselves.

The consequences of this betrayal led to the world's longest ongoing civil war. Almost 700,000 *Rohingya* people fled to Bangladesh in 2017 to avoid ethnic and religious persecution by Myanmar's security forces in their "clearance operations." The situation is ongoing, and it has devastated the tourist industry here. It's not just the fields that are now burning but also the village huts too.

When Myanmar finally regained its independence from its ruling masters it promptly restored its original name. Rangoon the capital city was also renamed to Yangon. And that's where I'm now headed to catch my flight over the *Bay of Bengal*.

But first back to joining up my dots. *Eric Blair* was the real name of George Orwell. He and Rudyard Kipling had a lot in common. They were both born in India to privileged families who were well connected to the British elite. They both went to posh public schools in England and both spent time in Burma. However, to me, they represent two very different sides of the 'Queens shilling.' Kipling clearly embraced his privileged connections and represented the worst aspects of the British Conservative elite class.

Orwell hated his private education and the bigotry and hypocrisy he experienced there. He became a Socialist and humanist and a rare role model for me when I was young. Some of his greatest works include *'Animal Farm'* and *'1984.'*

The seeds of this very British disease of power abuse and bigotry are perhaps still fostered in its top private schools and institutions. Dis -empowered people are often drawn to powerful roles. In 2015, *David Cameron, the British Prime Minister* was outed by his Oxford school chum for his depraved behaviour with a pig. Perhaps to divert attention from his public shame or simply to save his own face, he announced the Brexit referendum. The rest, as they say, is history.

Since then the true nature and behaviour of this ancient 'British Club' has been revealed to the world. The values they embrace are not mine. And they are not Scottish. I believe that it's now time for us to leave this club and let them deal with the sins of their own fathers.

This sombre song would drain the sun
But it won't shine until it's sung
No water running in the stream,
the saddest place we've ever seen
Everything I touched was golden
Everything I loved got broken
On the road to Mandalay."

Robbie Williams

South India: Inside the Golden Golf Ball...

May, Days 221-235: 46,834 miles

You know you're in India when people wobble their heads back and forth and it's hard to look them in the eyes without wobbling yours as well. Everyone calls you 'Sir'. Your morning toast is inside your curried omelette and the tea is sickly sweet. There are cows outside your hotel room door. They wander about the streets along with the goats, dogs, and chickens. The kids play cricket amongst the poo.

I intend to spend a month in this fascinating country travelling from the South to the North via the west coast towards Nepal. I've had to hop over *Sri Lanka* due to the bombings and come straight to *Chennai*. This city was originally called Madras and at 40 degrees, it's as hot as the curry.

I think that the Indians must have adopted their bureaucratic style from their English masters back in the day. Everything here is so very complicated. At the airport, someone checks your passport, someone else stamps it and then someone else checks that the stamp has been stamped most properly.

I try five different ATM's before I find one that actually dispenses cash. And getting a SIM card with a data plan takes me four days. At every stop there is another smiling, tutting head wobbler who explains the next requirement in this very, very tricky process.

Over 1.3 billion people live in the 29 states which make up India. That's nearly 20% of all the humans on the planet. Chennai is the capital of the State of *Tamil Nadu* and home to over 5 million. Yet it's only the sixth most populated city here. Over 30 million people live in Delhi which is the 2nd most populous city on Earth.

I book an air-conditioned luxury bus to *Puducherry*, but the taxi driver drops me off at the wrong location. I stand by the busy roadside with traffic speeding by, horns hooting and tooting, lost again. A group of young guys sense my dilemma, come to my aid, advise me that there is a bus station eight miles away and flag down a tuk-tuk to take me there. Indian people are so friendly and helpful.

This tuk-tuk is a cooperative one and it tuks on down the road weaving in and out of the busy traffic. How do folk tolerate this heat, noise, fumes and dust? When there are people by the roadside the driver swerves towards them and shouts 'Puducherry' and folk just pile in.

There are seats for four but somehow, we manage to squeeze in nine including the driver. An old lady puts my bags on her knees and climbs onto mine. An hour later I prize myself out of the vehicle at what I am assured is the bus station. It costs just 20p.

Throngs of people surround clapped out government buses and I ask a shopkeeper for help but don't understand what he says to me. He then grabs my suitcase and my arm, and we run to a packed blue rickety old bus just in the nick of time. The windows are wide open but it's still scorching hot. At every stop,

shouting street vendors jump aboard selling water, bags of fruit, nuts, and celery sticks.

My ordeal is lightened when *Vivek Anand* and his lovely daughter sit next to me on the torn plastic seats. He encourages her to talk and translate for him. At just 11 years old, her grasp of the English language is excellent, and her bright-eyed curiosity and intelligence is a delight. The miles speed by and I soon arrive at Puducherry bus station. It's another crazy 40-minute tuk-tuk ride to *Greens Guesthouse* in Auroville.

The next morning, I am sitting under the *Banyan Tree* in the heart of *Auroville*. We have been shuttled by free bus from the visitors' centre and now sit in silence before our guide leads us into the *Matrimandir* - the golden futuristic Holy Temple at the centre of this remarkable place.

All possessions must be left behind including cameras, so I only have these words to describe what's inside 'the mysterious and magical golden golf ball.'

The Banyan Tree itself is like a huge natural temple and hosts so much life. Crows, minor birds, lizards, squirrels, insects, and butterflies thrive in her sanctuary. A tiny owl flies out from one of the holes in the ancient trunk and watches me with big eyes in its swivelling head. "Who, who are you?" I imagine it says.

I am about to realise that I'm not who I thought I was.

This tree drops tendrils to the ground which then grow into new trunks supporting the massive branches growing horizontally from the central trunk. It's like a massive natural cathedral. A stark contrast to the magnificent golden structure which has been built intentionally next to her.

We walk in silence through one of the twelve inspirational gardens towards the Temple in solemn procession. There are twelve 'petals' surrounding the dome. Each houses a domed, coloured, and themed meditation room.

The Temple Ball is held upon concrete trestles and looks as though it is suspended in the air, floating. We leave our shoes on the path and are led up white marble steps from one of the four entrances. Inside everything is white. We sit to put on white socks before walking up a steep spiral ramp with soft white carpets. Water trickles down mosaic channels at each of the four segments to the white marble lotus petals below the globe.

As we climb slowly, reverently and in single file, we see others descending the opposite spiral like a double helix. This is dreamlike and yet it feels so familiar to me. I imagine this is what dying could be like.

Inside, the scene it's like a sci-fi set. Twelve huge white marble pillars appear to support the dome. There are no flowers, no incense, no paintings, and just smooth white marble walls. From the apex, a hundred-foot long silver shaft of sunlight forms a thirteenth column in

the centre of the chamber.

The light is guided by computers which track the sun and focuses the beam through mirrors and lenses downwards to the centre of a meter-wide solid crystal ball. I can see the entire room reflected inside the crystal including the crystal ball itself. In that reflection, I see a smaller version of this scene, to infinity. This is an absolutely stunning physical metaphor of the Soul of this place.

Someone coughs and the sound amplifies and reverberates around the room like thunder. Then silence with only the refreshing cool breeze of the air conditioning system to engage the senses. Seven of us sit between each column, making around eighty people here in this space. Strangers have come from all corners of the globe, all ages, and religions, from many walks of life, and are now sitting in a circle of silence on white cushions. We simply meditate and concentrate on the space inside from the space outside.

Many of us are moved to tears and the feeling is like coming home from a long journey to a place long remembered. No longer longing. Just belonging.

I am sitting between two women. Later, on the bus back we find ourselves sitting next to each other again and we talk for the first time. Lucy is from *Marseilles* in France and came here to convalesce after cancer surgery. Melanie came here from French-speaking *Quebec* in Canada to 'find herself' after her mother and grandmother recently died.

For the next few days, the three of us seem to meet up spontaneously everywhere we go. Literally finding ourselves at the same table in restaurants and at roadsides, by complete 'chance.' It's as if we are magnetised. It's remarkable and very magical. We become what I expect to be lifelong friends and we help each other with our life stories.

Auroville is an experimental community in southern India. It was founded in 1968 by the spiritual leader *Mirra Alfassa* as a town where people from all over the world could live in harmony. Half of its 3,000 residents are Indian and the other half from everywhere else. 52 Nationalities and every and no religion.

It has grown exponentially and now covers some nine square kilometers of its intended 20. It belongs to no one and everyone and now employs over 6,000 people. It has 17 schools with over 1200 students, two health centres and twelve dental clinics. There are over 500 alternative energy centres and 36 of its settlements are completely off-grid. It has reforested 1250 acres of forest and planted three million trees.

The entire region is alcohol-free and there are healthy vegetarian and vegan restaurants everywhere. For me, this place is as near to heaven on earth as I can imagine. I scoot around the hot, red dusty tracks on my electric scooter, rented for less than £3 per day.

I eat deliciously healthy food, do lots of yoga, visit some inspiring businesses, cooperatives and social enterprises and hang out at the nearby beach with the locals.

Auroville affects me so deeply like no other place I have ever visited. In a strange yet familiar way it feels like home which I know sounds crazy, but I also know that I must and will return here one day.

Goa is famous for its beautiful beaches and full moon parties. It has now become a staging post on the global hippy trail. I find a small guest house in the South of Goa at Bogmalo Beach. It's nearer the airport and less commercial and frantic than elsewhere.

Travelling is surprisingly hard on the mind and body and I need some relaxing holiday time for a few days to try and integrate and make sense of my experiences in Auroville.

Joets Guesthouse was created by Lynne from Lanarkshire, Scotland, and her husband Noola from Goa. In thirty years, they have grown a great business and many of their customers return here often. The staff seems like one big happy family. The kitchen has a refreshing Scottish flair, the food is great and the beer ice cool.

Most of the tourists have fled the hot season so I have the beach to myself most of the time. There is nothing more for me to do than socialise with 'The Joets Clan', bask in the sunshine, swim in the warm waters of the Arabian Sea, watch the locals shimmy up the coconut trees and play football on the beach.

Ah. You got to go to Goa.

"I believe I'm gonna shut down my chakra,
and shift Shiva off of my shelf...
Cause the righteous truth is
there ain't nothing worse than some fool
lying on some third-world beach
in spandex psychedelic trousers smoking damn dope
and pretending he's getting consciousness expansion."

Alabama Three

Delhi Delights and The Taj Mahal...

May, Days 236-244: 48,897 miles

Delhi is the political capital of India and the gateway for most international travellers. It's not the best first impression of this fascinating country. There are just too many people, the roads are gridlocked, and the pollution levels are often the worst in the world. As a result, everything is a bit grey and shabby.

The taxi I am in looks like it has been through a demolition derby and I have to close my eyes as the young driver weaves at high speed across the lanes and pushes his way through the tight traffic, horn blasting. There are no rules here and there could never be enough police to reinforce them, even if there were.

In the morning I take a walk around the block and I'm immediately surrounded by a gang of unwashed and unkempt street children shaking their silver begging bowls at me with big round pleading eyes and pointing at their tummies. "Money, give money" they demand.

The subcontinent of India has had a long history of conflict. Following the Vedic period, the *Maha Janapadas* were formed. Later, *Alexander the Great* added India to his extensive list of conquests and founded the *Macedonian Empire*. *Gupta* then established the *Mauryan Empire* which was taken over by *Ashoka*. *Dasaratha* then established the *Satavahana Empire* which was defeated by the *Nomads* who formed the *Kushan Empire*.

Then came the *Chola Empire* and the *Tamils*. The *Pandyan Dynasty* followed and then in 1300 AD, the *Khilji Muslim Dynasty* took over. The *Hindu Vijayanagar Empire* grew from the South of India but was conquered by the *Northern Sultans* who were overthrown by the *Moguls*. Then came the Europeans, French, Portuguese and finally the British.

The British divided, conquered and created lines; battle lines, boundary lines and railway lines. The latter helped to unify the country.

At last, came a leader in the form of *Mahatma Gandhi* who united his countrymen against the British with the simple slogan 'Get Out.' Without armies and much further bloodshed, his genius strategy of peaceful civil disobedience eventually succeeded, and in 1947, India finally achieved its independence from its British royal rulers.

It's a very complicated history but it helped to create a wonderful fusion of races, people, religions, architecture, cultures, and food which has resulted in the rich and diverse chaotic harmony which is now incredible and inclusive India. I visit the *Mahatma Gandhi Memorial* where he was cremated after his assassination and the *Gandhi Museum* paying tribute to his martyrdom.

In *Old Delhi,* I see the huge 17th Century *Red Fort* and India's largest mosque which can hold up to 20,000 people. Later I visit the Mogul King, *Humayun's Tomb* which is the predecessor of the *Taj Mahal* and was built by his wife after he died falling down the steps of his library.

The Qutab Minar is the landmark of Delhi and is 72 meters high. The stonework and carvings are astonishing when you consider that there were no cranes or power tools in those days. They did, however, have thousands of poor locals willing to work around the clock for food and lodgings.

New Delhi was built by the British and seems to be an exact replica of the *Champs-Elysees* in *Paris* including the *Royal Mile, Royal Palace* and the *Arch de Triomphe* look-alike, *The India Gate*.

The Palace is now home to the Indian President and his government officials who now live in the posh British styled mansions. My guide tells me that they are still corrupt power-seekers but at least they are now Indian corrupt power-seekers. It's election time here again and he shows me an indelible black mark on his fingertip which indicates that he has voted and can't vote twice.

I travel to *Agra* to view one of the wonders of the world, the majestic Taj Mahal. As I enter through the *East Gate*, the full panorama within the surrounding walled gardens opens to reveal this spectacular building in all its glory. It rises in perfect symmetry before me like an ivory ghost made from moonbeams. The beauty really is breath-taking.

It was built by the Mogul emperor *Shah Jahan* as a mausoleum for his wife *Mumtaz Mahal*, who died in childbirth. She had 14 children when she died at just 38 years old, so I'm not surprised. Her husband bumped off his brothers to get the throne and imprisoned his father for eight years in the nearby palace so that he could watch its construction without interference.

No expense was spared. The best architects and artisans in the world were commissioned and the white marble has been meticulously carved and inlaid with precious stones; rubies, emeralds, sapphires, and solid gold. It's precisely built on a north-south line and is identical on all four sides. It's meant to symbolise Heaven according to the Muslim faith.

A huge ramp 1.5 kilometers long was built so that bullocks could drag the massive marble stones to the top of one of the largest double domes ever built. They were glued in place with a special mixture of sugar cane, beeswax, honey, lemon juice, marble dust and lentils. They should have called it the Taj Ma Dahl.

It took just 22 years to complete and it's still perfect 387 years later. The Taj (or crown) of Mahal lies on the bank of the once very wide Yamuna River so that it would reflect its beauty to maximum effect. Sadly, the river has all but dried up these last three years due to climate change. It is said that he also planned to build a black Taj Mahal on the opposite riverbank but died before it could be started.

Inside there are only the crypts for his dead wife and his own body, which was later laid to rest on her right side with both of their heads facing West towards Mecca. The air cools as the sun sets and the colours change to soft pastel pink tones. There is such a peaceful

and calm feeling around. Everyone is smiling contentedly. Black kites soar gracefully overhead and tiny chipmunks chase each other around the acacia trees. The full moon is already high in the sky and I'm told that the building glows in the moonlight, but the gates close at 5 pm.

Jaipur is the capital of India's Rajasthan state. At the Amber hill fort, I take my first and last elephant ride to the top. This is a massive fortified complex which took just 15 years to build. However, it was abandoned 14 years later as someone forgot to check that the water source was clean and reliable.

In 1727, the successive royal family then founded what is now called the *'Pink City'* for its trademark terracotta building colour. At the centre of its stately streets stands the opulent, colonnaded *City Palace* complex. With gardens, courtyards and museums, part of it is still a royal residence.

Jai Singh was a keen scientist and astrologer and he designed the city around nine squares representing the nine planets. The sun and moon representing the King and Queen of course.

In its centre, he housed his 12 'wives', chosen from each sign of the zodiac to ensure that his children were 'full spectrum.' Each wife was given her own adjoining luxury apartment which she could not leave, and they were not allowed to speak to each other or be in the company of other men.

Instead, men were castrated to become eunuchs to look after them. The wives gave birth to his 99 children. He also had thousands of concubines for his pleasure. Yes, Jai was clearly a big man with a big appetite. In the museum, his silk underpants are on public display and they are at least five feet wide.

I learned that Black Magic (or Abracadabra as it is known here) was also practiced. Human sacrifice was believed to be powerful but only if the offering was a virgin and had no pierced skin. Women and men subsequently pierced their ears and noses to avoid being taken. This was the start of modern-day jewellery.

I have travelled far and seen some strange things, but I was not prepared for *Varanasi* known as *'The City of Light'* and the spiritual capital of India. It's a huge culture shock and it shakes my understanding of this world. It's mind-blowing.

I'm staying in the oldest part of this ancient city near the 'Ghats' or funeral sites on the banks of the *River Ganges*. It's jam-packed with so many unusual looking people wearing the strangest garments; Muslim women are hidden in black from head to toe, naked *Aghoris Sadhus* covered with just white paint and human ashes, Indian women wear beautiful saris in vibrant rainbow colours and hundreds of beggars with silver bowls lie or sleep by the roadsides.

The roads are nose to tail with ancient buses and cars, motorbikes, scooters, bicycles, rickshaws, camels, horses, and things with wheels that I just can't describe. The noise of their incessant horns is deafening. The lanes between these ancient buildings are too narrow for cars so I wheel my luggage over the dirty old bumpy flagstones to find my guest house.

These lanes are a labyrinth of winding, smelly, garbage-strewn dark passageways. I must take extra care to avoid the potholes and the cow poo. There are sleeping dogs, goats, cows, and horses everywhere. And it smells like a farm. Monkeys jump around like acrobats seizing every opportunity to get up to mischief. I patiently follow a cow as the lane is too narrow to pass.

A guy on a hooting motorbike suddenly appears behind me and the cow stops to let him pass. It lifts its tail and then deposits its runny excrement all over the street and my sandals. I take the opportunity to squeeze past as quickly as possible.

Humans and animals seem to co-exist here in harmony. Even the dogs don't fight. My GPS won't work here and there are no street signs that I can understand. Just as I start to doubt if I will ever find my way, a young guy with a jet-black handlebar moustache and a bright yellow suit calls me from a doorway. "*Safarnami* sir?" Yes, that's the name of the place I'm staying at and he is the manager. What a happy coincidence.

As I enter the guest house another guy starts banging a loud drum to welcome me. He then puts a garland of yellow and orange marigold heads around my neck. What a wonderfully strange welcome.

The managers' name is Raj and he brings me a silver tray with a glass of cold apple juice. He then shows me around the refreshingly cool and clean establishment. There are just six guest rooms here and I am the only guest. What a relief it is to get out of those crazy, hot, noisy, and smelly streets. And all this including breakfast for just £11 per night.

At dusk, I head up to the flat rooftop of this four-storey building. It's good to get away from the claustrophobic dark lanes below to see the sky again. It's a different world up here. Haphazard red brick and dirty concrete structures have been added on as families have grown. In the sky, there are dozens of small black paper kites flying high. Boys all over the city are flying them on mile-long pieces of string and showing off their tricks.

Large bats also whiz around, and I see lizards and dogs on the hot tin roofs, but no cats. There are lots of monkeys though, posing and leaping across the walls. As I turn my back, one of them scales up the wall and steals my glass of beer. It deftly downs it with both hands and puts the glass down before laughing at me and scuttling away. Beer is as hard to find in this city as a meat dinner. The Hindus worship Hanuman, the monkey god, as they do all living beings. It represents our mind of mischievous thoughts. So, the monkey in me laughs also.

Cheers, big ears.

Next day I book a tour with *Rishi Kant* and we travel to the local Hindu Temples through the hot chaotic streets in a tuk-tuk. I discover more about this ancient religion which predates all others. I learn that Hinduism is more of a system of understanding the cosmos and a collection of beliefs rather than a single religion. Its thousands of years old precepts are not out of touch with modern-day science and our recent understanding of quantum physics

Briefly, the Hindu trinity includes three fundamental forces and are characterised by *Brahma* (the creator), *Shiva* (the destroyer) and *Vishnu* (the preserver). These 'gods' overarch many other deities or qualities including the five elements of Sky *(Akash),* Wind *(Vayu),* Water *(Varuna),* Fire *(Agni)* and Earth *(Bhumi).* Each has its own character and quality.

There are also gods for each and every single quality of the cosmos. All co-exist in harmony and balance and there are sects which follow specific ones. We also visit Sarnath, where Siddhartha Gautama delivered his first teachings under the Bodhi tree at the monastery there. I am told that Buddhism is an inside job to help us realise that we are all 'godlets' - drops in the tidal ocean of the cosmos.

I play a game with the street beggars. I change £10 for 100 ten-rupee coins (worth just 10p each). I give two to one of them and suggest that he gives one to his neighbour. When he does so, I replace it with another. I keep doing this until he runs out of friends, then I turn to another and do the same until my money runs out. If they don't share the second coin, its game over and I ignore them.

They soon get the idea that only by giving do they keep receiving and I soon gather quite a large good-humored crowd. The bonus for me is that once my money is gone, they leave me well alone and they no longer hassle me on subsequent days either. Instead, they wave as they greet me and call me 'Baba Scottish.' Age has its advantages.

One of the Holy men is watching me intently and he invites me to walk with him to meet his friends. He seems to understand exactly what I am playing at and gives me his rosary necklace. He then dips into his little bag and puts orange saffron powder on my third eye. "This will protect you," he says. He wants nothing in exchange. He takes off his beautiful silver ring and hands it to me but I decline.

He then leads me down the steps of the Ganges to meet his friends, the Aghoris. These are a small group of ascetic Shiva Sadhus who are much revered here. They are believed to have great healing powers and even command the weather.

I see them sitting naked, covered in the white and grey ashes of the dead. Their practices are said to include cannibalism and other unspeakable acts of self-physical defilement. The Aghoris are highly respected here by the locals. They follow Shiva the destroyer, and they have a secret hangout on the steps near the funeral pyres.

I buy clean water and paper cups to share with them. One of them tests me and tries to scare me with his demon face, 'evil eye' and claw hand so I just hold his other hand and give him a hug until his smile

breaks through. They are a bit like our own Hells Angels back home; hard on the outside and soft on the inside.

I look deep into the eyes of one of the older men and behind the deathly pallor and insane expression, I see an intensely shiny soul, perhaps fully awakened to the ultimate reality of being.

It is said that the human soul finally completes its journey over many lifetimes, here in this Holy City of Varanasi. Perhaps the Aghoris are those of us at the end of the road, taking the ultimate step to fully release the material world, to laugh in the face of death and return to the source.

It's 5 am on my last day here and the streets are already buzzing with people. As the sun rises over the Ganges, people climb down the steps and enter the Holy water. Many have travelled far to be here. An old man shakes my hand and before I know it, I am on my back on the dusty, warm steps being given a thorough *Ayurvedic* massage by this sprightly 70-year-old. What a way to wake up. "You happy, then I happy," he says, wobbling his head with sparkly eyes.

For me, India is like a huge cake with so many diverse, colourful and sometimes seemingly incongruent ingredients. It's a melting pot for humanity where all races, religions and backgrounds have been mixed together to live mostly with tolerance and in harmony. The result is a country of diverse people, architecture, beliefs, cultures, and food.

A great recipe for the ultimate human curry.

As I post this blog, the results of India's election have just been announced. *Narendra Modi* was re-elected as the president of India. "Together we will build a strong and inclusive India," he tweeted after the country voted him in with a massive and historical margin from all of the States. I don't doubt his words.

Travel Tip No 23: To help combat food poisoning, the locals eat cardamom seeds coated in real silver. You can buy these in most street stalls for just 10 rupees (1p) per packet. Often in restaurants, you are offered tiny sugar-coated sweets containing liquorice and aniseed which also aids digestion and freshens the mouth.

Travel Tip No 24: Let sleeping dogs lie.

Travel Tip No 25: When passing a cow in a narrow lane, stay away from both the sharp end and the blunt end. Don't let it squash you against a wall.

"Thank you, India,
Thank you, terror,
Thank you disillusionment,
Thank you frailty,
Thank you consequence,
Thank you silence
Thank you. "

Alanis Morrisette

Nepal - On Top of the World...

May, Days 245-254: 49,496 miles

It's another grueling 20-hour bus ride to Kathmandu on a 'Super VIP' bus with hard torn fixed seats and a busted suspension. Vehicles just can't survive these potholed rocky roads and the journey is a real boneshaker. We squeeze past oncoming lorry convoys with sheer drops to the valley floor far below.

Next to me is Rico from *Capetown* and we quickly absorb ourselves in rich conversation. He is solo travelling on a low budget and a tiny backpack throughout Asia 'to just experience the world.'

"We are moving into a new realm of connected and shared consciousness from the simple 3 dimensions of the physical world into five dimensions which are beyond space and time," he explains. "Our solar system is now moving through higher frequencies of the universe which is causing our own sun to emit more light plasma. It's literally causing us to become more 'enlightened', illuminating the darkness from our past and the shadow of our limited egos."

"How old are you Rico," I ask. "My body is 26 years old, but my soul is eternal." he laughs. "How do you know all this stuff at your age," I ask. "Mushrooms man," he replies. "I don't do chemical drugs, just mushrooms and marijuana. Mushrooms contain the DNA of connectedness and they help me to join up the dots.

All knowledge is available once we are able to perceive it and really 'know' it. Opening the doors of perception allows me to discard what those who came before tried to teach me and I can see things as they are now more clearly for myself. It's really simple but people are freaking out with the changes. All they have to do is just chill and it's going to be just fine." he laughs again.

Lost in the conversation we stop noticing the bumps on the road and we time travel in our thoughts, meditation, and sleep. The miles speed by and in no time at all, we are at the border of Nepal.

Stepping off the bus is painful as my back and legs remind me of their physical confinement. Yes, we are back in 3D reality again - aches, heat, hunger, gravity and the need to find a toilet bring us back down to earth with a bump.

There is an entirely different vibe here. The roads, cows and shanty styled shops and houses look the same but there are fewer people and more smiles. After an effortless process through the friendly immigration and visa application hut, we are back on the bus and arrive eight hours later in Kathmandu, the capital of Nepal.

The temperature is a welcome 10 degrees cooler than in India. The air at 4,000 feet above sea level is clearer and the mountains show tantalising glimpses of the snow-covered Himalayas towering in the distance.

This massive mountain range is more than 450 million years old. The subcontinent of India is pushing against the continent of Eurasia and the mountains are slowly crinkling upwards under the pressure.

I'm back in my jeans for the first time in ages and explore the city. Kathmandu is more yuppie than hippie nowadays. They have learned a lot from the thousands of foreign tourists who come here every week, mostly from Europe and America. It's regularly voted as the best tourist destination but travelling from poorer India, prices have just tripled for me and are now on a par with the UK.

Bang goes my budget.

I'm staying in *Hotel Buddha* in the popular district of Thamel. The city centre is full of small shops open to the streets and the bazaars are a nomad's paradise. The smell of sandalwood incense wafts everywhere.

Souvenirs, cashmere, crystal balls, temple bells,
Tie-dye hippy bags, Himalayan prayer flags.
Shawls, sandals, bracelets, bangles,
Brass bowls, wooden masks, latest fashion handicrafts.
Kukri knives, cookery books, trippy thangka paintings,
Ashtrays, ding dongs, Nepalese hash glass bongs.
Rainbow scarves, beads in jars, tin flutes, trekking boots,
Pashmir, mountain gear.
Good prices, buy 'em here.

There are so many temples to see and every mountain peak has a stupa at the top. I visit the iconic *Durbar Square* and *Swayambhunath Temple*. The eyes of consciousness look down reminding us that everything we do and everything we think is observed. Later I meet more orange-clad holy men at *Pashupatinath Temple* and *Bodhnath Stupa*.

In April 2015 and in just 57 seconds, a devastating earthquake was followed by powerful aftershocks and avalanches. Nearly 9,000 people were killed, and another 22,000 others injured. Ancient buildings were destroyed. UNESCO is helping to rebuild these and now every tourist dollar helps the cause. The dust has yet to settle and the air is still badly polluted here in the city.

I am shocked at the sheer scale of the terrible air quality in this part of our planet. Thailand, Myanmar, North India, and Nepal record some of the most hazardous air pollution levels second only to *Beijing* in China. It's often 20 times the safe limit and there are now millions of premature deaths from respiratory diseases each year. I've heard it's the equivalent of everyone (including children) smoking 50 cigarettes a day. Everyone is coughing to fill their coffin.

I have wanted to go to *Tibet* ever since I read *'Seven Years in Tibet'* as a teenager. The Chinese government invaded the country in 1950, expelling the *Dalai Lama* and the Tibetan people from their homeland. Nepal is now full of purple-clad Tibetans and the message they live, and breathe is now spreading across the world. It's difficult to get a visa now so I settle for a flight around *Mount Everest* with Nepal's first

carbon-neutral *Yeti Airline*.

On the way to the airport, I notice that the streets are lined with gun bearing cops. "There must be a bigwig coming to town," says my driver. Later I read that there were three explosions here and three students protesting against Government corruption were killed. It's strange that the cops were on the streets hours before this happened.

I'm flying high with 12 teachers from *Colorado* and *Captain Khadka* invites me into the cockpit for the best view in the world. There are no words for me to describe the feeling I have around mountains such as these. They take me somewhere that words don't exist, nor need to. Three climbers died down there last week. Last year nearly 900 people attempted its peak and they sometimes had to queue up on the unforgiving ridges to take their turn. It just adds to the danger. One person in every 16 dies, ironically from overcrowding on one of the most remote places on Earth.

I travel on to *Pokhara* in the west of the country and I'm staying at *Peace Dragon Lodge* above the *Peace Pagoda*. It's a hard, hot hike up 200 rocky steps to the top of the mountain with my luggage. The views are worth it though.

As I arrive breathless, the frogs start to sing, the skies then darken, and the peace dragon awakes. Lightning flashes overhead sending out forked tendrils of spiky electric fire over the lake and the thunder claps its hands so loudly that the windows shake. Fierce winds lift the heavy marble tables on the terrace, smashing them.

The rain then comes down in heavy torrents. It's the first rain I've seen for months so I stand in awe on my balcony and just soak it all in. It will hopefully clear the air and the dusty streets. I might even see the Himalayas in the morning.

It's sunrise at 5 am and I throw open my curtains to be greeted by an awesome spectacle. From my balcony, I look down a steep mountainside lush with green vegetation resounding with the songs of the dawn chorus. Far below, Phewa Lake shines silver as the morning sun emerges, illuminating the valley.

On the other side of the lake there is another green mountain dotted with small white farm buildings. And beyond that, towering above everything is the *Annapurna* mountain range. The spiky fishtail of Annapurna One is like the tip of a knife piercing the sky. The snow-clad peaks seem to glow and sparkle in the light of this morning sun. My jaw drops and I gasp in awe at nature's beauty.

Below my guesthouse, I meet *Pra Kash*. He is the proud owner of a motorbike and he offers to be my tour guide. "I'm a great driver as I've been driving for six years ever since I was 16 years old," he tells me. "I am very safe and know everyone and everywhere around my hometown. You don't need to climb all of these steps when we can go up and down on my bike."

I later find out that at 14 years old he discovered that two of his teachers were engaged in an extra-marital affair. He unwisely decided to tell the world by writing it on the school wall. He was promptly expelled and blacklisted from attending any other school. Since then he has taught himself and speaks better English than his teachers. That's all the character reference I need so I hire him and tell him that if we crash or I fall off he will not get a tip. "Just take me to the places that you love," I tell him. "I'll pay for petrol, food and beer." "And don't forget the big tip," he replies with an enthusiastic grin.

I'm high on the back of his bike inching down a 50-degree incline on a rocky stream bed and I'm hanging on with my fingertips. We seem to defy gravity and I don't understand why we don't slide or go over the edge.

At the bottom of the valley, we join the main road and things don't get any better. The traffic is chaotic, and people just pull out in front of us to cross over. There are no traffic lights or rules here, just killer potholes. The heavy lorries churn up the sand as they pass us so closely and people just digest the dust. My eyes sting and I close them on most of the 25 km journey to another beautiful lake high in the mountains.

Trust and naive ignorance are two essential qualities of a traveller.

We visit Pras family and hang out with his mates. I meet his best friend Wiz who shows me around his round stone eco-house which he is building with his own hands. We take a boat around the lake and paddle past the island temple there. We watch the paragliders fly gracefully down the mountain. At night we hang out in his uncle's corrugated iron shop at the top watching the city of tiny lights sparkling below us and drink beer at £5 a bottle.

Down below I watch a bunch of tiny frail women pulverise a 20-ton mound of large rocks with sledgehammers. They then drop the broken pieces into wicker baskets on their backs held up by a sash around their foreheads. I reckon that there's at least a hundredweight in each basket, more than their own body weight for sure.

They then climb up the steep mountain path, one steady step at a time to rebuild the stupa which was damaged by an earthquake. I struggle just to lift my own body up these steps in this exhausting heat but the Nepalese people, although small in stature are so incredibly strong. My legs ache for several days to recover from just living here.

At 2 am I'm wakened by the sound of barking dogs. At breakfast, I'm told that they saw off a leopard which often prowls around at night looking for goats. Tigers have been spotted here too.

What is the drive that motivates humans to live at the top of these inhospitable mountains, exposed to the weather and defying gravity? Surely, it's the most dangerous place to be living on top of the world like this. Danesh, my guest house manager explains.

"At the top, there is nothing that can fall on you," he says. "And we can see the whole world from up here.

Perhaps we're even closer to God."

Travel Tip No 26: Those inflatable neck supports that you can buy in airports also make comfortable cushions to comfort your bum on long bumpy bus journeys.

Travel Tip No 27: Beware simple headline prices. In Nepal, a 10% service charge is added before 15% VAT. The final cost of everything is at least 25% more than stated on the menu.

Travel Tip No 28: It's always a good idea to travel with toilet paper and wet wipes, especially if you have diarrhea.

Travel Tip No 29: A great free app called AirVisual shows the current air quality where you are now.

"From a distance, the world looks blue and green
And the snow-capped mountains white
From a distance, the ocean meets the stream
And the eagle takes to flight
From a distance there is harmony
And it echoes through the land
It's the voice of hope
It's the voice of peace
It's the voice of every man."

Julie Gold

Qatar - Land of the Car...

June, Days 255-259: 51,585 miles

Qatar **is a halfway house between Kathmandu and** *Cairo*. **As I arrive, I realise that I'm now in an entirely different material world.**

This country has the highest per capita income on the planet, mostly shared between the wealthiest few in this country of just under 3 million people. It could not be more different from Asia.

The 12-lane motorway from the airport is immaculate and smoothly controlled by a sophisticated traffic system. The city road system is like graph paper. Six lane roads crisscross the city allowing the traffic to move extremely fast.

It's difficult for pedestrians though and I have to take long detours to find the underpasses. With zero taxation and petrol costing just 40p per litre, the car is definitely the king of the road. Mercedes and Porch are the favoured marques.

This economy is backed by the world's third-largest natural gas and oil reserves and it shows. The King, *Sheikh Tamim* has prioritised improving the domestic welfare of citizens, which includes establishing advanced healthcare and education systems, and expanding the country's infrastructure in preparation for the hosting of the 2022 World Cup.

There are no income or sales taxes and certainly no austerity. This King seems to be a good example of a benevolent dictator. It's a major culture adjustment for me. Everything here seems highly organised, clinically clean, and very sophisticated.

However, compared to colourful and chaotic Asia it's very monotone. Everything seems black and white. The buildings white and beige, the cars new and mostly white. Islam encourages people of both genders to dress modestly. The men and boys wear cool white long tunics or thaubs while the women must be cooking in this 40-degree heat inside their full-body black hijabs.

I'm strolling around the local *Souq Wakif*, the traditional marketplace. It's nearing the end of Ramadan, so most places are closed until sunset. Everything is for sale here including horses and camels and there is an entire area specialising in caged birds and hawks.

A crowd is gathered near the centre and as I walk to investigate, suddenly there is a massive bang and smoke rises above the crowd. I am startled and fear the worst but it's only the canon being fired to mark the end of this days fast. Surely a rousing chorus of "God is Great" would have been more appropriate than an explosion?

A toddler drops her ice cream cone. Immediately two smartly dressed young men appear to clean up the mess, washing it clean. The entire city including the side streets is spotless.

It's easy to notice things which are different from my own culture. There are many older men with small children, and I realise that they probably have more than one young wife. Men are openly affectionate, embracing, kissing each other's cheeks and holding hands but not with women who often walk behind the men like shadows.

It seems to me to be very much a 'man's world', at least in public places. However, I'm assured that in the privacy of their own homes, Muslim women are very fashionable. I meet with Bahija who explains an entirely different perspective.

"We pity your Western women", she says. "They must obey their own social norms of course - wearing fashionable clothes and expensive cosmetics to look good". Here we all look the same on the outside. There is no need to show off our status.

Also, here, the men provide so most of us don't have to go out to work. Don't think that we don't have fun though. We often have fashion parades around our private swimming pools and even wear bathing costumes. Just never in public or in front of other men", she laughs.

Bahija is one of three wives and they all look after the children as if they are their own. "Don't you get jealous of the other wives?", I ask. "Not at all". She says. "We are more like sisters and we all share the housework. We take turns sleeping with our husband and it's good to have a break", she laughs again.

"From my perspective, I see the West as lost in a sea of chaos. The Koran and the Bible both teach us about the seven deadly sins, but many Westerners seem to ignore this and are having to suffer the consequences. Envy, gluttony, greed, lust, pride, sloth, and wrath seem to be rampant and even encouraged in the West. It's so sad "

Human occupation of Qatar goes back over 50,000 years. Pearl diving was once one of Qatar's main industries. However, in the 1930s the Japanese succeeded in farming cultured pearls on a massive scale which destroyed the local economy. Even though pearling is no longer a thriving industry, it remains a beloved part of Qatari culture. Fortunately, the area struck oil and gas in the 1940s and it has prospered ever since.

At night, the City takes on a completely different appearance as it transforms into an illuminated wonderland. The hop-on bus takes me into the inner sanctum known as *'The Pearl of Qatar.'*

Here, buildings light up like coloured phallic popsicles and one even looks like it is wearing a golden condom. No expense has been spared here to make this the dream city of the desert - a 21st Century metropolis. Posters advertise the rollout of 5G, and it looks like Christmas all year round.

There is barely any rainfall, so all of the water is made from desalination plants at huge energy costs. Here they have reclaimed huge islands of sand on which have been built the most extravagant island communities. You can even buy your own personalised island,

although how long these will last for after the seas rise is debatable.

The shops here are the most expensive on the planet and showcase all the world's most expensive brands. There's a joke here that if you need to ask the price then you can't afford it.

I sit in an outside cafe with huge air conditioning units blasting into the hot open air. I am told that the football stadium is also cooled by these enormous gas-guzzling machines. Energy is cheap when you own the gas reserves.

In some of the friendliest places I have visited, people have the smallest wallets and the biggest hearts. I have found the opposite to be also true both here and in Las Vegas.

The people are very polite but seem to lack the open-hearted friendliness that I have experienced in some of the poorest countries.

Qatar for me is a land of darkness and light. Black and White like night and day.

All that glitters is not gold.

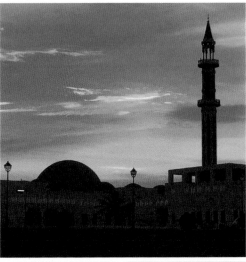

Travel Tip No 30: It's especially important to observe local customs. Men here are very warm, polite, and friendly but never stare, touch, or try to take a photograph of women

"Oh Lord, won't you buy me a Mercedes Benz?
My friends all drive Porsches, I must make amends.
Worked hard all my lifetime, no help from my friends,
So Lord, won't you buy me a Mercedes Benz? "

Janis Joplin

Nights over Egypt...

June, Days 260-266: 53,801 miles

I am staying in *Downtown, Cairo* just a few hundred yards from Tariq Square. It was here in 2005 that the Arab Spring started.

They still call it *'The Peoples Revolution'* and no one can forget the 967 people who were massacred by government snipers. My friend Achmed cries as he tells me how he held his dying school friend in his arms.

Tonight, is the end of *Ramadan* and the streets are buzzing with young people. Tourists are few these days and I am given a hero's welcome by these lovely kids. Everyone wants a selfie with me, and I am thronged by dozens of them who want to show me their city. The feeling in the air is palpable and with so much testosterone around, the cops are once again out in force.

I escape the madness with a night boat in Cairo. For just £12 I am treated to the best Arabian buffet followed by classic entertainment with some great performers including a belly dancer and a whirling dervish with his dwarf assistant.

Drinks are expensive but no one notices that my water bottle is pre-prepared gin and tonic. It keeps the mosquitoes away so there are no flies on me.

There is only one way to really see the *Great Pyramids of Giza* and that, of course, is on the back of a camel. *Lawrence of Arabia* makes it look far too easy.

This one is called Grumpy no doubt for its charming character. Camels are hard to get on and easy to fall off. When they stand, they push their front legs up and I am thrown backwards only to be pushed forwards again when it gets up on its hind legs.

Soon I and my camel are clomping through the sands of time. "If it goes too slow just hit it with the stick," instructs my camel man. But he is sitting low down on a friendly little white Arabian pony and I don't relish the idea of galloping off at 40 mph into the distance on this dromedary. And where are the brakes anyway?

The sand-flies really irritate Grumpy and he decides to lie down and roll over for a quick sand bath. I must leap off quickly. The locals call these animals 'leg breakers' for good reason. They also kick, bite and spit if they are in a bad mood so I whisper sweet nothings in its big ears. It seems to like my Scottish accent.

As I descend the steps into the tomb of *'Ka Omni Dyn,'* I feel the strangest sensation. It's like my arms are magnetised and want to defy gravity. I also feel light-headed. In the next chamber, there is a massive stone coffin cut from a solid piece of basalt.

Modern science still does not know how these precise cuts were made or how the 200 ton stones were moved to build these massive structures. It has been established that the three main pyramids at Giza were not mausoleums and were originally coated in three colours, white, red, and black.

Perhaps the ancients had knowledge of technology which we have yet to rediscover. My own belief is that these were giant machines which channeled geopathic energy to create powerful force fields which had a positive effect on the area.

This place, however, is full of secrets. Only the *Sphinx* knows the truth and it's not telling.

I follow the Nile down to *Luxor* and treat myself to a bit of luxury at the 5-star *Pavilion Winter Hotel*. For just £26 a night including breakfast, my balcony overlooks the Nile and the finest gardens in Egypt.

As I walk through the palm trees I am greeted by a flock of beautiful pink crested hoopoes, a bird I have always wanted to see. I make friends with Mustapha, a local guy who is happy to drive me around on his bike and on his horse and show me how the locals live.

I'm soon sitting in a dark and dusty back street surrounded by a herd of goats, horses, ducks, chickens, and barefooted naked toddlers. It's a far cry from my luxurious hotel.

We spend time together for the next few days and become good friends. This is his neighbourhood and he knows everyone. Mustapha gets me local prices and protects me from the scammers and I, in turn, look after him. Mutual respect is always a 'win-win' situation.

Finally, I achieve my long-held dream of flying in a hot air balloon. It's a 4 am start to catch the sunrise over the desert and soon we are floating effortlessly as silent as the wind over the fields and desert below.

On 26 February 2013, a hot air balloon crashed here, killing 19 out of the 21 people on board. It was the worst ballooning accident in history and the deadliest aerostat disaster since the Hindenburg went down in 1937 killing 36 people. I remind myself that it's not the falling that kills but the moment you hit the ground. I just have to remember to jump up at just the right moment.

All fears and negative thoughts quickly evaporate like the morning mist as we gently float upwards This is so silent and dreamy with only the occasional very loud blast of gas to take us higher. *Captain Bob* advises us that the breeze today is perfect as we glide above the West bank of the River Nile.

As the sun rises, I see the shadow of our balloon pass over Karnak and *The Valley of the Kings and Queens*, the mortuary temple of *Queen Hatshepsut* and the Tombs of Nobles and workers. This is a much more pleasant way to see the sights than being on the back of a camel.

On the descent we pass over farms and villages and the children wave at us as we land with a bump on the desert sands.

When visiting new places, it's always good to leave on a high.

Travel Tip No 31: There are lots of scams in Egypt and I found them to be the most aggressive types. Here are just a few...

1) Someone offers to take a picture of you with your phone. You think it's friendly until they ask for $10. If you don't pay, they run off with your phone.

2) Always check your change. It's common for some folk to try and pass a 100 Egyptian Pound as 1000.

3) Beware portable card scanners. I got stung when someone put through my transaction twice. (My bank later repaid me.)

4) Always agree on the full price including any hidden extras (Water for the camel, grass for the horse, hire of head dress etc.)

5) A friendly old gent asks me where I'm from. "I have a cousin in Scotland, come into my bar and have a drink." The beer costs $10 and then a pretty 'lady' sits next to me and asks for a drink. "How much?" I ask. "Only $20," she replies.

I realise that this is a 'club' and tell her that I'm not interested in 'extras', so I buy her a $10 drink for the chat. It's water in her glass.

Times are tough in Egypt as, since the revolution, tourism has dropped away. These folks are just trying to get by and feed their families. As the oldest son with an absent father my friend Mustafa must support eight people including his mother, wife, horse, two kids and four cousins. So be understanding, generous and kind but watch your wallet.

Trust in God but tie up your camel.

"Oasis in the sand where life once began
Under the moonlight
Your eyes won't believe what your mind can't conceive
Ooh...ooh...ooh...ooh...
Nights over Egypt."

The Jones Girls

A Greek Tragedy...

June, Days 267-275: 58,065 miles

The turquoise waters of the *Aegean Sea* sparkle invitingly as I land in *Athens*. The first thing I notice is .... legs and bare skin. It's almost pornographic after having spent so many months travelling through more modest countries.

Yes, I'm back in Europe, the land of bearded men, shops with familiar brands, cats, street cafes and the smell of freshly baked croissants and coffee. And it feels like home.

Unknown to me I would soon be back in Scotland much sooner than expected.

I spend a few days in Athens which I first visited in 2015 at the worst depths of Greek austerity. How things have changed in such a short time. There are less homeless people on the streets, the metro has fewer beggars and the streets are clean.

People here are in general agreement that things are slowly returning to 'normal' even though most of their national assets have been sold to foreign investors to pay off the debts.

Athens is the capital and was once the heart of ancient Greece, a powerful civilization and empire. The city is still dominated by 5th Century BC landmarks, including the *Acropolis*, a hilltop citadel and topped with ancient buildings like the colonnaded *Parthenon* temple.

Compared to the pyramids of Egypt and the Mayan temples of Peru, they look almost modern.

It has been 270 days since I left home and I'm now 270 degrees (or 3/4 of the way around the Earth). Including my wiggles north and south, I have travelled more than twice the circumference of the planet.

I haven't seen a familiar face for over four months but that's about to change. I'm soon skimming across the sea on a hydrofoil to visit my friend Jackie on the beautiful *Island of Egina*. We have known each other since primary school and it's great to catch up again.

Egina is a small triangular island just 45 km from Athens and many wealthy Athenians have second homes here. The population of just 20,000 residents trebles in the summer months.

At one time this place competed with Athens as the power centre of the area. We visit the *Temple of Aphaea* on the equilateral holy triangle of temples including the iconic Athenian Parthenon and The *Temple of Poseidon*.

Afterwards we wander through the arid dry hills to the ruins of *Paleochora* which was designated as the capital of the island. In the 8th Century the locals, threatened by pirates, began to move from the coast to the interior. Over 366 tiny churches once stood on this hillside, some no bigger than a garden shed.

We spend the next few days island hopping to *Agistri* and *Moni Island*. There are so many beautiful

small islands in Greece, and these are two little jewels. One is even home to dozens of peacocks, so I go on my first peacock hunt.

Egina is the island of the pistachio nuts but I discover that they prefer cake and soon have them eating out of my hand.

Just as I'm planning the last leg of my journey through Europe, I receive an e-mail informing me that my house sitter has to quickly move out so I must cut my journey short and head for home much earlier than I had planned.

I have a few days booked in Sicily and then a few more in Rome so sadly, the rest of my trip will now have to wait for another day.

I have very mixed feelings about this. I must cancel nonrefundable flights and hotel bookings and I was looking forward to meeting up with family members in Germany and old friends elsewhere.

However, I also feel exhausted from 10 months of travelling and am looking forward to being home again and spending some quiet summer time in my garden.

I feel that it may take some time to process the many experiences I have had. I do feel like a different person and am uncertain if I will ever get back to 'normal', whatever that is.

A week of sun, sandy beaches and floating in the clean blue sea is just the tonic I need. Along with gin of course.

Oh, and the best ice cream in the world.

Travel Tip No 32: Always expect the unexpected.

"I saw the light of ancient Greece
Towards the One
"I saw us standing within reach of the sun
Let go into the mystery of life
Let go into the mystery
Let yourself go."

Van Morrison

Sicily - Living on Lava...

June, Days 276-278: 58,631 miles

Arriving in *Sicily* from Athens is the easiest transfer from one country to another I have yet experienced. I am now used to my routine of getting a visa, converting my currency, queuing through immigration and security, getting new currency and a new sim card and then finding my transport on to my destination.

In Catania airport, I simply grab my bag and walk out of the exit door.

I'm home in Europe now and it feels so familiar, safe and easy. I feel so sad that Britain will soon be leaving this trusted arrangement and I am sure that many folks will soon regret the decision to leave.

There is no hassle at the taxi rank or from the street vendors and no incessant hooting in traffic. Ah!

As a schoolboy fascinated by maps, I always saw this island as a rock being kicked by the leg and boot of Italy. Now governed by Rome, most Sicilians will quickly assert that they are not Italian and many feel that Italy still kicks them around. It's a bit similar to how most Scots feel about Westminster.

Catania lies at the foot of *Mount Etna* which towers above the entire island like *Orodruin* in the land of Mordor *in Lord of the Rings.*

This however, is a relaxed and cultured place, refreshingly green with trees and plants growing on the verdant hillsides. The temples and mosques of Asia being replaced with Catholic churches and cathedrals.

The old town where I am staying has some of the best examples of baroque architecture in Italy. The avenues and open spaces are lined with blue flowering Jacaranda trees. It's very pretty.

At dawn and dusk, the skies are filled with thousands of swifts which reel over the orange terracotta rooftops. From my sixth-floor balcony, I watch them as they flap hard for a bit and then glide past me in pure joy as they swirl and skirl around the blue skies.

The town comes alive in the evening when the streets fill up with pavement cafes and restaurants offering the best seafood, pizzas, paellas, pasta and risottos. The wine is also quite fine.

The small town of *Taormina* is set in an idyllic location, perched high on a cliff overlooking the Ionian Sea. Besides the ancient Greek theatre, it has many old churches, lively bars, fine restaurants, antique shops and chic fashion shacks. It's been a popular tourist destination since the 19th century and the prices certainly reflect that.

I get the bus up to Mount Etna to 6,000 feet. There I meet Enrico who is a volcanologist and the perfect guide to show me around this black and foreboding mountain.

It's a live and active volcano which last erupted just four years ago. The lava blasted out 1 km into the sky

and the smoke cloud a further 2 km. Every 500 years or so a major eruption takes place which has created and reshaped this island. Many of the communities perched on its precarious slopes are now buried under rock.

"The mountain talks to us," explained Enrico. "We get to know its grumbles, tremors and earthquakes. It also shows how it is feeling by the colour of the plume of gases which rise from its peak. Sometimes it's sulphur-yellow, sometimes iron red. When it turns black, we run from it as fast as we can." Today thankfully, it's white and in a good mood.

The landscape seems like another planet with black dust and jagged molten rocks everywhere.   Enrico shows me some huge boulders which look like giant dinosaur eggs. "We call these bombs," he tells me. "They have been blasted half a mile into the sky and have landed here, forming their own mini craters."

We explore its caves through which the lava once flowed. Inside, the rocks have blistered, forming weird and wonderful shapes. It feels like we are inside the veins of the earth but instead of red blood, hot lava and gasses once flowed.

Life on our planet is awesome. Within just 70 years or so, the rich fertile minerals are colonised by grasses and vegetation. Yes, those hungry vegetables just love to gobble up those poor defenceless minerals. Trees and shrubs soon follow accompanied by insects, birds and finally, mammals.

We humans, as part of this food chain, then grow fruit orchards, olive groves and vineyards. In this way, black basalt rock from the bowels of the earth become transformed in time to spirit in the form of some of the finest wines in the world.

Great writers, poets, artists, and philosophers have been drawn to this place of outstanding power and natural beauty. *Goethe, Nietzsche, Wagner, D.H. Lawrence, Bertrand Russell, Roal Dahl* to name but a few.

Tonight, in the ancient Greek amphitheater overlooking the ocean, one of my favourite bands, *Jethro Tull* is performing. It's sold out and despite my best efforts to charm the sound and stage crew, I am unable to blag a ticket as a minstrel in the gallery.

Perhaps my luck has finally run out and it's time to head for home.

It's elemental, dear Watson.

*"Now I don't know I don't know
I don't know where I'm a-gonna go
When the volcano blows."*

Don Henley

When in Rome...

June, Days 279-281: 59,126 miles

I catch the train to *Rome*, a distance of almost 500 miles. At Messina, the train drives straight into a huge ferry and splits in two. Across on the Italian mainland, it drives off and couples back together. This is simply genius. Italians have always been very practical.

It's a beautiful 10-hour journey through *Pompeii* and *Naples*. The train hugs the west coast while offering magnificent views of the *Apennine Mountains* on the east side. The countryside here is green and lush. There are so many farms and neat rows of olive trees and vineyards line the tracks.

The fields are inter sprinkled with old baroque sandy coloured castles and other buildings alongside the hillside hamlets and small villages. It's clear that this is a very sophisticated part of the world.

Trains provide the best windows for appreciating the panoramic views.

I arrive after midnight at my long-term friends Luigi and Bibi. Luigi is making eco-friendly wax for surfboards and Bibi is creating leather shoes for tango dancers. The 'Tango Team' also travel the world teaching others this wonderful dance technique.

Italy is the place where words all seem to end with vowels, mostly o's, a's, and i's.

The Romans gave us Latin which is the main root of our own British language. It's, therefore, a relatively easy language for me to understand. But most folk here as elsewhere, speak English.

The Romans also gave us straight roads, planned cities, the calendar we now use, global currency in the form of coins, bureaucracy, plumbing and sanitation. The word plumb comes from the Latin word for lead.

It took another 2,000 years for us to discover that lead pipes cause lead poisoning.

The coastline near Rome is one long beach and it's filled with folk escaping the heatwave. It's over 35 degrees here just now and even the water is warm. On the way home, we stop at a farm shop for local organic fruit, vegetables, and cheese. The Italians love their food, wine, and still value local produce.

Before the Romans arrived, the Greeks and Etruscans ruled this part of the world. At night, we explore an ancient avenue of tombs carved out of stone. These people believed in life after death and made thousands of stone carved bedrooms with stone beds for their 'sleeping' relatives.

There are so many similarities between the ancient Egyptians and Mayans. As we explore the dark tombs, hundreds of fireflies appear to float around the trees. It's magical.

I get up early to catch the train into the capital. In *St Peters Church*, the square is filled with Catholics here on a pilgrimage to catch sight of *Jorge Mario Bergoglio*, the current Pope.

Vatican City is a separate state from Italy with its own laws and police force. It's exactly the same setup as the *City of London*. Their owners have known for a very long time how to avoid taxes and stay outside the law of the land.

It's quite a spectacle and at 10 Euros a head just to stand in the square, quite a money earner too. It's another 30 Euros to enter the *Sistine Chapel* with its famous ceiling painted by *Michelangelo*. The queues are exceedingly long, but it doesn't deter the packs of tourists who dutifully follow their flag flying guides around the city like sheep.

It's a very pleasant stroll walking through the ancient streets and they are filled with iconic landmarks including *The Castle of Saint Angelo* where I cross over the *River Tiber* via a white marble bridge. *Piazza Navori, Palazzo Madama, Fontana di Trevi* and the *Pantheon* are next on my list.

At lunchtime, I do as the Romans do and tuck into a plate of spaghetti carbonara washed down with a glass of Dolcetto before carrying on to the *Piazza Venezia* and the *Museum*. Finally, I stroll around the ancient Foro Romano ancient archaeological gardens and the *Palatino* before walking around the *Colosseum* which really is colossal. So is the entry fee.

It is with very mixed feelings that I must now return home and end this wonderful odyssey. Thanks for keeping me company dear reader and providing me with a purpose for my journey. I hope that you enjoyed the trip and like me, have learned something new.

"I laid my heart out
I laid my soul down
I'll always remember
Three days in Rome."

Sheryl Crow

Epilogue...

June, Day 282: 60,884 miles

I have visited 24 countries which means that there's 171 still left to see. I've travelled the equivalent of 2.4 times around our Earth. That's 51 flights, 30 bus journeys, 29 road trips, 13 train rides and 10 boat trips. I also travelled on motorbikes, tuk-tuks, electric bikes, a horse, an elephant, and a camel.

I slept in 87 different beds plus 2 couches, in 3 overnight buses, on top of a boat and in the back of a car. No wonder my back aches. I also walked 1,215 miles and climbed the equivalent of 6,202 floors. I lost 10 pounds in weight and feel as fit as a fiddle and younger than I was when I left. My hair grew 5 inches and I have a nice suntan. It rained only twice in 10 months.

England is by far the most expensive country I have visited. It cost nearly £1 per mile to travel from Gatwick to Heathrow by *National Express*. My spaghetti carbonara cost double what I paid in Rome for the real deal. £8.50 for a pint in Gatwick is also the most I have ever paid for a beer anywhere in the world.

Still, it feels good to be back in this very green and pleasant land. As I fly north over Scotland, I look west to witness a beautiful sun setting over *Ardnamurchan, Skye and the Islands*. As beautiful a landscape as you will see anywhere in the world. It's still light at 11 pm and surprisingly warm.

Stepping back into my house of familiar sights and smells is strange and I wonder now if my journey was just a dream. I awake to wonder where I am.

It seems that not much has changed since I left. The grass on the roadsides and public areas is much longer due to the local council cutbacks. That's good for the birds and the bees but I doubt if the locals are happy about it. L.E.D. streetlights have been installed which look rather nice and should allow us to see the stars more easily.

Along the way, folk I have met have tended to ask me the same questions. It dulls my experience to repeat these often so that's one reason that I write. Here are the most frequently asked questions but please feel free to ask me others...

What's your most and least favourite country?

This is hard to answer as everywhere has its own appeal for various reasons. It's very subjective and obviously based on my limited time and personal experience there. So, this table is my attempt to help me find a definitive answer. It may also help you to decide on your own possible future travel destinations.

1. Safety: A general feeling based on the danger from people, nature, and the environment.

2 Transport: How easy and affordable it was to get into the country and travel around.

3 Fun: How happy people were and how happy I was to be there. (Yes, I even counted smiles).

PLACE		Transport	Fun	Food/Health	Comms	Value for money	Values	TOTAL
North Thailand	9	7	9	10	9	8	10	62
Indonesia, Bali	8	7	9	8	7	9	9	57
New Zealand (South Island)	10	9	7	8	10	3	8	55
Scotland	9	10	7	8	10	3	8	55
New Zealand (North Island)	9	9	8	7	10	2	8	53
Italy, Sicily	9	9	8	9	8	4	6	53
Canada, Montreal	9	9	8	8	9	3	6	52
Australia (West Coast)	9	9	8	8	9	3	6	52
Italy, Rome	9	9	7	8	8	5	5	51
USA, San Clemente	9	9	8	8	9	2	5	50
Greece	8	9	7	9	7	4	6	50
USA, Monterey	9	9	8	7	9	2	5	49
Canada, Vancouver	7	9	7	8	9	3	6	49
USA, San Francisco	8	7	8	7	10	2	6	48
USA, Oregon	8	8	7	7	9	3	6	48
USA, Yesemeti	8	9	7	8	8	3	5	48
Chile	8	8	8	8	8	3	4	47
Peru, Cusco	8	6	6	8	5	7	7	47
Australia (East Coast)	9	8	6	6	9	3	5	46
Mexico, Quintana Roo	8	5	7	7	5	7	7	46
Canada, Rockies	8	8	5	8	9	3	5	46
Nepal	8	5	7	7	7	4	8	46
Canada, Toronto	8	9	5	8	7	3	5	45
England	7	9	4	8	9	2	6	45
Peru, Machu Pichu	7	4	8	6	4	7	8	44
India, South	7	3	5	5	6	9	9	44
USA, New York	7	9	4	5	9	4	5	43
Canada, Calgary	9	8	4	7	9	3	3	43
Singapore	9	10	3	8	7	2	3	42
Cuba	6	4	8	5	3	7	8	41
Mexico, Tulum	6	6	6	7	3	6	7	41
Indonesia, Java	6	5	5	6	5	8	5	40
India, North	6	4	4	4	5	9	8	40
USA, Niagara	7	9	4	6	8	3	2	39
Indonesia, Flores	7	5	4	3	3	9	7	38
USA, Las Vegas	5	8	3	7	9	2	2	36
Qatar, Doha	6	9	2	5	8	3	1	34
Egypt	3	5	3	4	5	7	4	31
Mynamar	3	3	3	3	4	9	5	30
Vietnam	5	3	4	3	4	7	3	29
Mexico City	2	4	3	3	3	7	2	24
Kampuchea	3	2	3	2	2	8	3	23
Colombia, Bogota	1	3	1	2	2	6	1	16

4 Health: How easy it was for me to stay healthy due to food quality and the environment. Access to affordable quality health care is also considered.

5 Communication: How easy was it to dialogue with the locals and access the internet.

6 Value for money.

7 Values: How comfortable I felt with the behaviour of the people I met.

Generally speaking, I found Buddhist countries to be the happiest and friendliest. However, Auroville in India is the place where I felt most at home, inspired, and connected. As a 50-year-old experimental community, I think it's really shaping the future for a fully integrated humanity, living sustainably and in harmony with nature. I hope to return there someday.

What did you miss the most?

Apart from friends and family, surprisingly little. My guitar, my garden, a good cup of tea, my morning healthy smoothie and 'proper' bacon and eggs. I missed the cold when it was too hot and the heat when it was too cold. I'm glad I missed Brexshit.

What are your best insights?

1) People with the biggest wallets have the smallest hearts. The wealthiest places I visited were Las Vegas and Qatar. People there seemed too preoccupied with themselves or their stuff to be interested in others. Maybe they had more things to worry about or lacked a life of useful hardships. Conversely, the poorest people I met were the kindest and the most generous. Perhaps empathy is developed through suffering and helps us to care more for each other?

2) Don't believe what you see on television or in the movies. Some of the loveliest people I met were Muslims or other groups who I have been indoctrinated to fear.

3) The outside world I experience reflects how I feel inside. When I was ill in Colombia and in Vietnam, the people and places seemed sad and frightening. When I was happy and healthy, I met lovely people and had great experiences.

4) I tend to get what I give. I experimented with this idea. I gave away 10% of my travel budget to deserving people who could use it and it was always refunded from a different source. The first 10 times I gave money to help others it came back to me on the same day! This then became a habit and I stopped counting.

When I was friendly and kind, I met kind friends. When I was shy and introspective, I felt lonely. When I helped others, others helped me. Karma is real.

5) Being alone and not seeing a familiar face for almost five months, pushed me to connect with strangers. This was as simple as looking into the eyes of others and smiling. Children especially always notice this and smile back. Doing my clumsy best to communicate always gained respect and made people laugh. It helped me stay connected, sane, and never lonely. People seemed genuinely interested to talk with me and help me, everywhere.

6) Climate change is real. Everywhere I travelled, older people told me that the weather had intensified over their lifetime. Snow came two months early in the Rockies. More wildfires in the USA. Species disappearing in South America. More earthquakes and eruptions in Asia. Record temperatures in Australia. Droughts with lakes and rivers drying up in India. Life-threatening smog across half of the planet. Our Earth is definitely in transition.

It's not all gloomy though. Nature is more resilient than humans. Many countries are becoming greener, more eco-conscious, clearing up their waste and reducing their use of oil, chemicals, and pharmaceuticals. Most governments need income from tourism and therefore must behave now. The internet is helping us to inform each other and allows us to share problems and solutions. Human populations are naturally declining in most places. There is still hope but not much time for many of us.

7) Living in the UK is very expensive. However, I now feel so lucky to live in Europe and especially Scotland (which is more beautiful than I previously realised.) Understanding more fully Britain's colonial history makes me feel ashamed to be British. Scottish and Irish people are loved across the entire world. Everyone from everywhere I travelled wants Scotland to break from Westminster and to remain a partner in Europe. Many countries I visited have done this already and are thriving.

What mistakes did you make?

Lots! But I learned from them and about myself. I'm proud that I never missed a flight or a departure time. I travelled through some dangerous places but was oblivious to the threats at the time. 'Trust in God but tie up your camel' is a great truth. There is no such thing as too much research. Google is great. So are Booking.com and AirBnB. There are also some great nomad Facebook pages and websites for travellers to share information. We are an emerging global community.

What were your best experiences?

There were so many but my most enduring memories are Machu Pichu, getting to the top of Rainbow Mountain in Peru and being kissed by an alpaca, cuddling a tiger, getting up close to a whale and a Komodo dragon, seeing hummingbirds and other exotic creatures, being alone in the jungle, riding a camel through the desert, flying in a hot air balloon, seeing the Himalayas, being on stage at The Fillmore, seeing Carlos Santana, getting lost and finding my way out of scrapes, surprising myself, falling in and out of love (again), making new friends for life, experiencing awesome sunrises, sunsets and natural wonders.

Solo travelling is very empowering. It will build your character, broaden your mind, expand your heart, and feed your soul. You can experience so much in just one year. History comes alive.

I realise now that when I lost my fear of death, I also lost my fear of life. I no longer fear heights, darkness, dogs, snakes, and other animals with sharp teeth including scary people. Maybe this is easier as I get older because there's less to lose. I'm still here.

My time in Varanasi, India was the most mind-blowing and made me review so many of my preconceived ideas about life, death, and everything in between. I quite literally saw birth, death, and procreation on the streets. It puts things into an unfamiliar perspective. I lost my ability to judge others. Life is utterly amazing, humans especially so.

And the worst experiences?

Being ill, vulnerable, and alone and thinking that if I died, no-one would know.

Losing my iPhone and realising how utterly dependent I was on it. I couldn't use an ATM to get cash, access my tickets, arrange transport, translate language, contact friends, or know where I was or how to get somewhere else. The difference between life and death can be the dollar you need for a phone call. I now have huge respect for those early pioneers who travelled without modern-day technology.

How much did it cost?

I spent an average of £420 per week including all equipment, transport costs, tours, accommodation, food, and entertainment. I could have done this on half of that quite comfortably. Younger backpackers I met are travelling for a fraction of that, couch surfing and working as they go.

Factoring in what I saved on expensive UK prices if I had stayed at home including car, electricity, food, and taxes etc. it only really cost me an extra £280 per week.

If I had leased out my home this could have been reduced to around £100 per week or just £15 per day. That's about three weeks of wages for many people I met. Prices in Asia are roughly one-fifth of prices in the UK. So that goes a long way. My experiences and memories are priceless.

Any regrets?

I wish I could have done this when I was younger. Having said that, I met many solo travellers much older than myself. It's never too late. I also wish I could have flown less and travelled in more trains, buses, cars, and boats. Next time I will travel slower and go deeper.

What's your Top Tips for solo travellers?

1) Talk to other travellers and to the locals. Do your research on the move and before you arrive. Read the reviews. Shop around to get the best deals. Use paper maps. Carry two debit cards and keep them separate.

Don't carry too much cash. (For long journeys, ask a trusted friend or family member to transfer cash to you at regular intervals). It's essential to have an emergency contact and to check in regularly.

2) Travel light and you will have fewer things to carry, to clean, to lose and to worry about. Aim for 10 Kg to avoid most carry-on fees at airports.

3) Invest in good shoes and a quality backpack with sturdy wheels. (I recommend *Keen* shoes and *Osprey* luggage.)

4) Carry a compass, a torch, a whistle, and a power pack for recharging your phone.

5) Back-up all your documents and photos to the cloud daily. Write important things down in a notebook (NOT passwords). Keep spare photocopies of your passport and extra passport photos.

6) Travelling is hard on your body, emotions, mind, and spirit. Self-discipline and developing healthy routines are essential. (Good diet, drink lots of water, meditate and do yoga). Take a holiday and just chill on a beach if you get too exhausted. It's easy to burn out.

7) Have fun. Be curious. Take risks but keep your eyes open. Stay sober.

8) Be respectful of others customs, don't flash your cash and don't be a dick.

9) Travellers redistribute wealth so spend your money wisely with those who need it most. You are an ambassador of your country and you can do a lot to dispel false judgments and help to create world peace between nation, race, and gender. Be a friend and help others.

10) Take lots of photos and keep a diary or write a blog. It's easy to forget experiences with so much going on and it may help, inform, and inspire others.

And remember that life is a journey and not a destination. Enjoy your adventures, one step at a time and two feet wide.

The End

"The colours of the rainbow so pretty in the sky
Are also on the faces of people going by
I see friends shaking hands saying how do you do
They're really saying I love you.
I hear babies crying, I watch them grow
They'll learn much more than I'll ever know
And I think to myself what a wonderful world
Yes, I think to myself what a wonderful world."

Louis Armstrong

HAPPINESS
around our world

01 NEW YORK: Happy Hour

02 MONTREAL: Happy protestors

3 TORONTO: Happy in the confetti dome

4 CALGARY: Happy cowboys and cowgirls

5 LAKE LOUIS: Happy catching babies

6 TORONTO: Happy with mom on the bus

7 PORTLAND: Happy humming bird

8 YOSEMITE: Happy to met this majestic being

9 MONTEREY: Humpback whale jumping for joy

10 SAN FRANCISCO: Happy drummer

11 SAN CLEMENTE: Happiness is golden

12 LAS VEGAS: So happy to see Carlos Santana

13 MEXICO CITY: Happy on the day of the dead

14 BACALAR: Happy in a hammock

15 XULA: Happy sweat lodge family.

16 TULUM: Happy climbing this Mayan Temple

17 TULUM: Happy to meet you too

18 CUBA: Happiness is a bottle of Havana Rum

19 BOGOTA: No Happiness found here

20 CUSCO: Happy kids, lambs and alpaca

21 RAINBOW MOUNTAIN: Happy at 17,600 feet

22 CHILE:: Happy hillside houses

23 PALMERSTON, NZ: Happy samba band

24 HOBBITON NZ: Happy hobbitsss

25 FIELDING NZ: Happy Christmas

26 PAHORA, NZ: Happy beach bum

27 SYDNEY: Happy New Year

28 BLUE MOUNTAINS: Happy to see this sun rise

29 REDHEAD BEACH: Happy surfer dude

30 BYRON BAY: Happy hippies on the beach

31 BREMER BAY: Happy re-union with a friend

32 KALGOORLIE: Happy Sheila the barmaid

33 BALI: Happy Hindus on holiday

34 FLORES: Happy hill climbers

35 BANDUNG: Happy and hopeless romantics

36 BORUBUDOR: Happy Muslim schoolgirls

37 YOGYACARTA: Happy students

38 SINGAPORE: Happy at 'Gardens by the Bay'

39 KUALA LUMPUR: Happy dancers and diners

40 VIETNAM: Happy devotees at Cao Dai temple

41 CHU CHI TUNNELS: Happy survivors of war

42 SIAGON: Street life

43 LAOS: Orange happiness on a long boat

44 ANGOR WATT: Happy sightseers

45 KAMPUCHEA: Happy wedding party

46 CHIANG MAI: Happy Karen tribe kids

47 THAILAND: Happy massage therapists

48 CHIANG MAI: Happy ladyboys in the final

49 CHIANG MAI: Happy new year Songkrat 2562

50 MANDALAY: Happy pink monks (both genders)

51 BAGAN: Happy puppets hanging around a shop

52 NGAPALA: Happy fish sellers at the market

53 CHENNAI: Happy to be here and now

54 AUROVILLE: Happy flowers floating in water

55 GOA: Happy watching football on the beach

56 DELHI: Happy gardeners in the sunshine

57 AGRA: Happy to see the Taj Mahal in the distance

58 JAIPUR: Happy school holidays at the Pink City

59 VARANASI: Happy Hindus on the steps of Ganges

60 KATHMANDU: Happy kids at Pashupatinath

61 NEPAL: Happy teachers flying around Everest

62 : POKHARA: Happiness on a boat on Phewa Lake

63 DOHA: Happy in the back of daddy's car

64 CAIRO: Happiness is a cool new pair of trainers

65 LUXOR: Happy the balloon didn't burst

66 ATHENS: Happiness is a beach bar in Paradise

67 EGINA: Happy with those special friends

68 CATANIA: Happy on a toy train

69 ROME: Happy gladiators at the Colosseum

70 VATICAN CITY: Happy statues

71 LONDON: Happy fridge magnets

72 FORRES: Happy to be home

To me this old world is a wonderful place
I'm just about the luckiest human in the whole human race
I've got no silver and I've got no gold
But I've got happiness in my soul

Happiness is a field of grain
Turning its face to the falling rain
I see it in the sunshine, breathe it in the rain
Happiness, happiness everywhere

A wise old man told me one time
Happiness is a frame of mind
When you go to measuring my success
Don't count my money count my happiness

Oh, happiness, happiness, the greatest gift that I posses
I thank the Lord I've been blessed
With more than my share of happiness

Ken Dodd

About the Author ...

Stewart Alexander Noble was born in Bucksburn, Aberdeen in the fifties. In the seventies he gave up his job in the local paper mill to become a famous guitarist. He failed the famous bit but still loves his guitar.

In the eighties he became a newspaper publisher. In the nineties he found himself self-employed as a marketing consultant. This led to a brief foray into the world of commercial property sales which ended abruptly on 'Black Wednesday' - the first major financial crash in his lifetime.

That's when he flipped, and woke up to the realisation that the key problem in the world was down to the way its money was designed. So, he created a new interest free version known as LETS. (Local Exchange Trading System).

In the noughties he helped many local groups setup their own local currencies; he became a director of EarthShare - a collective organic growing Co-op; ShopShare - a shared retail Co-op. He was then awarded the grand title of 'Scottish Social Entrepreneur of the Year'. Finally, he had a job title which impressed his mum. Various other co-operatives and social enterprises followed.

He gave up his last voluntary job as Chair of Forres Community Council to embark on this solo journey around the world. He has now become a travel writer but plans to become a time traveller in the near future to do it all over again.

One last step ...

Thankyou for buying my first (and best book)
And congratulations for getting all the way
to the end.
Please take a few minutes to rate and review it.
This helps other people to get an idea what it's all
about. Your feedback really is important to me and
I read every one.
It will also help me to improve on the next one.

Other Publications...

in 'The Two Feet Wide' Series:

Before the World Changed - The Novel
ISBN: 9798683673246

Before the World Changed - Digital Kindle Version
(To view on your e-reader, tablet or phone.)

Available on Amazon

United Kingdom
USA, Canada, Brazil, Mexico
Italy, France, Germany, Spain
Australia, New Zealand
Japan

Stewart Alexander Noble
Two Feet Wide

Printed in Poland
by Amazon Fulfillment
Poland Sp. z o.o., Wrocław

63365294R00105